The Missional Church in Context

Helping Congregations Develop
Contextual Ministry

Edited by

Craig Van Gelder

WILLIAM B. EERDMANS PUBLISHING COMPANY
GRAND RAPIDS, MICHIGAN / CAMBRIDGE, U.K.

© 2007 Wm. B. Eerdmans Publishing Co.
All rights reserved

Published 2007 by
Wm. B. Eerdmans Publishing Co.
2140 Oak Industrial Drive N.E., Grand Rapids, Michigan 49505 /
P.O. Box 163, Cambridge CB3 9PU U.K.

Printed in the United States of America

12 11 10 09 08 07   7 6 5 4 3 2 1

Library of Congress Cataloging-in-Publication Data

The missional church in context: helping congregations develop contextual ministry /
    edited by Craig Van Gelder.
        p.   cm.   — (Missional church series)
    Includes bibliographical references.
    ISBN 978-0-8028-4567-2 (pbk.: alk. paper)
    1. Mission of the church.   2. Church.   3. Missions — Theory.
    I. Van Gelder, Craig.

    BV601.8.M595   2007
    266 — dc22

                                                            2007029058

www.eerdmans.com

Contents

SECTION II

Preface

The missional church conversation continues to make a vital contribution to thinking about congregations and their contexts. This conversation is now in its second decade, and new insights are continuing to emerge. A primary issue that the church confronts in our context today — in the midst of the emerging postmodern context — is the need to re-examine and re-envision what it means to be church. It is the issue that the missional church conversation keeps inviting us to address.

This conversation had its primary beginning with the work of missiologist Lesslie Newbigin and the publications that came from him during the decades of the 1970s through the 1990s. His focus was on the relationship of gospel and culture, and the particular context that he sought to address was the late-modern culture he experienced in England when he returned in his retirement from global mission and ecumenical work in the 1970s. Newbigin helped to develop a particular Gospel and Culture programme in England in the 1980s, and that soon found its counterpart in the United States, where it became known as the Gospel and Our Culture Network (GOCN).

What is proving to be a seminal publication, *The Missional Church: A Vision for the Sending of the Church in North America* (1998), was written by six missiologists of the GOCN in the United States. The "missional church" conversation has now spread into many venues and has provided language that is being picked up by numerous denominations and faith traditions. It is clear, however, that the use of the word "missional" often means different things to different groups. The most common problem is the tendency among some to assume that it is just another way of framing the historical understanding of missions in the life of the church. But the use of the word "missional" within the missional church conversation has something much more basic in view: it is about the very nature or essence of what it means to be church.

This book is intended to help bring further clarity to the word "missional" and to contribute to this ever-widening conversation in the church. It is the result of the Missional Church Consultation that is now being sponsored each year by Luther Seminary in Saint Paul, Minnesota. The first of what would become annual consultations was held in December 2005 and engaged the theme "The Missional Church in Context." The background/theoretical chapters and the case studies that make up this volume are the studies that were prepared for discussion at that consultation.

Luther Seminary has been engaged in thinking about the missional church for several years, especially since it adopted its strategic plan, entitled Serving the Promise of Our Mission, in 2000. This plan envisioned the development of a strategic initiative in the field of Congregational Mission and Leadership; concentrations in this field are now available in the degree programs of Master of Arts, Master of Divinity, Doctor of Ministry, and Doctor of Philosophy. Part of the vision of this strategic initiative is to create an ongoing center for research concerning the missional church that is framed biblically and theologically while being informed by insights from the social sciences. The annual Missional Church Consultation is designed to bring scholars together on a yearly basis to contribute to this research.

The Wm. B. Eerdmans Publishing Company has graciously agreed to serve as the publisher for the new Missional Church Series that Luther Seminary is taking the lead in developing. We anticipate that this series will include both monographs and edited volumes of essays that come out of these annual consultations. It is our prayer that the church of Jesus Christ will be more deeply informed, and be built up and strengthened, by our contributions in this series.

CRAIG VAN GELDER
Editor, Missional Church Series

Contributors

Mark Lau Branson holds an Ed.D. degree from the University of San Francisco and is presently serving as the Homer L. Goddard Associate Professor of the Ministry of the Laity at Fuller Theological Seminary, where he has taught since 2000. His most recent book is *Memories, Hopes, and Conversations: Appreciative Inquiry and Congregational Change* (2004), published by the Alban Institute.

James Tzu-Kao Chai holds a Ph.D. degree from Luther Seminary in the field of congregational mission and leadership. He grew up as a Southern Baptist in Taiwan. Following his completion of graduate studies in the United States, in 2006 he returned to Taiwan, where he is now serving as assistant professor of missiology at the Logos Evangelical Seminary.

Mary Sue Dehmlow Dreier holds a Ph.D. degree from Luther Seminary in the field of congregational mission and leadership. She is ordained in the Evangelical Lutheran Church in America (ELCA) and has extensive pastoral experience in a variety of settings, the most recent of which was the starting up and developing of a new church over the past decade. She is now serving as associate professor of congregational mission at Luther Seminary.

Terri Martinson Elton holds a Ph.D. degree from Luther Seminary in the field of congregational mission and leadership. She is a member of the

Evangelical Lutheran Church in America (ELCA), and she has extensive leadership experience working with the Changing Church initiative at Prince of Peace Lutheran Church in Burnsville, Minnesota, and also served as a staff member of the Saint Paul Area Synod of the ELCA. She is now serving as an affiliated faculty member at Luther Seminary in the area of children, youth, and family, with a focus on contextual theology.

Scott Frederickson holds a Ph.D. degree from Luther Seminary in the field of systematic theology and is presently serving as pastor of discipleship at Good Shepherd Lutheran Church in Bismarck, North Dakota. He also serves as an adjunct faculty member in the field of congregational mission and leadership in the D. Min. program at Luther Seminary.

Joon Ho Lee is a Ph.D. (ABD) student at Luther Seminary and is working in the field of congregational mission and leadership. He is an ordained minister in the General Assembly of the Presbyterian Church in Korea (GAPCK), and he served in a number of ministries in Korea in that denomination before pursuing graduate work in the United States. He is now serving as assistant pastor at the Open Door Presbyterian Church in Herndon, Virginia.

Gary M. Simpson holds a Th.D. degree from Christ Seminary-Seminex and is presently serving as professor of systematic theology at Luther Seminary, where he has taught since 1990. Prior to teaching, he served for fourteen years as a pastor in several Lutheran congregations. His most recent publication is *Critical Social Theory: Prophetic Reason, Civil Society, and Christian Imagination* (2002), published by Fortress Press.

Craig Van Gelder holds a Ph.D. degree in mission from Southwestern Baptist Theological Seminary, and a Ph.D. in administration in urban affairs from the University of Texas in Arlington. He has served as professor of congregational mission at Luther Seminary since 1998; before that, he taught for ten years at Calvin Theological Seminary. His recent publications include *The Evangelizing Church: A Lutheran Contribution* (Augsburg Fortress, 2005), co-edited with Richard H. Bliese, and *The Essence of the Church: A Community Created by the Spirit* (Baker, 2000).

Engaging the Missional Church Conversation

These are exciting yet challenging days for the church of Jesus Christ as it continues to face massive shifts that are taking place throughout the world. To those of us living in the West, one of the more interesting shifts is the growing recognition by churches in the United States that they are now in their own mission location. This awareness is generating fresh opportunities for new ministry, but is also introducing the disruption of long-standing practices. It is no longer possible for congregations in the United States to conduct business as usual. As a result, many historical denominations are now in serious decline. Alongside this development, significant new movements are emerging: the rapid expansion of megachurches; the significant increase in the number of immigrant congregations; and the dramatic expansion of the number of congregations along generational lines.

It is profoundly important, in the midst of such shifts, to keep returning to the foundations of what it means to be the church of Jesus Christ in the world. This involves the issue of ecclesiology (a theological term that refers to the "study of the church": *ecclesia* — church, and *-ology* — the study of). In the mist of our changing world, we constantly need to continue to engage in *the study of the church*: to explore its nature, to understand its creation and continuing formation, and to carefully examine its purpose and ministry.

The past several decades have seen the emergence of a significant discussion that is helping us focus our attention on this ongoing study of the church: it is known as the "missional church conversation." This discussion has a number of generative sources, but by far the most influential have been the contributions of the late missiologist Lesslie Newbigin, whose writings from the 1970s and following decades gained wide circulation and growing influence after his retirement from the mission field and his work in the ecumenical movement.

The Influence of Lesslie Newbigin

Returning home to England, Newbigin took up the challenge of trying to envision what a fresh encounter of the gospel with late-modern Western culture might look like. The issue he raised is probably best focused in his book *Foolishness to the Greeks,* in the form of a question: "What would be involved in a missionary encounter between the gospel and this whole way of perceiving, thinking, and living that we call 'modern Western culture'?"[1]

A movement emerged in England in the 1980s with the goal of addressing this issue: it came to be known as the Gospel and Our Culture (GOC) conversation. While the GOC discussion first surfaced in England, it soon spread to the United States, where it was taken up by a new generation of missiologists; they focused their attention on addressing the U.S. context as its own unique mission location.

Newbigin's missiology was shaped largely by the mission theology that was born within the International Missionary Council (IMC) conferences during the three decades of the 1950s-1970s. This was a trinitarian understanding of mission, or what is commonly referred to as the *missio Dei.* Influenced by the biblical theology movement of the 1930s-1940s, a trinitarian foundation for mission theology began to take shape at the Willingen Conference of the IMC in 1952. This understanding was later formulated as the *missio Dei* by Karl Hartenstein,[2] and then was given fuller expression by Johannes Blauw in his 1962 publication *The Missionary Nature of the Church.*[3] Newbigin articulated his own expression of this

1. Lesslie Newbigin, *Foolishness to the Greeks* (Grand Rapids: Eerdmans, 1986), p. 1.

2. H. H. Rosin, *'Missio Dei': An Examination of the Origin, Contents and Function of the Term in Protestant Missiological Discussion* (Leiden: Inter-university Institute for Missiological and Ecumenical Research, Department of Missiology, 1973).

3. Johannes Blauw, *The Missionary Nature of the Church: A Survey of the Biblical Theology of Mission* (Grand Rapids: Eerdmans, 1962).

mission theology in his 1978 book *The Open Secret*.[4] Central to his understanding of mission is the work of the Triune God in calling and sending the church through the Spirit into the world to participate fully in God's mission within all of creation. In this theological understanding, the church is understood to be the creation of the Spirit. It exists in the world as a "sign" that the redemptive reign of God's kingdom is present. It serves as a "foretaste" of the eschatological future of the redemptive reign that has already begun. It also serves as an "instrument" under the leadership of the Spirit to bring that redemption reign to bear on every dimension of life.[5]

The British GOC Programme

The British version of the GOC conversation, as noted above, was a movement developed during the 1980s that came to be known as a "programme." It was shaped largely by the writings of Newbigin during that period: *The Other Side of 1984* (1983), *Foolishness to the Greeks* (1986), and *The Gospel in a Pluralist Society* (1989).[6] Newbigin's intellectual leadership of this programme was joined by the administrative and organizational contributions of Dr. Dan Beeby and Bishop Hugh Montefiore. An occasional newsletter began publication in 1989, but the programme culminated in many ways in 1992 with the National Consultation at Swanwick. A volume of essays edited by Montefiore, entitled *The Gospel and Contemporary Culture*, served as the agenda for discussion at that consultation.[7]

During the early 1990s, the British GOC programme floundered somewhat, due primarily to its failure to secure sufficient funding and to find an institutional home within the church. A move to merge the GOC programme with the C. S. Lewis center in 1994 proved to be short-lived, and the programme was disbanded in 1996.[8] Lesslie Newbigin's death in

---

4. Lesslie Newbigin, *The Open Secret* (Grand Rapids: Eerdmans, 1978).

5. Newbigin, *The Open Secret*, p. 124.

6. Lesslie Newbigin, *The Other Side of 1984* (Consul Oecumenique, 1983); *The Gospel in a Pluralist Society* (Grand Rapids: Eerdmans, 1989).

7. Hugh Montefiore, ed., *The Gospel and Contemporary Culture* (Cassell Academic, 1992).

8. A brief history of the British GOC Programme is available online at www .deepsight.org/articles/engchis.htm.

1998 brought an additional sense of closure to his substantive as well as symbolic leadership of the movement in England.

The GOC Network in the United States

As the British programme began to gain public recognition, a U.S. version of the Gospel and Our Culture conversation also began to emerge. Several consultations sponsored in the mid-1980s by the Overseas Ministries Study Center stimulated interest in the question Newbigin had posed in his Warfield Lectures at Princeton in 1984 (later published as *Foolishness to the Greeks*). Growing out of these early events, a *network* began to take shape in the mid-1980s under the leadership of George Hunsberger.

By the early 1990s, the Gospel and Our Culture Network was publishing a quarterly newsletter and convening a yearly consultation. By the mid-1990s, the U.S. movement began to find its own voice — beyond the influence of Newbigin — when the Wm. B. Eerdmans Publishing Company began issuing a series of books under the moniker The Gospel and Our Culture Series. Included in this series to date are the following volumes:

George Hunsberger and Craig Van Gelder, eds., *The Church Between Gospel and Culture: The Emerging Mission in North America* (1996)

Darrell L. Guder, ed., *Missional Church: A Vision for the Sending of the Church in North America* (1998)

George R. Hunsberger, *Bearing the Witness of the Spirit: Lesslie Newbigin's Theology of Cultural Plurality* (1998)

Craig Van Gelder, ed., *Confident Witness — Changing World: Rediscovering the Gospel in North America* (1999)

Darrell L. Guder, *The Continuing Conversion of the Church* (2000)

James V. Brownson, ed., *StormFront: The Good News of God* (2003)

Lois Y. Barrett, ed., *Treasure in Clay Jars: Patterns in Missional Faithfulness* (2004)

This literature focused on understanding the United States as its own unique mission location and the church as being missional by nature, and the above books continue to stimulate a very important conversation. A number of other books from several different publishers have also contributed to this conversation:

Craig Van Gelder, *The Essence of the Church: A Community Created by the Spirit* (Grand Rapids: Baker Book House, 2000)

Richard H. Bliese and Craig Van Gelder, eds., *The Evangelizing Church: A Lutheran Contribution* (Minneapolis: Augsburg Fortress, 2005)

Alan J. Roxburgh and Fred Romanuk, *The Missional Leader: Equipping Your Church to Reach a Changing World* (San Francisco: Jossey-Bass, 2006)

The strategic importance of the missional church conversation is taking on an increasing consequence in the United States as this genre of literature continues to expand. More and more denominational and congregational leaders are becoming aware of the need to explore deeper issues about the church regarding its nature and identity. This awareness is stimulated largely by the increased recognition that the multiple late-modern strategies and programs that have been generated to make the church more effective have significant limitations in addressing systemic issues. This awareness, plus the need to continue to extend the missional church conversation, are the primary impulses that have given birth to this book, which is the first in a new series to be published by Eerdmans and to be known as the Missional Church Series.

The Missional Church Series

The purpose of this book is to help extend the missional church conversation by attempting to build on the contributions that have already been generated. Substantive developments in theology continue to offer new insights for this conversation; in addition, efforts to bring the missional church conversation into direct discussion with particular contexts is now gaining traction.

This book is the result of the first — of what will be an annual — Missional Church Consultation, whose theme was "The Missional Church in Context: Developing a Contextual Missiology," hosted by Luther Seminary in Saint Paul, Minnesota, in December 2005. The plenary essays and case studies from that consultation make up the chapters of this volume. They are organized into two primary sections: first, there are four chapters that explore more deeply the engagement of the missional church in relation to contextualization: they pay attention to exploring biblical, theolog-

5

ical, and historical dimensions of how the church is to engage in ministry within and to a specific cultural context; the second set of four chapters are case studies that provide the reader with perspectives on how a missional understanding of the church can be brought to bear on particular denominations and particular contexts.

How to Read and Use This Book

As I have noted above, the primary purpose of this book is to extend the conversation about the missional church by taking it in some new directions. The reader will find that the authors draw deeply on the literature that has been generated to date. But in the midst of drawing on this extant literature, the authors represented here also contribute some fresh new insights into how we might think further about the missional church.

The first four chapters are intended to contribute to the development of a constructive argument for the missional church. In the first chapter, Craig Van Gelder sets up the discussion regarding the missional church in context by bringing insights from the discipline of missiology to bear on the conversation, suggesting a number of inherent aptitudes that the missional church needs to cultivate in order to live out its missionary nature in particular contexts. In the second chapter, Scott Frederickson explores the interrelationship of congregations and their specific contexts. Drawing on insights from a trinitarian understanding of the social reality of God, Frederickson suggests that congregations have an inherent reciprocal relationship with their contexts, and they need to attend to it. In the third chapter, Gary Simpson returns the reader to the Protestant Reformation in a search for fresh insights that can inform our understanding of the missional church. He develops five themes that provide critical perspectives toward developing a deeper understanding of how a missional church lives in the world. In the fourth chapter, Mark Lau Branson moves the conversation about the missional church into the specific practices of particular congregations within their specific contexts. He uses insights from this interaction to help inform the practices of leadership within the missional church.

The second section of four chapters is intended to help the reader understand how a missional church perspective can be brought to bear on particular denominations in particular contexts. Terri Martinson Elton's chapter takes up the question of denominations and denominationalism in the United States: she explores how this particular form of the church might benefit from engaging the missional church conversation, especially as denominations now find themselves within an emerging postmodern condition. Joon Ho Lee's chapter takes Korea as its context and the General Assembly of the Presbyterian Church in Korea as its denomination for investigation. Lee engages in a critical analysis of how this denomination might profit from interacting with the contributions that a missional church perspective can provide. Mary Sue Dreier's chapter explores the challenges facing the Evangelical Lutheran Church in America by bringing the missional church perspective into critical conversation with that church's approach: she examines ways in which the increasing diversity within the denomination might be addressed to help it more effectively engage its present context. James Tzu-Kao Chai's chapter brings the Southern Baptist Church in Taiwan into discussion with the missional church conversation, exploring the challenges and opportunities facing this Western transplanted denomination within the unique context of Taiwan.

The reader will observe that a number of common themes surface throughout these essays. The reader will also observe that, while these essays are intended to complement each other, the diverse perspectives of the authors also introduce some points of tension that need to be addressed. I have provided an overview of some of these themes and points of tension in the brief introductions that precede each of the two sections in this volume.

SECTION I

Introduction

As I have noted in the introduction, these first four chapters explore more deeply the biblical, theological, and historical dimensions regarding how the church is to engage in ministry within and to a specific cultural context. There are a number of issues that the reader will want to be aware of in working through these essays.

First, all four of these essays engage the issue of how we should understand the trinitarian foundations for mission. They seek to address how recent trinitarian studies shape and inform our understanding of the missional church. Lesslie Newbigin was part of a mid-twentieth-century shift in formulating a trinitarian foundation for mission theology. What became known as the *missio Dei* in the aftermath of Willingen in 1952 shifted the theological foundations for mission from a high Christology to a trinitarian perspective. This perspective was primarily related to the Augustinian tradition of understanding God as it was retranslated by Karl Barth into the twentieth century. But it focused primarily on the work of the three persons of the Godhead in light of the oneness these persons share in common. This led Newbigin and others to emphasize the *called and sent* aspects of the church. Over the past few decades, contributions from the Eastern Orthodox tradition, which emphasizes the in-relationship social reality of the three persons, have begun to make their way into the larger conversation about the trinitarian foundations for mission. The interrelationship of the persons of the Godhead is often referred to by the term *perichoresis*. Readers will want to note the significant ways in which all four of these essays bring these two views of the trinitarian foundations for mission into an understanding of the missional church.

Second, there is the issue of the discipline of missiology. Interestingly, the perspectives and insights from this discipline have only recently been brought to bear on thinking about ecclesiology. Van Gelder explores the reasons for this in providing a survey of the historical development of this discipline. He notes the Copernican revolution that took place in mission theology in the mid-twentieth century with the shift to a trinitarian understanding as the foundation for mission. Rather than the church having a mission, it is God who has a mission in the world, and it is God who calls and sends the church to participate in this mission. This introduces the perspective that the church is missionary by nature. If this is the case, then what are the characteristics of how missionary congregations should live within their particular contexts? This essay identifies seven aptitudes that inherently characterize congregations when they come to live into their identity as a missional church.

Third, there is the issue of how the missional church should respond to the reality of consumerism within our cultural context. To what extent should the missional church use this cultural reality as a part of its practice of contextualization, and to what extent should it confront this reality as part of the brokenness within our culture? Scott Frederickson engages this question by drawing on the analogy of a perichoretic understanding of the Godhead to think about the interrelationship of a congregation and its context, noting that these are always inherently interrelated. While not being naïve about the power of evil embedded within cultural realities, he takes a more positive approach to a contextualization of the faith within particular contexts. However, the reader will want to note the critique of consumerism that the third and fourth essays bring to this part of the discussion. Some contrasting points of view between these chapters provide helpful insights toward better framing and exploring this complex issue.

Fourth, there is the issue of how to read the historic Christian faith when using a missional church lens. To what extent are the confessional insights from historical theological developments, such as the Protestant Reformation, congruent with or do they help inform the missional church conversation? Gary Simpson provides a rereading of five key confessional themes of the Protestant Reformation from a missional church perspective, particularly with respect to his Lutheran tradition. When read from this perspective, these themes open up powerful new insights into our conceiving of the missional church in context. Simpson's work suggests that mission and confession always need to be kept in a healthy tension as polarities, and it invites other theological traditions into a rereading of their own confessional heritage for similar insights.

Fifth, there is the issue of understanding how leadership is formed and how it is to function within a missional church understanding. How are we to understand the practices of leadership within the missional church? Mark Lau Branson provides a powerful critique of our cultural context by using the Sermon on the Mount as a hermeneutical lens. He argues that the alternative understanding that Jesus was inviting his disciples to use as their interpretive framework for life is still relevant for the missional church today. This understanding has profound implications for how leaders are formed and for how they are to lead missional communities of faith in the world. The reader will note the importance that this essay places on the role of the leadership to provide for interpretive sense-making within communities of faith.

CHAPTER 1

How Missiology Can Help Inform the Conversation about the Missional Church in Context

Craig Van Gelder

Congregations are the location where the vast majority of church members and their leaders live out their relationship with God. In this regard, congregations represent the primary location for understanding the work of God, both within Christian faith communities and in relationship to the world.[1] Unfortunately, congregations have not historically tended to be of primary interest to the theological academy, except with respect to learning the arts of ministry. Over the past several decades, however, an interest in congregations has re-emerged within several disciplines: congregational studies;[2] practical theology;[3] re-envisioning theological education;[4] and

1. David H. Kelsey, *To Understand God Truly: What's Theological About a Theological School* (Louisville: Westminster John Knox Press, 1992).

2. Nancy Tatom Ammerman, *Congregation and Community* (New Brunswick, NJ: Rutgers University Press, 1997); Nancy Tatom Ammerman et al., eds., *Studying Congregations: A New Handbook* (Nashville: Abingdon Press, 1998); Mark Chaves, *Congregations in America* (Cambridge, MA: Harvard University Press, 2004); Carl S. Dudley and Nancy Tatom Ammerman, *Congregations in Transition: A Guide for Analyzing, Assessing, and Adapting in Changing Communities* (San Francisco: Jossey-Bass, 2002); Cynthia Woolever and Deborah Bruce, *A Field Guide to U.S. Congregations: Who's Going Where and Why*, 1st ed. (Louisville: Westminster John Knox Press, 2002).

3. Don S. Browning, *Practical Theology*, 1st ed. (San Francisco: Harper & Row, 1983); Gerben Heitink, *Practical Theology: History, Theory, Action Domains: Manual for Practical Theology*, trans. Reinder Bruinsma (Grand Rapids: Eerdmans, 1999).

4. Robert J. Banks, *Reenvisioning Theological Education: Exploring a Missional Alternative to Current Models* (Grand Rapids: Eerdmans, 1999); Edward Farley, *The Fragility of*

leadership and organizational theory.[5] Patrick Keifert summarizes this point well when he notes that what we are experiencing is, in fact, a return of the congregation to theological education.[6]

The purpose of this chapter is to bring resources from the discipline of missiology into conversation with this emerging focus on congregations. I wish to do so by using the recent emergence of the missional church conversation within missiological circles to reframe the relationship of congregations and their contexts.[7] It is interesting that the discipline of missiology, as it emerged in Western theological education, did not tend to focus its attention on congregations — at least not those at home. The missional church conversation offers a corrective to that focus. This chapter argues for the construction of what might be called "a missiological framework for thinking about congregations in context." My primary focus is on congregations in the United States, since this is my social location; but this framework should also be applicable, at least to some extent, to congregations in other parts of the world.

A Short Interpretive History of the Discipline of Missiology

The church of Jesus Christ, and particularly churches within this world-wide church, have always been involved in conveying the message of the good news to others, and in engaging in the development of congregations as communities of faith. In this sense, churches have always participated in God's mission in the world. Literature on the history of missions clearly documents the expansion of the Christian movement over the past two

---

Knowledge: Theological Education in the Church and the University (Philadelphia: Fortress Press, 1988); Farley, *Theologia: The Fragmentation and Unity of Theological Education* (Philadelphia: Fortress Press, 1983); Kelsey, *To Understand God Truly.*

5. Norman Shawchuck and Roger Heuser, *Leading the Congregation: Caring for Yourself While Serving the People* (Nashville: Abingdon, 1993); Shawchuck and Heuser, *Mangaging the Congregation: Building Effective Systems to Serve People* ((Nashville: Abingdon, 1996).

6. Patrick R. Keifert, "The Return of the Congregation: Missional Warrants," *Word & World* 20, no. 4 (2000).

7. This conversation has its roots in the work initiated by Lesslie Newbigin in Britain in the 1980s and brought into the U.S. in the 1990s through the work of the Gospel and Our Culture Network.

thousand years.[8] Much within this unfolding story contributes to the content of the discipline of missiology. However, we should note that a systematic formulation regarding how churches are to participate in God's mission emerged rather late — at least a formulation that relied on critical reflection.

The Roman Catholic Church developed such a focus in the several centuries following the Protestant Reformation, especially with the formation of the Sacred Congregation of the Propagation of the Faith in 1622.[9] Protestants, on the other hand, did not develop a formal or systematic approach to the study of missiology until the early nineteenth century. The primary reason for the development of the discipline at that time was as a response to the expansion of what became known as "foreign missions." These "missions" were conducted by most Protestant churches in the West, and they largely functioned within the milieu of the expanding system of colonialism.

The modern missions movement carried out by Protestants required churches to be more intentional in the training of personnel who would serve as missionaries. At first, much of this training took place outside of formal theological education; but by the mid-1800s there were signs that a discipline known as "missiology" would become part of the theological curriculum. Over the next 150 years, this new discipline underwent significant changes — not to mention a few challenges to its very validity. A brief review of this history will help to provide perspective on the significance of the recent emergence of the missional church conversation, as well as on the importance of developing a missiological framework for thinking about congregations in context.

Some Important Precursors

As I have noted above, the formal discipline of missiology began to develop during the nineteenth century. But, prior to that time, there were numerous

---

8. Sydney E. Ahlstrom, *A Religious History of the American People* (New Haven, CT: Yale University Press, 1974); Kenneth Scott Latourette, *A History of the Expansion of Christianity*, 7 vols. (New York: Harper, 1937); Stephen Neill, *A History of Christian Missions,* The Pelican History of the Church, 6 (Baltimore: Penguin Books, 1964).

9. Stephen Neill, *A History of Christian Missions,* rev. ed. (New York: Penguin Books, 1986), p. 152.

contributing movements and persons that offered some missiological perspective regarding the church's participation in God's mission in the world. Illustrative examples of such contributions include: (1) Pope Gregory the Great sending Augustine and company in 596 on an intentional missionary engagement to Britain; (2) the indigenous missionary work of the Irish monastics from the fifth to eighth centuries that reflected the founding influence of Patrick; (3) Ramond Lull, in the early fourteenth century, who was the first to develop a theory of mission that included the study of context and the translation of texts; (4) Justinian von Welz, in the mid-seventeenth century, who went against consensus opinion in claiming that the Great Commission was still valid; and (5) the pietist Count Zinzendorf, in the early eighteenth century, who helped mobilize the Moravians as a missionary community.

Though seeds for the development of a discipline of missiology were planted by earlier precursors such as those noted above, the flowering of a formal discipline was still missing. It was William Carey who significantly contributed, as a transition figure, to the framing of a larger conception of the missionary task. In his *Enquiry,* published in 1792, and in the later writings of the Serampore Trio (Carey, Ward, and Marshman), he formulated a fuller theory and practice of mission.[10] But missiology was still not conceived of as an academic discipline.

Missions — A Missiology for
Foreign Missions, Phase I: 1811-1910

The development of a formal discipline of missiology finally began to emerge during the nineteenth century. This history is detailed in the foundational two-volume work of Olav Myklebust, first published in the 1950s; it was also summarized several decades ago in a series of essays in *Missiology: An International Review.*[11] Some of the important develop-

---

10. William Carey, *An Enquiry into the Obligations of Christians* (Leicester, UK: Printed by Ann Ireland, 1792); John Clark Marshman, *The Life and Times of Carey, Marshman, and Ward Embracing the History of the Serampore Mission* (London: Longman Brown Green & Roberts, 1859).

11. William Richey Hogg, "The Teaching of Missiology: Some Reflections on the Historical and Current Scene," *Missiology* 15, no. 4 (1987); Olav Guttorm Myklebust, *The Study of Missions in Theological Education; an Historical Inquiry into the Place of World*

ments of the formal discipline of missiology during the nineteenth century include the following:

- the conception of F. D. Schleiermacher's 1811 proposal for a theological curriculum of placing missions within the study of theology as a subdiscipline within practical theology;
- the appointment in 1836 of Charles Breckenridge at Princeton as the professor of "Practical Theology and Missionary Instruction" (the post was discontinued in 1839);
- the creation in 1867 of a chair of "Evangelistic Theology" at Edinburgh for Alexander Duff, which he held until 1878 (that chair ended with his death);
- the appointment of Gustav Warnack in 1896 to a chair of "Missionary Science" at the University of Halle, a position he held until 1908. This was the first official chair in missiology on the European continent.

It is important to understand that the Protestant version of the modern missions movement emerged largely outside the established, institutional church. It was conducted primarily by mission societies in Europe, which operated alongside state churches, and through a combination of parachurch organizations and denominational boards in the United States. Most of these boards had been added for this explicit purpose to the growing national denominational organizations that had been formed in the late 1700s and early 1800s. The recruitment of future missionaries, especially in the United States, was largely the work of voluntary associations of students who networked across the various theological schools.[12] The focus was on developing efficient practices to support the training and sending of mission personnel to other parts of the world. Some denomina-

---

Evangelisation in Western Protestant Ministerial Training, with Particular Reference to Alexander Duff's Chair of Evangelistic Theology, Egede-Instituttet, Oslo (Oslo, Norway: Egede instituttet; hovedkommisjon Land og kirke, 1955); James A. Scherer, "Future of Missiology as Academic Discipline in Seminary Education: Attempt at Reinterpretation and Clarification," *Missiology* 13, no. 4 (1985); Scherer, "Missiology as a Discipline and What It Includes," *Missiology* 15, no. 4 (1987).

12. Michael Parker, *The Kingdom of Character: The Student Volunteer Movement for Foreign Missions (1886-1926)* (Lanham, MD: American Society of Missiology and University Press of America, 1998).

tions in the United States also established "home mission boards," but these tended to focus on starting new congregations as denominational franchises on the expanding frontier, and they tended to pay little attention to matters of context. The theology undergirding these movements was largely shaped by an understanding of the necessity to obey Christ in seeking to fulfill the Great Commission (Matt. 28:18-20).

This formative period in the development of the discipline of missiology paid little attention to congregations, either theologically or theoretically, whether at home or abroad. Congregations at home were assumed to be the primary constituents for supporting the work of foreign missions. Substantial denominational organizations for supporting this work were developed — especially by women. Congregations on the mission field were, for the most part, the byproduct of the primary work of evangelism that focused on winning converts to the faith. This lack of attention to the development of indigenous congregations was complicated by the fact that missionaries often maintained primary leadership roles for decades within those newly growing churches. Those same missionaries also tended, somewhat uncritically, to bring into the new congregations many of the practices of traditional church life that existed back home.

There are a few exceptions of leaders who formulated other ways to develop new congregations in seeking to avoid the problem of Western domination in the various mission fields. For example, by the mid-1800s, Henry Venn in England and Rufus Anderson in the United States had independently proposed a "three-self" formula for establishing new churches: self-governing, self-supporting, self-propagating.[13] Also remarkable was the late-nineteenth-century work of John Nevius, who proposed what became known as the "Nevius method," which emphasized the development of local indigenous leadership from the very beginning of a congregation's life.[14] The newly forming discipline of missiology was beginning to think about the formation of congregations, at least on the mission field. Overall, though, foreign missions throughout this period tended to transpose predominantly Western forms of congregational life into the various mission fields as the *younger* churches and their congregations began to take shape.

13. Wilbert R. Shenk, "Rufus Anderson and Henry Venn: A Special Relationship?" *International Bulletin of Missionary Research* 5, no. 4 (1981).

14. John Livingston Nevius, *The Planting and Development of Missionary Churches*, 4th ed. (Philadelphia: Presbyterian and Reformed, 1958).

Church and Missions — A Missiology
of Foreign Missions, Phase II: 1910-1950

The world conference on mission held in Edinburgh in 1910 clearly represents a major transition both for the foreign missions enterprise and for the further development of the discipline of missiology. That conference was to be a staging ground for planning the last major thrust for what was the watchword of the Student Volunteer Movement: "the evangelization of the world in our generation."[15] In reality, it represented more of a culmination point of what had been the success of the nineteenth-century foreign missions enterprise.

The devastation experienced by the Western world in World War I, along with the massive changes that it introduced, including the gradual dismantling of the colonial system, brought substantial changes to the enterprise of foreign missions. Ironically, at the same time that these changes were being introduced, the theological academy was just beginning to expand courses, as well as the number of teaching positions, for the newly emerging discipline of missiology. The following examples are illustrative of this development:

- In 1910, about half of the theological schools in the United States offered courses in missions, although most of these were elective offerings.
- In 1910, there were three full professors of missions in theological schools — Southern Baptist in Louisville, Episcopal in Cambridge, and Yale Divinity School.
- Significant expansion of the discipline of missiology occurred with the development of missions programs and professorships at Union Theological Seminary in New York in 1914; at Princeton Theological Seminary in 1914; and with the merger of the Kennedy School of Missions into Hartford Seminary in 1913.
- By 1934, the vast majority of theological schools offered at least some courses in missions, and about half of them required students to take these courses; in addition, significant numbers of these schools created at least one chair in the field of missions related to the teaching of these courses.

15. W. H. T. Gairdner and John Raleigh Mott, *Echoes from Edinburgh, 1910: An Account and Interpretation of the World Missionary Conference* (New York: Fleming H. Revell, 1910).

Just as the discipline of missiology was gaining viability in the academy, the whole climate of the field of foreign missions was shifting. The very validity of the foreign missions enterprise was increasingly being called into question, as illustrated in the report edited by W. E. Hocking in 1932, entitled *Rethinking Missions: A Layman's Inquiry after One Hundred Years.*[16] Compounding this shift were two other realities: (a) most of the advocacy for including a chair in missiology within seminaries was coming primarily from denominational agencies and volunteer student associations, making its inclusion somewhat suspect among the more established theological disciplines; and (b) missiology continued to focus primarily on foreign missions, while the academy was turning its attention to either ecumenism or world religions. Missiology as a discipline within theological education was being increasingly marginalized at the very time it was becoming increasingly institutionalized.

The role of congregations in the United States during this period remained largely the same: providing support for the enterprise of foreign missions. The development of congregations on the foreign mission fields, however, encountered substantial changes. The rising tide of national movements within many colonies, and the eventual dismantling of the colonial system, increased the attention that was being given to developing indigenous churches under local leadership. In response, the newly emerging discipline of missiology focused more attention on church planting, leadership development, anthropology, and local cultures. The language differentiating the churches in the West from those on the mission field also began to change. At the beginning of this period, the missiological literature spoke of "older churches" and "younger churches."[17] At the end of this period, a phrase like "Partnership in Obedience," used at the IRM meeting in Whitby in 1947, illustrated a growing awareness of the need to reconsider the worldwide church in new terms.[18]

16. William Ernest Hocking and Laymen's Foreign Missions Inquiry, Commission of Appraisal, eds., *Re-Thinking Missions: A Laymen's Inquiry after One Hundred Years* (New York: Harper, 1932).

17. T. V. Philip, *Edinburgh to Salvador: Twentieth Century Ecumenical Missiology: A Historical Study of the Ecumenical Discussions on Mission* (Delhi: CSS & ISPCK, 1999).

18. International Missionary Council, *The Witness of a Revolutionary Church: Statements Issued by the Committee of the International Missionary Council, Whitby, Ontario, Canada, July 5-24, 1947* (New York, 1947).

Church and Mission: A Missiology
of Mission versus Missions, 1950-1975

The colonial systems that had served as a holding environment for the modern missions movement began to be dismantled following World War II. This introduced tremendous changes into both the work of foreign missions and the teaching of missiology in seminaries in the United States. R. Pierce Beaver led the way in 1950 in the formation of the Association of the Professors of Missions (APM) to help address these changes. This effort built on an earlier association that had been developed on the Eastern Seaboard among people teaching missiology at key theological seminaries. Beaver intended the APM to serve "not as an expression of the old missionary triumphalism, but as an attempt to build a lifeboat for floundering brothers and sisters."[19] This new association faced challenges that were indicative of the problems that the discipline of missiology was also encountering in the academy by midcentury.

There was clearly a need to reconceive the discipline beyond preparing persons to participate in foreign missions. Less evident, but more substantial, there was a need to develop a more substantive theological foundation for the discipline. The meeting of the International Mission Council (IMC) at Willingen in 1952 provided such a framework for the latter, and this, in turn, helped reshape the former. A major shift took place in the conception of a trinitarian understanding of mission as a result of the work done at Willingen, which was first formulated by Karl Hartenstein as the *missio Dei*.[20] This shift was from an understanding of missions as flowing largely out of Christology, which emphasized the obligation of churches to participate in fulfilling the Great Commission, to an understanding that a trinitarian God is involved in mission in the world in which the church participates. The conception of the *missio Dei*, though not without controversy, has proved to be a Copernican revolution within the discipline of missiology.

This new conception of mission was developed primarily in ecumenical circles and mostly within the IMC. In 1961, under the leadership

19. As quoted by Scherer, "Future of Missiology as Academic Discipline in Seminary Education," p. 448.

20. H. H. Rosin, *'Missio Dei': An Examination of the Origin, Contents and Function of the Term in Protestant Missiological Discussion* (Leiden: Inter-university Institute for Missiological and Ecumenical Research, Department of Missiology, 1972).

of then director Lesslie Newbigin, the IMC merged into the World Council of Churches as the Commission on World Mission and Evangelism (CWME).[21] Critical to this early conception of the *missio Dei* was its connection to the theme of the *kingdom of God* as announced by Jesus, a theme that was receiving a growing consensus in biblical scholarship as being at the center of understanding the message of Jesus.[22] God has a mission in the world that looks toward the whole of created existence, and the church participates in this mission by living into and announcing the redemptive reign of God in Christ (the kingdom of God). This framework keeps a strong Christology tied to the larger horizon of God's redemptive activity within the broader context of the world, and it keeps an understanding of the gospel as being for the sake of the world.

There was a brief period, the early 1960s, when this understanding of mission as *missio Dei* tied to the kingdom of God became connected to a conversation about ecclesiology in general, and congregations in particular.[23] This conversation was a precursor in many ways to the missional church conversation that has surfaced in the past decade. Representative of Roman Catholic thinking along these lines was the Vatican II document *Ad Gentes,* which conceived of the church as missionary by nature. Unfortunately, a shift in the late 1960s diverted the attention and energy of this emerging connection between missiology and ecclesiology in regard to congregations.

21. Ironically, the mission movement that gave birth to the modern ecumenical movement now became only one unit within the World Council of Churches. The daughter became the mother and lost what was a unique opportunity to place the newly emerging discipline of missiology directly into conversation with ecclesiology on equal footing.

22. John Bright, *The Kingdom of God: The Biblical Concept and Its Meaning for the Church* (Nashville: Abingdon-Cokesbury Press, 1953); Oscar Cullmann, *Heil Als Geschichte: Heilsgeschichtliche Existenz Im Neuen Testament* (Tübingen: Mohr, 1965); Herman N. Ridderbos, *The Coming of the Kingdom* (Philadelphia: Presbyterian and Reformed, 1962).

23. Representative of this work among ecumenical Protestants are Johannes Blauw, *The Missionary Nature of the Church: A Survey of the Biblical Theology of Mission,* 1st ed., Foundations of the Christian Mission (New York: McGraw-Hill, 1962); Johannes Christiaan Hoekendijk, *The Church Inside Out,* trans. Isaac C. Rottenberg (Philadelphia: Westminster, 1966); H. Kraemer, *A Theology of the Laity* (Philadelphia: Westminster, 1958); World Council of Churches, Dept. on Studies in Evangelism (Western European Working Group) and World Council of Churches, Dept. on Studies in Evangelism (North American Working Group), *The Church for Others, and the Church for the World. A Quest for Structure for Missionary Congregations. Final Report of the Western European Working Group and North American Working Group of the Department on Studies in Evangelism* (Geneva, 1967).

This shift was the increased focus on secularization, which led some to begin to conceive of the church as needing to give up its life for the sake of the world.[24] One problem with this emphasis was that it failed to keep an ecclesiology clearly connected to the missiology of *missio Dei*. Another problem was the diminished emphasis of redemptive dimensions of the kingdom of God being dynamically connected to the *missio Dei*. This resulted in conceiving of the work of God in the world largely in social and political terms. As this emphasis came to a peak at the 1968 World Council of Churches meeting in Uppsala, and at the 1972-1973 meeting of the CWME in Bangkok, many evangelicals began to question whether it was a helpful framework for the discipline of missiology.[25] This suspicion was compounded by the increased influence of liberation theology, which came primarily from Latin American Roman Catholic theologians, who called for the church to adopt a proactive stance on social and political action.[26] This movement was also perceived by many evangelicals as being discontinuous with the historical understanding of mission.[27]

In this context, evangelicals organized in new ways, being fueled by those who were disaffected by the WCC and the merger of the IMC into that body. Beginning in 1966, with conferences at Wheaton College and in Berlin, evangelicals began to find a new voice for continuing to emphasize world missions.[28] This came to a fuller expression with the formulation of the Lausanne Covenant at the International Congress on World Evangelization held in 1974.[29] Deeply embedded in this resurgence of an evangelical emphasis on missions was a nineteenth-century understanding of the priority of evangelism that was now largely reframed within the theology

---

24. See, for example, Hoekendijk, *The Church Inside Out*.

25. Peter Beyerhaus, *Shaken Foundations: Theological Foundations for Mission* (Grand Rapids: Zondervan Publishing House, 1972), pp. 34-48.

26. Gerald H. Anderson and Thomas F. Stransky, *Liberation Theologies in North America and Europe*, Mission Trends, No. 4 (New York: Paulist Press, 1979).

27. See, for example, David J. Hesselgrave, ed., *Theology and Mission: Papers Given at the Trinity Consultation No. 1* (Grand Rapids: Baker Book House, 1978).

28. Carl F. H. Henry and W. Stanley Mooneyham, *One Race, One Gospel, One Task; Official Reference Volume: Papers and Reports* (Minneapolis: World Wide Publications, 1967); Harold Lindsell, ed., *The Church's Worldwide Mission: An Analysis of the Current State of Evangelical Missions, and a Strategy for Future Activity* (Waco, TX: Word Books, 1966).

29. J. D. Douglas, *Let the Earth Hear His Voice; Official Reference Volume: Papers and Responses* (Minneapolis: World Wide Publications, 1975), pp. 3-9.

and methodology of what was becoming known as the "church growth" movement.[30]

The discipline of missiology went through several major shifts during this period:

- A new missiology society was formed in 1973, known as the American Society of Missiology. It was made up of people from ecumenical, Roman Catholic, and evangelical streams, and it served for a time as an arena for the reconception of missiology.
- Many of the former mainline and flagship seminaries that had first established chairs of missiology either terminated those chairs or changed their focus substantially — to such things as interreligious studies or ecumenism (note, for example, the ending of the programs at Hartford, Union, and Yale seminaries, and the changing of the program at Princeton Seminary to ecumenism).
- Some mainline schools sought to revise the conception of missiology consistent with the *missio Dei* understanding by turning it into a conversation with the whole of their curriculum (note, for example, the curricular revision at the Lutheran School of Theology at Chicago in the early 1980s[31]).
- Many evangelical seminaries and educational institutions expanded their departments of missiology and the various programs offered, but these tended to reflect the more classical understanding of missiology rooted in a high Christology and the fulfillment of the Great Commission (note, for example, the start-up of the School of World Mission and Institute of Church Growth at Fuller Theological Seminary in 1969, and later the E. Stanley Jones [ESJ] School of World Mission & Evangelism at Asbury Theological Seminary in 1983).

The discipline of missiology began to conceive of congregations both at home and abroad in new ways during this period. With the shift in understanding mission as God's mission, churches and their congrega-

---

30. Donald A. McGavran, *Understanding Church Growth* (Grand Rapids: Eerdmans, 1970).

31. Scherer, "Future of Missiology as Academic Discipline in Seminary Education," pp. 453-54.

tions everywhere began to be conceived as being in a mission location. The growing evidence of the decline of Christianity within European state churches increasingly placed a focus within missiology in those locations on the need to revitalize such churches and their congregations. The suburban success in the United States, accompanied by the urban failure in the central cities (described so well by Gibson Winter[32]) began to raise deep questions about the core identity of congregations and their unwillingness or inability to engage in God's mission in this context. In addition, what had been the former foreign mission fields were now reconceived as being both sending and receiving locations,[33] with indigenous churches and their congregations assuming a more active role in contributing to this work. The discipline of missiology struggled, however, to bring its resources to bear to adequately address these strategic changes. This failure appears to be largely related to its earlier heritage of being closely aligned with the modern missions movement.

Convergence and Divergence, 1975-1995

Some interesting developments within the discipline of missiology took place during the latter several decades of the twentieth century. On the one hand, the larger world church community experienced an amazing convergence of thinking regarding the basic understanding of mission around the concepts of the *missio Dei* and the kingdom of God.[34] On the other hand, especially in the United States, the distance between ecumenicals

32. Gibson Winter, *The Suburban Captivity of the Churches* (New York: Macmillan, 1962).

33. Robert O. Latham and World Council of Churches Commission on World Mission and Evangelism, *God for All Men: The Meeting of the Commission on World Mission and Evangelism of the World Council of Churches at Mexico City, December 8th to 19th, 1963* (London: Edinburgh House, 1964); Ronald K. Orchard and World Council of Churches Commission on World Mission and Evangelism, *Witness in Six Continents: Records of the Meeting of the Commission on World Mission and Evangelism of the World Council of Churches Held in Mexico City, December 8th to 19th, 1963* (London: Published for the Division of World Mission and Evangelism of the World Council of Churches by Edinburgh House Press, 1964).

34. David Jacobus Bosch, *Transforming Mission: Paradigm Shifts in Theology of Mission*, American Society of Missiology Series, No. 16 (Maryknoll, NY: Orbis Books, 1991); James A. Scherer, *Gospel, Church, and Kingdom: Comparative Studies in World Mission Theology* (Minneapolis: Augsburg, 1987).

and evangelicals continued to grow even in the midst of an increasing convergence of thinking in the understanding of mission. Quite a few people from the two-thirds world, in the midst of this, viewed themselves as evangelical ecumenicals: they found value in both streams of the multiple conferences and congresses sponsored by the CWME of the WCC and the movement that became associated with the Lausanne Committee on World Evangelization.[35] But illustrative of the growing divergence in the United States was the gradual withdrawal of numerous evangelical missiologists from the American Society of Missiology during the 1980s.[36] Also illustrative was the failure of the ecumenicals and Roman Catholics in the ASM to replace their aging cadres of missiologists with people from younger generations.[37]

Church growth during this same period tended to serve as the key theological and methodological framework for dealing with congregations among many of those teaching missiology in evangelical seminaries. In contrast to this, many mainline seminaries, while getting out of the business of focusing on a missiology that engaged in foreign missions, did develop an interest in congregations by focusing on the growing discipline of congregational studies, which is probably best illustrated by the work being done at the Hartford Institute of Religious Research.[38] Drawing largely on social science methodologies, this discipline engages in the systematic study of congregations in trying to understand their dynamics and to explain their changing patterns. The little emphasis on mission that did remain in mainline seminaries was usually redefined in terms of ecumenism, intercultural studies, or partnerships with other churches in the worldwide church.

Few additional developments took place during this period in the field of missiology regarding congregations. The focus of the discipline seemed to be devoted primarily to the development of missions theology

35. Examples of such people include Emilio Castor, a Methodist from Peru who was director of the CWME during this time, as well as Orlando Costas, from Latin America, and David Gitari, from Africa.

36. For example, the author recalls professors from various Southern Baptist Seminaries withdrawing from active participation in the early 1980s as that denomination took a more conservative turn theologically.

37. This is the author's personal reflection regarding the past decade of ASM meetings.

38. Refer to http://hirr.hartsem.edu/.

and the reconception of the world church. The exception to this, as I have noted above, was what became known as the church-growth movement. Drawing on social science insights, the operative theology and the methodological framework of this movement were anchored primarily in what had been the logic of the modern missions movement of the nineteenth century.

In the academy, "church growth" was largely discredited by the early 1980s because it was found to be problematical on theological grounds, as illustrated in *Exploring Church Growth,* the 1983 volume edited by Wilbert Shenk.[39] However, with its emphasis on applied technique and the continued drive for success in the midst of rapid cultural changes, church growth took on a life of its own among numerous congregations in the United States. This emphasis, in turn, has gone through various phases over the past few decades: church growth, church effectiveness, and church health.[40] Within much of the broader church in the United States today, the ethos of church growth is still very much present and represents the functional missiology of many congregations, especially evangelical congregations, although increasing numbers of ecumenical congregations are gravitating in this direction as they struggle to survive within dramatically changed contexts.[41]

Missional Church: Reconnecting Missiology and Ecclesiology, 1995 to the Present

A new conversation has emerged over the past decade that is beginning to capture the attention of many congregations across diverse confessions and theological positions: it is the missional church conversation. This conversation stems largely from the work of Lesslie Newbigin, who brought a missiological perspective to bear on thinking about the West when he

39. Wilbert R. Shenk, *Exploring Church Growth* (Grand Rapids: Eerdmans, 1983).

40. Craig Van Gelder, "Missional Challenge: Understanding the Church in North America," in Darrell L. Guder et al., ed., *Missional Church: A Vision for the Sending of the Church in North America,* The Gospel and Our Culture Series (Grand Rapids: Eerdmans, 1998), pp. 72-73.

41. Craig Van Gelder, "The Gospel and Our Culture Views of Church Growth," in Gary McIntosh, ed., *Evaluating the Church Growth Movement: 5 Views* (Grand Rapids: Zondervan, 2004).

raised the question, "Can the West be converted?"[42] This conversation is finally making a clear connection between missiology and ecclesiology in developing what has become known as a "missional church," or what might also be identified as a missional ecclesiology, or missiological ecclesiology.[43] Though it has some parallels to the work done in the early 1960s, this new movement is much more explicit about bringing the connection of the *missio Dei* with the kingdom of God into conversation with particular congregations with respect to the emerging postmodern context.[44]

It is worth noting that the adjective "missional" reframes the whole discussion of what had previously been referred to as "church and mission." The latter formulation tends to introduce a dichotomy from which it is impossible to escape without tending to give precedence to one over the other. But the missional church invites a different conception: it sees the church as being missionary in its very nature. It is also a perception that views every context as a missional context, and every congregation as a missional congregation that is responsible to participate in God's mission in that context.[45] Developing this understanding as a missiological framework for thinking about congregations in context is the focus of the next section of this chapter.

Developing a Missiological Framework for Congregations in Context

Trinitarian Foundations for Missional Congregations

The missional church conversation draws deeply from the significant developments in the past few decades in trinitarian studies concerning an understanding of mission. Ironically, during the last half of the twentieth

---

42. Lesslie Newbigin, *Foolishness to the Greeks.*

43. Craig Van Gelder, *The Essence of the Church: A Community Created by the Spirit* (Grand Rapids: Baker, 2000).

44. Guder et al., ed., *Missional Church: A Vision for the Sending of the Church in North America.*

45. Richard H. Bliese and Craig Van Gelder, eds., *The Evangelizing Church: A Lutheran Contribution* (Minneapolis: Augsburg Fortress, 2005); Darrell L. Guder, *The Continuing Conversion of the Church,* The Gospel and Our Culture Series (Grand Rapids: Eerdmans, 2000); Guder et al., *Missional Church;* Van Gelder, *The Essence of the Church: A Community Created by the Spirit.*

century, at the same time that many churches in the West were beginning to drop words like *missions* or *mission* from their ecclesiastical vocabulary,[46] developments in trinitarian studies began to reshape the understanding of mission by directly connecting missiology with ecclesiology.

Several important theological contributions to understanding mission, ideas that grew out of the strong biblical theology tradition that was emerging in the 1930s and 1940s, became evident shortly after mid-century.[47] As I have noted above, one such development was represented in the work done by the former International Missionary Council (IMC). The 1947 conference at Whitby placed a focus on the kingdom of God, and the conference at Willingen in 1952 helped foster the creation of a framework for understanding the mission of God in the world as being in relationship to all three persons of the Godhead — Father, Son, and Holy Spirit. The result was to call the church to understand the church as being missionary by its very nature, and that this missionary nature is expressed as the church is sent by the Spirit into the world to participate in God's mission. This understanding was similar to that articulated by the Catholic Church at Vatican II in its document *Ad Gentes*,[48] but mission scholars on the Protestant side also contributed to this growing discussion.[49] What is intriguing is the remarkable level of convergence that was emerging by the 1980s toward these concepts among ecumenical, evangelical, Orthodox, and Roman Catholic missiologists.[50]

Now, after the Christian church has wrestled with these issues for fifty years, their fuller implications for understanding the missionary nature of congregations have begun to come into play. The extensive insights of trinitarian studies regarding mission are now being directed toward the

46. It is interesting to note that many previous doctoral programs in missiology have now changed their nomenclature to "intercultural studies" in order to move past the appearance of Western imperialism that is often associated with the word *mission*. This is now also the case at Fuller Theological Seminary.

47. This movement emerged as part of the neo-orthodox reaction to late-nineteenth-century liberalism and was greatly influenced by the work of Karl Barth, Emil Brunner, and the Niebuhr brothers.

48. See, especially, the "Decree on the Church's Missionary Activity, *Ad Gentes Divinitus*," as available in Austin Flannery, ed., *Documents of Vatican II* (Grand Rapids: Eerdmans, 1975).

49. Blauw, *The Missionary Nature of the Church*.

50. Scherer provides a helpful discussion of this convergence in *Gospel, Church, and Kingdom: Comparative Studies in World Mission Theology*.

field of ecclesiology — an understanding of the church. But it is important to note that there are two primary streams within trinitarian studies that inform this conversation.

The Oneness of God and the Economic Trinity

One stream is represented by the theological tradition that tends to focus on the one nature within the Godhead in relationship to the work of the three persons: the economic Trinity. This approach draws deeply from the Western Augustinian tradition, which re-emerged in the twentieth century substantially through the work of Karl Barth, and which stands behind the reconception of mission at Willingen. A key representative of this stream is Lesslie Newbigin.[51] The focus is on the *sending* work of God: God's sending the Son into the world to accomplish redemption, and the Father and Son's sending the Spirit into the world to create the church and lead it into participation in God's mission. This stream of trinitarian emphases comes directly into the missional church conversation in the United States through the work of the Gospel and Our Culture Network,[52] especially in the widely read volume produced in 1998 by six missiologists in that network, *Missional Church: A Vision for the Sending of the Church in North America.*[53]

The Interrelatedness of the Three Persons and the Emphasis on Perichoresis

Another emphasis, especially among those within the Eastern Orthodox tradition who draw on the Cappadocian Fathers, deals with the interrelatedness of the three persons within the Godhead. Recent trinitarian studies coming from this stream have worked with the social reality of the Godhead as being foundational for understanding the work of God in the world.[54] Created humanity reflects this social reality of God through the

51. Lesslie Newbigin, *The Open Secret: An Introduction to the Theology of Mission*, rev. ed. (Grand Rapids: Eerdmans, 1995), pp. 19-64.

52. Refer to http://www.gocn.org.

53. George Hunsberger, "Missional Vocation: Called and Sent to Represent the Reign of God," in Guder et al., *Missional Church: A Vision for the Sending of the Church in North America*, pp. 77-109.

54. John Zizioulas, *Being as Communion: Studies in Personhood and the Church* (Crestwood, NY: St. Vladimir's Seminary Press, 1985).

imago Dei: humans being created in the image of God.[55] The church, through the redemptive work of Christ, is created by the Spirit as a social community that is missionary by nature in being called and sent to participate in God's mission in the world. A recent work that reflects this trinitarian approach is Miroslav Volf's *After Our Likeness: The Church as the Image of the Trinity.*[56]

These two streams of trinitarian studies are contributing today to a renewed understanding of ecclesiology in relation to missiology. The fuller mission of God, understood as the *missio Dei* and related clearly to the redemptive work of God — as best expressed in the kingdom of God — is now being focused on congregations in context. This relationship provides the framework for understanding the nature, ministry, and organization of missional congregations.[57]

Missional Congregations Minister for the Sake of the World

It is clear from even a cursory reading of the book of Acts that God is passionate about getting the message of the good news about Jesus Christ out to the world. The Acts of the Apostles (it might better be titled "The Acts of the Spirit") provides an account of what the followers of Jesus experienced after the Spirit came upon them. The author structures this book around the Spirit's activities of ensuring that the gospel would be taken to everyone, all the way to the ends of the earth, and that it would address all of life — everyone, everywhere, everything. Jesus had made it clear that this was God's intention (Matt. 28:19-20; Acts 1:8), which should have introduced the regular activity of *wisdom/planning* to develop strategy for this purpose into the life of the early church. But the church struggled to bring this intent of God into its shared practices. This led to new voices, often from the margins, calling for *faith/discernment* to understand the working of the Spirit in leading the church into the world (see, especially, the church at Antioch).

---

55. Stanley Grenz, *The Social God and the Relational Self: A Trinitarian Theology of the Imago Dei, The Matrix of Christian Theology* (Louisville: Westminster John Knox Press, 2001), pp. 23-57.

56. Miroslav Volf, *After Our Likeness: The Church as the Image of the Trinity* (Grand Rapids: Eerdmans, 1998).

57. This is the position that I argue in *The Essence of the Church.*

Under the Spirit's leading, and often in spite of the church's reluctance, the gospel continued to cross boundaries and become contextualized within new cultural settings: the picture that begins to unfold is that of a church that is always *forming,* even as it also seeks to be *reforming.* The hermeneutic used by the author of Acts to shape the content of the book makes a direct connection between the sharing of the good news about Jesus with three results: (1) the spreading of the gospel message; (2) the growth of the church; and (3) the influence of the gospel and the growing church within various cultural contexts. There are regular references to growth taking place, both in terms of people coming to faith in Christ — *evangelizing* — and the broader redemptive influence of the gospel coming to bear on the social and cultural settings into which it became contextualized — *mission.*

Engaging in Discernment/Faith: Conflict, Disruption, Interruption, Surprise It is interesting to note that the expanded mission and growth of the church, under the leading of the Spirit, is characterized in Acts as much by conflict, disruption, interruption, and surprise as it is by any planned strategy. The Spirit empowers, teaches, and leads the church even when the church fails to discern, understand, or engage the fuller purposes of God in living out its missionary nature. Examples of this stand out in the book of Acts, including: (1) conflict between groups in the church that led to the recognition of the need to appoint more leadership (Acts 6); (2) a severe persecution that scattered the believers (Acts 8); (3) challenges to the dominant theology that came from the margins — from the church at Antioch (Acts 11); (4) a conflict between key figures Barnabas and Paul that led to the emergence of Paul as the primary leader (Acts 15); and (5) the Spirit redirecting the mission team to Macedonia through a vision (Acts 16).

In each of these situations the church encountered significant change that was neither planned nor anticipated. No strategy was in place that directly led to the growth of the church from these influences. Yet the church was led by the Spirit to move in new directions, which resulted each time in new growth taking place. The church in general, and congregations in particular, had to engage in faith/discernment to sort out issues related to the changes taking place in their contexts.

Question One: What is God doing? The issue of faith/discernment Working within the reality of the incomprehensibility of God, the church confesses that the world belongs to God: the world is God's creation, and it is the location where God's work continues to take place. With this in mind, congregations must seek to discern what the Spirit of God is doing in relationship to the dynamic changes taking place within a particular context; congregations must also discern where and how God's mission is unfolding. These activities of the Spirit often present congregations with fresh opportunities for ministry. But it is also important to note that God is at work in the world beyond the specific activities of congregations. Discerning this work of God is foundational for effective ministry as congregations are called and sent to participate in God's mission in the world.

Engaging in Wisdom/Planning: Developing an Intentional Strategy
There are indications that the new church in the Acts story used some intentional strategies within its evangelizing and mission. Being sent necessitates making strategic choices. For example, the twelve chose to go to the temple daily to proclaim the good news about Jesus, even when they were forbidden to do so. In a similar way, Paul and those working with him made it a regular practice to try to win converts in the synagogues from among Jews of the Diaspora as the foundation for planting reproducing churches in the key commercial centers of various provinces of the Roman Empire. As they would plant churches, they would move on to the next province, working their way westward.

The church's use of an intentional strategy for evangelizing normally results in expanded mission and the growth of the church, though the church may have been redirected in how it actually carried out the strategy. For example, Paul and his companions had an intentional plan to get to Ephesus in Asia at the beginning of the second journey, but they were redirected by the Spirit to Macedonia. Once there, they continued with the same strategy of entering synagogues in major cities of key provinces as the basis for starting new congregations.

Question Two: What does God want to do? The issue of wisdom/planning
God desires to bring all of life into a reconciled relationship. A congregation must seek to understand how the intent of God as expressed in the gospel can work itself out in a particular context to contribute to this ministry of reconciliation. Many changes in a context present challenges that the church must seek to address, and that requires careful planning. Con-

gregations need to be stewards of the good news of the gospel as they engage in focused missional planning in considering how to participate in what God wants to do in a particular context.

Two patterns are evident in the book of Acts. There is intentional, planned activity that leads to growth, a *strategy* illustrated in the work of the apostles and Paul's mission team. But there is also the *Spirit's leading* of the church in and through conflict, disruption, interruption, and surprise — into new and unanticipated directions that result in growth. It is essential for missional congregations to use *wisdom/planning* to develop a strategy, but it is also essential for them to consistently exercise *faith/discernment* in the midst of unexpected change. Those congregations will experience the leading of the Spirit through both processes.

The Gospel as Good News in Every Context

Evangelizing is the verbal sharing of the good news about Jesus Christ with others. It is to be engaged in both corporately and individually by the community of faith as that community seeks to participate fully in God's mission in the world. But in order to be good news, the gospel must make sense to those who are hearing it. It must reflect the promise that is embedded in the Incarnation: that the Word becomes flesh. In becoming flesh, Jesus Christ as the living Word became understandable, knowable, and accessible. The Incarnation is foundational to an understanding of the inherent translatability of both the gospel and the church.

Inherent Translatability of the Gospel   Jesus took on the particularity of his context as the incarnate good news. But even in his particularity, he retained his universal relevance.[58] This is part of the mystery of the good news of Jesus Christ. We find in its particularity the promise and the reality of its universality, what Newbigin refers to as the "scandal of particularity."[59] Just as Jesus, the living Word, took on the particularity of a specific context, so also is his gospel of good news inherently translatable into every particular cultural context with a view toward being universally appli-

---

58. This point is ably argued by Lesslie Newbigin in *The Gospel in a Pluralist Society*, pp. 80-115.

59. Newbigin, *The Gospel in a Pluralist Society*, p. 72.

cable.[60] This means that it can become good news to *everyone, everywhere,* and about *everything* in language and within cultural expressions that are understandable, knowable, and accessible. Through this inherent translatability, this same gospel of good news invites people to come to know the living and true God and to become enfolded into the worldwide church.

Inherent Translatability of the Church and Congregations   Just as the gospel is inherently translatable into every cultural context, so also the church and its congregations are inherently translatable in the same way. The church that is professed to be catholic (universal), as stated in the Apostles' and the Nicene Creeds, is able to find expression *everywhere.* Thus this same catholic church, through its multiple congregations, has the inherent ability to live *every place,* to become contextual within any and every setting. That point is developed in Lutheran theology this way: the finite is capable of the infinite *(finitum capax infiniti).*[61] A church, and its congregations, that is missionary by nature inherently seeks its contextuality: it seeks to become adaptive to every context in which it finds itself.[62]

These premises regarding the inherent translatability of the gospel and church have profound implications for congregations with regard to mission and evangelizing. Congregations are responsible for translating the good news of the gospel along with their own organizational reality into every cultural context they encounter. To do so requires that congregations plan strategically for this work even as they seek to discern the leading of the Spirit.

---

60. I use the concept of "translatability" here to describe the way in which the message of the gospel comes to expression within a specific culture, where it becomes embedded in and is expressed in relation to the language, worldview, and customs of that context. A helpful resource in understanding this point is Lamin O. Sanneh, *Translating the Message: The Missionary Impact on Culture,* American Society of Missiology Series, No. 13 (Maryknoll, NY: Orbis Books, 1989).

61. See a discussion of this in Carl E. Braaten and Robert W. Jenson, *Christian Dogmatics* (Philadelphia: Fortress Press, 1984), pp. 508f.

62. I develop this point in *The Essence of the Church: A Community Created by the Spirit,* pp. 118-20.

Spirit-Led Ministry in a Specific Cultural Context

A missiological framework is helpful to congregations as they relate to their contexts because contexts are always changing. Change is the very nature of life, and it is important for congregations to anticipate change in their contexts so that they can intentionally continue to recontextualize their ministries to address new conditions as they emerge. But the process of change in congregational contexts often varies in both scope and speed. Some contexts tend to change slowly over a long period of time, while others go through rapid change. Congregations need to rely on the leading of the Spirit in order to be prepared to address both kinds of change.

What is it about the church that it can, on the one hand, be creative and innovative in seeking out new opportunities for ministry, yet, on the other hand, can often be reactive and resistant to change? How are we to understand these dimensions as being part of the same church of Jesus Christ? It is helpful to examine some of the strategies that congregations often use in responding to changes that take place in their context. There are several approaches.

Relevance

Typical of many congregations is a response strategy to change that attempts to incorporate elements of the new cultural patterns into the life of the church. This can be a helpful instinct to pursue in working at contextualizing — or recontextualizing — a congregation's ministry as changes take place. However, this strategy can become problematical if a congregation relies on it too heavily to provide the solution for effective ministry. This is evident today in the pattern among many congregations who are always seeking for what might be called the "new and the next," for example, adding a contemporary worship service, creating projection capability in the auditorium, developing a small-group ministry, moving to a gift-based deployment process, and so forth.[63]

The tendency is to look for methods that work or to find models of ministry that can be applied in different locations. Most of these efforts are filled with good intentions and are usually informed by biblical perspec-

---

63. A helpful introduction to this concept can be found in Charles Trueheart, "Welcome to the Next Church," *Atlantic Monthly* 278, no. 2 (Aug. 1996): 37-52.

tives. But they often fall short of becoming adequately grounded in sufficient biblical and theological foundations. Furthermore, they often fail to take into adequate consideration insights from the historical Christian faith that can help guide them in responding to their changing context.

Resistance

Many congregations, in the face of significant change in their contexts, seek to stave off change via strategies of resistance. Depending on the changes that are taking place, this response often takes on a reactive character and style. Typically, these congregations make efforts to maintain the status quo or even, at times, to recover a former approach to ministry from another historical time. For example, some congregations continue to emphasize strict adherence to particular confessional standards as being the true interpretation of the faith. Typically, these congregations define themselves in opposition to other congregations that they perceive as having departed from the purity of the faith.

The manifest logic they use to justify an approach of resistance is that maintaining things the way they are is a function of being faithful and obedient to the call and purpose of God. The embedded logic of this approach is that familiarity with "our way of doing things" represents a biblical fidelity that will be protected at all costs. Congregations that take this approach to change usually fight an endless battle of retrenchment, and usually they are able to attract only similar disaffected people from other churches.

Adaptation

Another pattern among some congregations is to pursue a strategy of gradual adaptation: this is an impulse to navigate a mediating pathway between the polar opposites of *relevance* and *resistance*. The primary approach here is to attempt to steward the history and traditions of the congregation or the denomination in order to maintain the genius of the tradition while responding to a changing context. Unfortunately, the adaptation strategy usually tends to be too internally focused and thus ends up responding too slowly to effectively engage a changed context.

While tradition always carries insights into how God's truth was understood and applied in other contexts, the church that is being led by the

Spirit recognizes that any tradition must be a living and dynamic reality, and that it must take account of new realities. It is a complex matter to sort out the dynamics of a living tradition in such a way that it can continue to adapt to new circumstances while also being faithful to the values embedded in the tradition. This introduces the important relationship between the gospel and culture where the church is always both *forming* and *reforming.*

Missional Congregations as Always Forming and Reforming

Related to but different from the strategies of relevance, resistance, and adaptation is another approach, one that I am proposing in this chapter to be inherent to the missional church. It helps to address the problems inherent in these other responses to change in which the church either tends to overcontextualize (relevance or adaptation) or undercontextualize (resistance) its identity within a particular context. This alternative approach is based on the reality that the church is always both forming and reforming, and it reinforces the logic that the church always needs to be both confessional and missional. I propose that the historical Reformation watchword for the church needs the complement of another perspective:

> The church is always forming (missional) — *ecclesia semper formanda.*
> The church is always reforming (confessional) — *ecclesia semper reformanda.*

This is the deeper truth about the church and the ministry of the Spirit that needs to be emphasized, a truth that draws together the better impulses of the other strategies and places them within a polarity.[64] This polarity creates a dynamic and healthy tension between change and continuity, and between mission and confession. In this polarity the leading of the Spirit maintains the tension line between the challenge of recontextualizing a congregation's ministry in the midst of a changing context and the challenge of continuing to maintain the truths of the historic Christian faith as understood by the congregation. The issue is really one of finding

---

64. Barry Johnson, *Polarity Management: Identifying and Managing Unsolvable Problems* (Amherst, MA: HRD Press, 1992).

the right balance between the two logics of *outside in* and *inside out:* the former deals with forming, while the latter deals with reforming.

On the one hand, congregations forming even as they engage in reforming means that they seek to become contextualized even while they seek to maintain the historic Christian faith; this is an outside-in logic. In doing so, they invite change even while they seek to maintain continuity. The ministry of the Spirit helps congregations engage in both processes simultaneously. This is a polarity, with the actions of one informing the actions of the other. In fact, a congregation's ability to effectively reform will usually be in a direct relationship to its ability to form a renewed identity with regard to the changing context.

On the other hand, congregations are always reforming even as they are continuously forming. This is one of the great insights of the Protestant Reformation. The direction of this effort is to make congregations more responsive to their heritage by focusing on the inside-out logic. It is assumed that the church, by recovering something from its past through reform, will become more responsive to its present. While this can be profoundly true, as was demonstrated in the Protestant Reformation, the insight can become misdirected if the focus becomes too inward — too much toward what has been. There needs to be a balance between the two.

Aptitudes of Missional Congregations in Context[65]

The Spirit of God not only creates the church by calling it into existence, but also leads the church by sending it into the world to participate fully in God's mission in all of creation. This means that congregations are missionary by nature, and this nature requires them to develop a number of aptitudes as they engage in ministry.

Missional Congregations Learn to Read a Context as They Seek Their Contextuality   It is critical that congregations develop the ability to read a context. This is an aptitude that is inherent within the church that is mis-

---

65. A helpful introduction into practices is provided by Dorothy C. Bass, ed., *Practicing Our Faith: A Way of Life for a Searching People,* 1st ed. (San Francisco: Jossey-Bass, 1997); see also Miroslav Volf and Dorothy C. Bass, eds., *Practicing Theology: Beliefs and Practices in Christian Life* (Grand Rapids: Eerdmans, 2002).

sionary by nature. This means that the church will always seek to be contextual in engaging the context wherever it is located. To do so faithfully and effectively, the church must understand its context. The importance of this aptitude for reading a context has become increasingly recognized in recent years, and many tools have been developed to assist congregations in this task.[66] The key to *reading the context* should not be limited, however, to the sociology of a context; it should also include a theological reading of this sociology. This is where the faith/discernment task of answering the question "What is God doing?" comes into play. But the analysis of the context also brings the other responsibility into focus, the responsibility of wisdom/planning, which asks the question regarding a context: "What does God want to do?"

Missional Congregations Anticipate New Insights Into the Gospel As the gospel engages new cultures within various contexts, and as the translation of the gospel takes place in these new cultures, missional congregations anticipate new insights into the fuller meaning of the gospel. The very act of translating the gospel into new vernacular languages often opens up fresh understandings regarding its meaning. This was certainly the case in the New Testament church when the gospel was translated into a Hellenistic worldview at Antioch. The Hellenized version of understanding the gospel helped break Jewish Christianity out of its provincialism, and it later became the normative expression of the faith for centuries to come.[67]

Lamin Sanneh makes this same point regarding the translation of the gospel into the African context, where, despite all the transposed Western forms, the gospel found its indigenous voice within the cultures of the African peoples and gave new expressions to the faith and new forms to churches and their congregations.[68] This aptitude of missional congregations for anticipating new insights into the gospel flows out of the fact that

---

66. Ammerman, *Congregation and Community;* Ammerman et al., eds., *Studying Congregations: A New Handbook;* Bass, ed., *Practicing Our Faith;* Jackson W. Carroll, Carl S. Dudley, and William McKinney, *Handbook for Congregational Studies* (Nashville: Abingdon, 1986); Dudley and Ammerman, *Congregations in Transition: A Guide for Analyzing, Assessing, and Adapting in Changing Communities.*

67. Andrew F. Walls, *The Missionary Movement in Christian History: Studies in the Transmission of Faith* (Maryknoll, NY: Orbis Books, 1996).

68. Sanneh, *Translating the Message.*

they are also *forming* within their context. In doing so, they often release fresh resources for understanding the faith.

Missional Congregations Anticipate Reciprocity   One of the interesting things about the leading and teaching of the Spirit in congregations is that, over time, the gospel often brings about reciprocity. Reciprocity occurs when the cultural group that has brought the gospel into another context is itself changed by those who have received the gospel.[69] An example of this is the story of Peter's encounter with Cornelius (Acts 10): it is as much about the continuing conversion of Peter as it is about the conversion of Cornelius. Another example is the spillover effect of the persecution in Acts 8 that resulted — circumstantially, it would seem — in the development of the gentile church in Antioch (Acts 11). Given time, the gospel that was proclaimed at Antioch as "salvation by grace through faith plus nothing" came to be accepted as the gospel of the entire church (Acts 15).

In the latter example, what began on the margins came to the center. This is often the case with reciprocity. A current example of this in the United States can be seen in many of the newer immigrant communities. Coming from churches in what were former foreign mission fields, many new immigrant congregations are now relocating in established Anglo communities, both urban and rural, across the United States. These congregations are often inviting people to a deeper level of understanding of the gospel's call for reconciled unity between Christians; they also often bring their own missionary activity into the United States, where they see their new location as needing to hear the gospel, once again, for the first time.

Missional Congregations Understand That They Are Contextual, and Thus Also Particular   Our language illustrates this point whenever we refer to a congregation as a *local church*. Local means that, of necessity, a congregation is particular to its time and place. While it is also catholic, bearing the full marks of the church universal and the historic Christian faith, it is profoundly local in contextualizing these realities to the community it seeks to serve. The church, as a local church, can only come into existence in its relationship to the reality of culture and cultures within a particular context.

---

69. Sanneh, *Translating the Message.*

This means that there is always a certain provisional character to the church as it lives within a context. As contexts change, the church should expect to change, even as it attempts to live out the tension inherent within being faithful to the gospel while being responsive to the context. This point introduces the important issue of how *models* function with regard to congregations. In reality, there can be no model congregation. While there can be illustrative examples of contextualized congregations that might help inform others, no congregation can function as a model for others. It is important to remember that it is the work of the Spirit to lead a congregation to contextualize itself within its particular location.

Missional Congregations Understand That Ministry Is Always Contextual, and Thus Also Practical   Missional congregations understand that the practice of ministry is always normed by Scripture, but they also understand that this takes place in the particular contexts that they serve. Just as congregations are always contextual, their ministries are also always contextual: the Spirit leads congregations within particular contexts. Ministry can take place only in relationship to a particular context, and, as ministry takes place, congregations develop specific practices for that context.

This means that all forms of ministry are going to bear the patterns and shape of the culture in which a congregation is ministering. The necessary practices that it develops are the practical outworking of the ministry. This point introduces the important issue of how *programs* function in congregations. In reality, there can be no common program that works the same in each congregation and context. While a basic programmatic framework may inform the development of ministry, each congregation is best served by thinking carefully about how such a program might need to be adapted to fit its particular ministry and the context it serves.

Missional Congregations Understand That Doing Theology Is Always Contextual, and Thus Also Perspectival   Congregations articulate their confessed faith in what is generally referred to as "theology." This is an understanding that is usually shaped by historical confessional perspectives, but missional congregations understand that these perspectives have embedded within them elements of the culture and context in which they were formulated. While theological expressions bear witness to the larger reality of God's truth, they must always be understood as being tied to time and place. And while the theological expressions of a particular time

41

and place can have great relevance for many other contexts, there is always a need to engage in interpreting and translating them when moving from one context to another.

This point introduces the important issue of how *confessions* function in congregational life. In reality, there can be no universal confession: every congregation needs to learn how to confess the faith in its particular context. While it needs to draw on historical confessions to engage in confessing the faith, a congregation needs to actively engage in translating the themes and insights of historical confessions in order to address the issues within its own context.

Missional Congregations Understand That Organization Is Always Contextual, and Thus Also Provisional   As a missional congregation develops organizational forms to carry out its ministry and to structure its life, it must understand that these forms also bear the imprint of particular contexts. Therefore, organization in congregations is always contextual and provisional in character. While there are biblical principles that function across a wide range of contexts, the particular forms that emerge must be seen as being particular to specific contexts. This is part of the good news of the gospel that congregations are able to relate to any culture and to any context.

The challenge is for the church to bring the gospel into diverse contexts as it allows the leading of the Spirit to give birth to approaches that are informed by the historic Christian faith, while it also reflects the realities of the context in which congregations are planted. This point introduces the important issue of how *polities* are to function in congregations. In reality, there can be no standardized polity. Polity needs to focus more on guiding principles rather than prescribed practices, because polities need to be adaptive and flexible as they consciously take context and culture into consideration in the midst of the processes of forming and reforming.

Summary

Today we are experiencing the return of the congregation to theological education. We are also experiencing the connection of missiology to ecclesiology within the missional church conversation. These two developments offer the promise that we as Christians will think more carefully about congregations in context; they also offer the promise that we will reconceive the discipline of missiology. In this chapter I have argued that missiology in the twenty-first century needs to mine its rich heritage and draw on its multiple resources in order to develop substantive theological foundations and focused strategies as it helps congregations understand and engage the contexts in which they are located and which they seek to serve. The result will be a focus on the missional church in context and on congregations developing contextual missiologies.

CHAPTER 2

The Missional Congregation in Context

Scott Frederickson

The relationship between a congregation and its context usually works between the two polarities of, on the one hand, being *undercontextualized* or, on the other hand, being *overcontextualized*. The former leans heavily, if not exclusively, toward privileging the congregation; in the latter, the congregation tends to become subsumed under its context. In this chapter I will draw out some of the implications of an authentic relationship between what I will refer to as a "missional congregation" and the context in which it is located.

The following two examples show the intricate relationship between the three realities of congregation, mission, and context. The first is from the early nineteenth century, when mission often had a barely discernible relationship to context. In the early history of Christian missions in the Pacific Northwest of the United States during the early 1800s, when missionaries came into a new context of the indigenous people, many of the native tribes held to their belief that god continued to live and be born each year with the running of the salmon. When the missionaries arrived, they ignored this part of the native religious context and tradition; they proceeded to try to convert the natives with the crucifix. Since the cross was not part of their context and was foreign to their religious beliefs, the natives did not respond; so the missionaries advocated their destruction. Lost in this struggle over the symbolic meaning of the cross, however, was the parallel between the Native Americans' symbolic understanding of the salmon as reflecting religious power and the Christians' use of the fish for centuries as the prime symbol of the Christian community. Instead of choosing dialogue and reflection along this parallel path, the missionaries flexed their power. This is an example of a context being underused by a mission, that is, an "undercontextualized church."

The second example is much more recent: Lakewood Church in Houston, Texas. In July 2005 the congregation opened a new worship facility that had formerly housed a professional basketball team and could seat well over 19,000 people at one time. It is presently the largest worship venue in the United States. According to published reports, its leader, Joel Osteen, had this to say about it when it opened: "How do you like our new home? It looks pretty good, doesn't it? This is a dream come true." He later remarked to reporters that the facility is a "Texas-sized sanctuary."[1] And in order to help people attend concerts at the new facility, the church placed a direct link to Ticketmaster on the front page of its website. What was interesting about its inaugural publicity was the absence of any references to God, Jesus Christ, the Holy Spirit, or any of the other traditional ways in which a congregation does mission in context. There is little doubt that this congregation is Texas-sized, but perhaps it is also a bit overcontextualized.

By setting up these examples as polarities, I wish to argue that attending to the distinction between a missional congregation and its context is a key to understanding how God works in the world. A missional congregation has for me a different and more useful value than does a congregation in mission. Often the word "mission" is used in the sense of a project or something that a congregation does, a view summed up by Wolfhart Pannenberg:

> the church calls itself apostolic not only in the sense that it was founded by the message of the apostles but also in the sense that it partakes of the spirit and mission of the apostles, and that in spite of the unrepeatable nature of the apostolate and the apostolic age it continues this mission through history. . . .[2]

"Mission" here seems to indicate something that is being done by the apostles and, more importantly, something somehow separate from "message."

---

1. www.msnbc.msn.com [accessed July 17, 2005].

2. Wolfhart Pannenberg, "The Significance of Eschatology for an Understanding of the Apostolicity and Catholicity of the Church," in *The Church* (Philadelphia: Westminster, 1983), p. 48.

I want to argue that a missional congregation tries not to have such a bifurcation of its message and mission. To be missional in this way is to understand that message and context are intricately related. Missional congregations live out their identity as Christian communities in close relationship to their contexts without, on the one hand, succumbing to the context or, on the other hand, denying the context on the basis of their identity, history, or tradition. To be missional in this sense is to understand how God works within a context without destroying the context. Beyond the question "What is the relationship between the missional congregation and context?" is the more important question: "What does it mean for the missional congregation to be contextual?"

For its resources, the missional congregation has at least two extremely valuable and central theological doctrines that begin to provide a basis for developing a contextual missiology, and that arise from the very life and being of God: an understanding of the Triune God and a radically deep Christology. From the outset we should note that mission is never ancillary to the missional congregation; rather, it is the very heart, the flaming center, of its own life and being. The missional congregation, regardless of its various contexts, cannot be other than what it is — missional — because it arises from the very being of its God, and from how it understands God to live in and for the world. The missional congregation does not "do mission" after its identity and life have been set; rather, the missional congregation is defined precisely both *in* and *as* the mission of God for the sake of the world.

A Perichoretic Understanding of God

The recent surge of trinitarian theology, loosely encapsulated under the rubric of a "social doctrine of the Trinity," has not been lost on the missional congregation.[3] One of the most helpful models for the missional congregation has come out of the work of the Orthodox theologian John Zizioulas and his understanding of the being of God in communion. Zizioulas's work, based on the trajectories of the early Greek fathers, provides the missional congregation with a doctrine of God intricately related

---

3. Scott Frederickson, "Ecclesiology of God: The Divine and Human Congregation" (unpublished dissertation, Luther Seminary, St. Paul, MN, 2001); see, especially, ch. 1 for a review of significant theological literature on the social doctrine of the Trinity.

to God's own being. In this way the missional congregation understands the importance of relationship in the being of God, and the congregation can use its own relationship with its context as a way to participate in God's mission for the sake of the world.[4]

God is one being in three persons. Zizioulas uses the word "person" in a way that differs from the usual psychological conception. A person is not an individual per se, but is by definition someone who exists within relationships. He says: "Being a person is fundamentally different from being an individual or a 'personality,' for a person cannot be imagined in himself but only within his relationships."[5] It is important to note that this definition of personhood goes a long way toward extrapolating a doctrine of the Trinity. Since God is three persons, not three individuals or personalities, we must note that all three persons of the Trinity, whether the Creator Father, the Son, or the Holy Spirit, are defined within their relationships, primarily their relationships with each other.

These relationships do not meld them into some other person; rather, they maintain their uniqueness within the relationship. "The mystery of being a person lies in the fact that here otherness and communion are not in contradiction but coincide. Truth as communion does not lead to the dissolving of the diversity of beings into one vast ocean of being, but to the affirmation of otherness in and through love."[6] Within the Triune God, Je-

---

4. I wish to note the irony of using an Orthodox theologian for the discussion of missiology. Without a doubt, missiology is the forgotten child of Orthodox theology. Even now the Orthodox Church struggles to grow in its capacity to be a vessel of God's work in the world (see Vigen Guroian, "The Crisis of Orthodox Ecclesiology," in Carl E. Braaten and Robert W. Jenson, eds., *The Ecumenical Future*). This is a shame, because they have beautiful theological resources in which to thrive. But the absence of an ethical drive in its theology has led Orthodoxy to leave these resources unused. What the Orthodox Church — and other churches that suffer from the same malady — need in order to reinvigorate is the sense of "sentness" by God to the world. God has sent congregations into the world to participate in the world (this is Pannenberg's definition of apostolicity above), and many congregations do not live from that sentness; rather, they choose to cleave only to themselves. Any sense of mission, expansion, sentness, or growth is completely lost on them. I have argued elsewhere (see my dissertation, ch. 2) that the theology of the Orthodox Church needs to expand to include this missiological perspective. In my work I often use the phrase "life and being" in order to expand on the Orthodox understanding of God's being: this is to note that there is a purpose for God, and that purpose is to bring life from God to the world.

5. John D. Zizioulas, *Being as Communion* (Crestwood, NY: St. Vladimir's Seminary Press, 1985), p. 105.

6. Zizioulas, *Being as Communion*, p. 106.

sus is still Jesus, the Spirit is the Spirit, and the Creator Father the Creator Father, but now constituted as one God. "Otherness" is the distinction that allows us to identify one from the other; "communion" is how we see them to be related. Zizioulas uses St. Basil to highlight how this can be: "The *nature* of God is communion. This does not mean that the persons have an ontological priority over the one substance of God, but that the one substance of God coincides with the communion of the three persons."[7]

This "coincidence" is the key to understanding a doctrine of the Trinity that maintains both an identity of the persons involved as well as the experience of the persons' relationships. The "coinciding" provides affirmation of Rahner's famous trinitarian rule: the immanent is the economic trinity.[8] In reality, we experience only the economic Trinity, that is, in Zizioulas's terms, the "communion of the three persons"; however, we do understand that distinctions and differentiations in God are important (how else can we explain Luke 4:1?).[9] So the persons of the Triune Godhead do not dissolve when they relate, but they hold to their uniqueness within the relationships we experience as God. Because Jesus coincides so deeply with the Holy Spirit and the Creator Father, the concepts that "God saves" and "Jesus saves" have the same economic result for God, though we understand that the immanent God is more than just the economy of salvation.

The Eastern Church has at its disposal a term for this coincidental understanding of the three persons of God in one being: *perichoresis.* John of Damascus seems to have first coined the term that points to such a deep-seated, intricate relationship of the three persons being one. Perichoresis understands that God so coincides in the three persons as to live and act as one being. Alister McGrath defines this in English as "'mutual interpenetration' . . . . It refers to the manner in which the three persons of the Trinity relate to one another."[10] This perichoretic understanding of the triune life and being of God will go a long way toward setting parameters regarding how we can understand that the missional congregation is contextual.

---

7. Zizioulas, *Being as Communion,* p. 134.

8. Karl Rahner argued famously that how God is (immanent Trinity) is how God does (economic Trinity); see *The Trinity* (New York: Seabury Press, 1974).

9. See Zizioulas for his analysis of St. Basil the Great's work in this area, *Being as Communion,* p. 134.

10. Alister E. McGrath, *Christian Theology: An Introduction,* 2nd ed. (Malden, MA: Oxford Publishers, 1997), p. 298.

Both the context and the missional congregation exist as "persons," albeit in the general sense of a community: that is, they have their own unique ways of living and being as communities. But the missional congregation *is* the context in the same way that the context *includes* the missional congregation. This is a key concept to grasp if we are to understand the importance of *perichoresis,* which I am arguing for in this chapter. God loves context (as it is an outcome of a radical Christology, I will argue below), and a missional congregation is one of the ways God uses to reveal that love to the context. But this means that the missional congregation is part and parcel of the context: it can provide the discernment the context needs to live out its God-createdness.

The missional congregation also carries with it the distinctiveness of bearing God's love as its raison d'etre and becomes the catalyst within the compound, to borrow an analogy from chemistry. Some of their behaviors and attitudes may be similar, some may not; but in each case there is enough distinction to note that a context does not equal a missional congregation. Nor does the missional congregation equal the community of the context in which it resides. The results of that relationship between a missional congregation and its context provide a new way of living and being for each community. It is not necessary for the symbiosis to work perfectly. In fact, given the examples I have begun with, there is often too much of one side or the other, so that there is no coinciding at all. This coinciding result comes about as each community (the context and the missional congregation) lives from itself in direct relationship with the other. On the one hand, neither community subsumes the other completely; on the other hand, each community avoids the coinciding.

Consider Luke 4 to see how this works for God, and analogously the missional congregation and its context. At the beginning of the story of Jesus' temptation, it is clearly the Spirit who leads Jesus to the wilderness; but it is Jesus, not the Spirit, who is tempted in the story. Yet the catalyst for Jesus' conquering of temptation is the Spirit, and Jesus consistently acknowledges that in his quotations of Scripture. Who is tempted here? The Spirit? Jesus? Both? Luke seems to argue that at this point it is almost impossible to distinguish Jesus from the Spirit in terms of motivation, though Jesus does do the actual speaking to Satan.

It is this "mutual interpenetration" that best explains the relationship between a missional congregation and its context as they coincide together in space and time. The God of Jesus Christ, in the power of the

Spirit, has created and redeemed this coinciding. The very incarnation of God into the Son and the resurrection of the Son to God is the way Christianity claims the context. This means that a missional congregation and its context are related. The missional congregation claims the reality of the context (the Incarnation) while not being subsumed wholly beneath it, in order to show the context a deeper reality (the Resurrection), namely, that God is constantly at work in the world.

Notice what this does to both the missional congregation and the context and its community. After a while it becomes difficult to discern which partner in the relationship is responsible for the coincidental results. Has the missional congregation had such an effect on the context that the community at large now seems to be a result of the missional congregation? Or has the context and the community at large so influenced the missional congregation that there no longer seems to be any distinction between the two?

The doctrine of *perichoresis* that I assert (following the leads of St. Basil, John of Damascus, and John Zizioulas) is that there are real distinctions and differences that lead to our ability to distinguish between the Creator Father, the Son, and the Holy Spirit. At the same time, the experience of oneness prevails because the three so deeply coincide with each other. In conversation and discernment, the missional congregation and its context relate to each other — at times positively, at other times negatively — but in neither case does this allow one or the other to dominate completely. The context can be challenged by the missional congregation, and the context can "hear" the challenge because the congregation is part of the context. At the same time, the context can challenge the missional congregation and the congregation can "hear" the context because it understands itself to be part of the context. A missional congregation and its context may behave in the same way: there are real differences and distinctions between the two, but the experience of their engagement provides the opportunity for the Triune God to be at work for the sake of the world.

A Radically Deep Christology

"The Word became flesh and dwelt among us" (John 1:14). With this brief phrase the life and being of the second person of the Trinity — Jesus the Christ, the Son of the Creator Father, advocate with the Holy Spirit —

opens a world of possibility and hope to the missional congregation. This radically deep Christology, centered in a thoroughgoing doctrine of the Incarnation, becomes the impetus for the missional congregation to exude what I refer to as its "missionality." The life and being of the missional congregation receives its formation and call from the activity of the Triune God, which is focused in the Son, Jesus Christ.

A strong emphasis on the Incarnation has been a hallmark of Christian theology since its earliest days, most notably in the work of Athanasius. His famous dictum ("He was made human so we might be made God") is not only an understanding of *what* God wished to do in Jesus but also *how* God accomplished God's goal.[11] Assuming from this radically deep, incarnational Christology that God continues to work in that same way of entering into reality in order to make it new, the missional congregation is free to explore the newness it has received. The missional congregation lives through God's remaking of it in Jesus Christ; and, by extension of that relationship, the context also experiences a remaking.

Baptism within a missional congregation reveals the understanding of how God works in the world. Calling on God to enter into the lives of its people, through the power of the Holy Spirit of Jesus Christ, the missional congregation understands its formation as a community to be grounded in the life, death, and resurrection of the Son. Each person who comes to the baptismal font comes expecting to meet God.[12] And when God *condescends* (incarnates) to a person, the world of that person — and by extension the world of the congregation — expands to infinite possibilities. These possibilities, depending on the diverse gifts and callings, will seek to be enacted. Not all possibilities will be enacted, as probability must also enter the picture; but there is no theoretical limitation to what the person, and persons within a community (the missional congregation), can attain. Baptism is the affirmation by the missional congregation that such possibilities, activated by God, promised in the resurrection of the Son, and empowered by the blessing of the Spirit, can now be realized by that congregation.

What happens to missional congregations that do not realize all of their possibilities, or perhaps only a few? In the midst of such ambiguity

11. Athanasius's "On the Incarnation," in *Christology of the Later Fathers*, ed. E. R. Hardy (Philadelphia: Westminster, 1954), p. 107.

12. For those traditions that practice infant baptism, this assumption is carried by those other than the baptismal candidate.

and despair, the promise lives again in the celebration of Holy Communion. The missional congregation gathers around the Lord's table in order to re-energize and refocus on the unlimited possibilities granted to each partner of the congregation in his or her own baptism. For the missional congregation, Holy Communion is more about moving into the future to experience realized possibilities than it is about re-enacting the death of the Son. Though the future of the missional congregation can be realized only through the death of the Son, the promise that is highlighted in the words "for as often as we eat from this bread and drink from this cup, we preach the Lord's death until he comes again" (1 Cor. 11:26) is the cornerstone and foundation of the community. Without participating in the possibilities God has granted in baptism to each partner within the community, the missional congregation loses the anchor to its deepest reality. Holy Communion frees the missional congregation to continue to explore its possibilities both positively and negatively within the world as it lives in the promise God has granted in Christ Jesus.

From these theological resources — a deeply relational understanding of the Triune God and a deeply incarnational understanding of God's activity in Jesus Christ — we can begin to address the relationship that a missional congregation may have with its context. Again, my goal is to open up possibilities for how the missional congregation might be contextual without sacrificing its identity as a *missional* Christian community. The congregation in mission has too often succumbed to complete enculturation, so that that community is no longer defined by its mission but is swallowed up completely by its context. We must maintain the distinctive clarity of these two theological resources that reveal how God has addressed context, and we must do so without being completely overwhelmed by or lost in it. And that should go a long way toward lighting a path for missional congregations to more adequately live in, with, and against their context.

Three Components of Context — and a Fourth Estate

There are actually two components to a context that I wish to highlight. We could add many more, but a significant part of one is so important to North America that it deserves to stand by itself as a component of context. The "fourth estate," as I have called it, is not so much an actual estate in political and economic terms as it is a state of mind, particularly concerning the question of leadership. The components of a context that I want to emphasize are the demographics of the people involved in the community, especially the economic indicators and the ways they influence attitudes and behaviors within a context. The other piece of a context is its ecclesial landscape — and how religious demographics are spaced within it. Along with these variables, the developer's mindset plays a part in the context, and we will address a couple of issues that a missional congregation should be aware of as it strives for relationship with its context.[13]

The demographic component, broadly construed, defines much of a context with regard to a particular community. Since the missional congregation lives in relationship with God at work in the world through the Spirit, the congregation is free to assess the demographics. The questions addressed by demographics reveal areas where missional congregations can have a deep and abiding impact, regardless of how they understand the possibilities granted to them by God. As congregations continue to discern their callings in relationship to their contexts, they will begin to see which demographic patterns of their community have greater importance for them. The reader should note that I am advocating the largest definition of community possible, and in this sense I prefer to speak of *communion*, that is, what all communities experience together. However, I do hold that there are also distinct, specific communities to be discerned. Although a missional congregation would see itself as a "communion of communities," we should also remember that a missional congregation itself is a community of a larger communion, namely, of God's ongoing creative enterprise in the world.

As an example, Michael Slaughter, in his book *Unlearning Church*, refers to a certain congregation that has sensed a ministry to a particular demographic community within its own communion. The congregation is Mission Hills Church of Littleton, Colorado. The leader, Doug Zerbst, offers this reflection:

> At the Edge, a worship and teaching ministry designed to reach the
> twenty-something generation, we've had to unlearn the idea that ev-

---

13. In my own tradition, the leader of a mission congregation is often called a "mission developer." Although I think the term "developer" is fine for an understanding of leadership, the use of "mission" in this way does not do justice to my argument as seeing mission, not as something ancillary to a congregation, but rather as something that is institutional and constitutional to a congregation's very life and being.

erything has to be polished and produced. Postmoderns do not trust things that are slick. They want authenticity above other values. For postmoderns, process is as important as product, if not more so. We are always struggling to meet people where they are and help them go with Jesus to where they need to be without seeming contrived.[14]

Zerbst and his communion have made some demographic choices for one of their communities. Whatever the actual definition of "postmodern" is, the communion of Mission Hills Church is offering a ministry that they believe will appeal to a particular community, a twenty-something cohort that has become their focus. It is important to see that demographics have played a key role for this congregation in understanding what kind of ministry it is offering. Presumably, people in older generations, those who value "product" over "process," will probably not find the Edge worship to their liking, nor will it resolve their spiritual yearning.[15] This is a key value in understanding the importance of the demographic component in a particular context. Demographics are not only about race or ethnicity; they also include the moral and spiritual values that a group of people hold. Missional congregations will pay attention to such demographics in order to better read their particular context. In reading its context, the congregation of Mission Hills was not only reading itself but was also reaching beyond itself to those who were not yet part of its communion.

It's true that, given a big enough context, every demographic might be represented to one degree or another. The point of understanding demographics is never to encapsulate an entire context but to reveal the tendencies that a context has. The Edge worship, for example, is obviously not designed for the local senior-citizen housing complex. But we can see how congregations can pick and choose from various demographics in order to offer ministry within a particular context. How the particular demographics of a context are dispersed can go a long way toward helping a missional congregation live within it. The missional congregation living from its creation in a Triune God deeply committed to the world would do well not to limit its context in order to achieve an idol such as "success" or to blas-

---

14. Michael Slaughter, *Unlearning Church* (Loveland, CO: Group Publishing, 2002), p. 125.

15. In my experience, generations often overlap, and some of the people most seeking after the experiences designed for "twenty-somethings" have long since passed that decade of life.

pheme God by ignoring those on the margins of the context. Though the God of Jesus Christ deeply cares for the world and all that it is, the biblical witness is clear that caring for those on the margins of contexts is what makes up our living from the being and life of God (Mark 12:29-31).

Economics, though technically within the realm of demographics, plays a huge part in the missional congregation's relationship to a context. And the United States of America, even though it is supposedly classless, places great value on wealth as a way to distinguish various groups within society, culture, and various contexts. Missional congregations would do well to discern the economic realm of the context in which it finds itself. This particular component of a context is not only involved in how money is spent and made but also in how it is valued and used as social currency. Wal-Mart and McDonald's and other corporations of their economic power have gone a long way toward standardizing communities in this country. As Wal-Mart brings its service jobs and blue smocks into communities across this country, and McDonald's brings standards of cleanliness and economy to restaurants worldwide, they have brought the world together in a rather strange way: we are all consumers of the same products. With such similarity, it would seem that economics would not be much of a distinguishing factor for a congregation in discerning its relationship with its context. However, what is astounding is the difference in the value placed on economics in particular contexts, something the missional congregation must pay attention to.

All contexts, especially in the Western world, seem to be driven by monetary issues — entertainment, sports, leisure, tourism, and so forth. Contexts where survival is of the utmost importance can (and I emphasize *can*) live without a fixation on money, though admittedly these are becoming less and less visible. Certain contexts, by virtue of their status on Maslow's hierarchy of needs, have the luxury of dealing with money; other contexts, threatened by starvation, poor health, and lack of sanitation, must deal with more basic needs.

In his recent book *Congregations in America*, where he reviews the data of the National Congregations Study, Mark Chaves points to an interesting statistic that shows the importance of economics. He reports on what congregations in the United States actually do in spending their money, and, even more significantly, he surveys with some accuracy the numbers of people involved in congregations. Information provided by the survey is revealed in two ways: first, it can include all the individuals in congregations (using statistical sampling with its attendant correctives); second, the statistical information can be grouped by congregations. Thus, according to Chaves, if you take all the congregations in the United States, the median income of each congregation is $60,000; but if you look at the income statistics based on individuals, the median income of congregations of individuals who actually attend church rises to $258,000.[16]

What does this mean? This statistic means that most people in the United States attend worship in congregations whose budget is a quarter of a million dollars. Note this distinction: there are many congregations that do not have budgets that approach this figure, but the actual number of people who attend these congregations make up less than half of all people who attend congregations. In other words, there may be plenty of congregations that do not have quarter-million-dollar budgets, but fewer than one-half of people who actually go to church attend them. Also note that the quarter-million-dollar budget is more than enough, in most cases, to supply the congregation with a full-time, fully credentialed leader of their choosing. This is a key to understanding a particular context for a missional congregation. Most of the people in a context will attend worship in a congregation whose budget approaches the median of $258,000. For a congregation just beginning its ministry in a particular context, this could be daunting. For a congregation seeking to live out its missional nature, this will be important to note as people will participate based on how stable the congregation's finances are. Living out a congregation's missional nature seems to require, at some point, a quarter of a million dollars.[17] A missional congregation does not have to be defined by its finances, but its finances are part of why people are in the congregation. Whether this is a positive or negative thing is a question we will leave for another time.

Besides demographic — and especially economic — indicators, a

16. Mark Chaves, *Congregations in America* (Cambridge, MA: Harvard University Press, 2004), p. 232.

17. It is true that Chaves's work does not say when the median (and it is a median number, and no congregation is required to attain it) must be reached; but it is interesting to note that most people attend worship in well-established, funded congregations in this country. Whether a missional congregation chooses to minister in spite of that, or in collusion with that, it behooves the congregation to note that most people worship in congregations that can support themselves. They may not attend because of money, but money does seem to allow them to attend.

missional congregation must note the ecclesiastical landscape of its particular context. In the heyday of denominationalism, this was a fairly easy landscape to survey. A denomination looked at a growing area — a new suburb of Philadelphia, say — and asked whether they had a congregation located there. If they did not, they would designate the location a "domestic mission field," and they would start up a congregation there and encourage it to grow. Where to place a congregation was decided by asking questions such as, Are there people of our denomination living there? Do Roman Catholics have a parish there? How about the Methodists, Presbyterians, and the Episcopalians? Finding a space for a localized franchise of the denomination's brand was deemed a relatively easy task. Even easier to answer was the question of what kind of ministry the new congregation would offer.

The answer to that question was quite simple: everything. Anything and everything that a Christian congregation ever would or could offer was to be the ministry program of that new congregation. What would make it different from the other congregations would be its denominational branding. So all congregations would offer the same ministries of worship, educational indoctrination for children, ministry experiences for youth, and fellowship and service opportunities for adults. The differences between them would be those that reside within the confessional traditions of the congregations. Church historian Martin Marty has called this effect "multitudinism": every congregation offers every ministry conceivable, each according to its own theological and ecclesiological principles.[18] That was all there was to surveying the ecclesiastical landscape until the late 1970s and early 1980s.

Over the last several decades, however, something has changed in the ecclesiastical landscape of the United States. Although the decline of denominationalism is a part of that change, the change is much broader than that. Various thinkers have suggested that the change is characterized by a "flight from authority" to "small-group renaissance" to conservative, nondenominational communions.[19] While these descriptions, among

18. See Martin Marty, *The New Shape of American Religion* (New York: Harper Books, 1959), for his take on congregations and their ministries through the early part of the twentieth century.

19. See Jeffrey Stout, *The Flight from Authority* (Notre Dame, IN: University of Notre Dame Press, 1981), for a philosophical treatment of the change; Robert Wuthnow, *Restructuring of American Religion* (Princeton, NJ: Princeton University Press, 1988), for a sociologi-

many others, of the direction churches have been taking may be accurate to a point, the major change in the ecclesiastical landscape over the past three decades may be summed up in one word: consumerism. Religion in the United States went from something into which one was born to something that one chose. Religious faith and belief went from being a family and communal heirloom into a product that was treated like any other product in the marketplace. Just as the people of the United States are nothing if not able consumers, religion, de facto, became a consumer product. And when it did, the ecclesiastical landscape changed.

For the missional congregation, this change has brought about significant opportunities as well as significant challenges, especially to any categories of its identity outside of *consumer* categories. As I will discuss below, the missional congregation may today explore new communities within its communion, both at the largest and smallest levels, because it is no longer necessarily constrained by tradition. But there is a less positive note as well: the very things tradition brought with it, of which community and communion are not the least important, now must be asserted, defined, and discerned. This includes determining everything else that goes along with choosing a product rather than accepting a given heritage, including how those on the margins of the community fare, which is not a trivial matter. The missional congregation undoubtedly works harder to maintain where it is than any congregation did before the advent of consumerism.

It becomes much more difficult to minister within a congregation in a world such as ours. It is no longer enough to provide worship for our own people in the ways the tradition has come down to us. Now we must view worship as the means by which people can receive enough value to retain their loyalty to our congregation. It is no longer enough to provide care and concern for people who are members; now we must make care and concern available to all people, regardless of their status in the community. It is no longer enough to push the latest denominational program or ministry; now we must provide programs and ministries that connect to people and their lives. This has led to a great change in the ecclesiastical landscape across all contexts and communities in North America.

---

cal treatment of the change; and Dean Kelley, *Why Conservative Churches Are Growing* (New York: Harper Books, 1972), for a theological treatment. No one specific idea can carry the entirety of the change, including the concept of "consumerism."

The Reawakening of the Great Commission

At times the use of Jesus' Great Commission in Matthew is nothing more than biblical lip service to indiscriminate growth for crass reasons. But one of the major positive advances for congregations in this shift toward consumer Christianity has been the focus on growing disciples, and on introducing people back to Jesus Christ. Consumerism has asked questions of Christian identity, vision, and mission, and many people have discovered that the age of denominationalism did not do a good enough job of leading them to live as followers of a living God. This reawakening does not make evangelizing from the Great Commission another task, or job, that a congregation must perform. Rather, as congregations have understood themselves to be missional in their very being and life from the radical Christology of the in-relationship Triune God, the Great Commission can now be an active component of the congregation's life.

For example, congregations that understand themselves to be missional — rather than opting to be in mission — may be prepared to take seriously the religious and spiritual needs of people who were previously overlooked in a particular context. I remember that, during my first tour of Willow Creek Church in Barrington, Illinois, in 1988, I asked where the cross was in the worship service, and was told: "We found people didn't like that. So we don't have one." What was interesting about that response was not that people do not like the cross (even Luther knew that!), but that they had taken the time to discover that people didn't like it. More astonishing was the fact that they had tried to address the needs of those people rather than any need of God or the cross. There is a danger here of overcontextualizing the Christian faith so that it becomes wholly subsumed within the culture. I should note, however, that Willow Creek, regardless of how one feels about its accommodation to culture, understands this to be who they are, not what they have to do. It certainly can run the risk of homogeneity, of complete capitulation to culture, and thus of a disregard for the universal yet diverse aspects of traditional Christian faith. But it can also offer the freedom of the gospel in Christ Jesus to people who need it and have never heard it before.

Though many may disagree with Willow Creek's choice and those of others, congregations everywhere have begun to ask questions about their traditions, beliefs, and values, their heritage, architecture, rituals, and practices. The upshot of this discernment is that, as congregations have made choices, they have begun to move away from providing all kinds of ministries to providing those that seem most compelling or useful. In discerning their context, congregations have begun to offer certain new kinds of ministries, certain new kinds of worship music and styles, certain new projects and programs — at the same time that they began to drop other ministries. The question is never whether a congregation can offer a specialized ministry of one kind or another, but whether a congregation offers those ministries out of the core of who God has created it to be in its particular context.

A congregation often seeks to reach out to families with young children because, as everyone seems to say, "that's the way to survive," even if they have no young families with children in their context, which stands in contrast to a congregation that reaches out to families with young children because those families are in its context. These two congregations are not the same: one is living out the Great Commission, while the other is ignoring its context in favor of living out of something it is not. What makes this problematical is that a congregation that tries to minister to a demographic that does not exist in its context often ignores the real ministry in the context to which God is calling it. If a congregation has only senior citizens in its context, and it ignores them in favor of ministry to a context of young families, it is not living out the Great Commission, but rather a greater omission.

My touring of congregations in Minneapolis and Saint Paul during the early 1990s led me to some interesting observations. Large and affluent suburban congregations focused on reaching out to those in their neighborhoods, as did the smaller interracial and urban congregations that were financially strapped. Both of them offered worship; but even if they were of the same denomination, it took a keen eye and ear to recognize the similarities. Youth ministry in the one community involved young people having pizza around a campfire, whereas it involved a GED course for young mothers in another community. But both kinds of congregations were seeking to live out their mission to make disciples, based on their context. Invariably, a focus on Jesus and his call to reach out to people became the theme in which the congregations reached a simultaneity.

This reawakening of the Great Commission is a great boon to the missional congregation seeking to address its context. Energized by the calling of God in Christ Jesus and by the power of the Holy Spirit to reach out to people, the missional congregation can authentically live as a witness to the life that Jesus brought into the world. No longer does a congregation go into a context to offer the denomination's alternative to the Christianity that already exists there; rather, the congregation can seek to live out its unique calling to share the message and deed of Christ in, with, through, and against the context. It is precisely here that the missional congregation can draw on the resource of how the intricacy of God's three-personed relationship can seem as one.

Living in its context, the missional congregation heeds the call of Christ to make disciples, regardless of whether it finds itself in an urban situation or a rural one (or a rich one, poor one, strong one, sick one, and so forth). What is important for the missional congregation is its understanding of how to best live within its particular context and take seriously its questions, while at the same time maintaining its own identity. Being able to maintain its identity as a congregation that is called by the Triune God in Jesus Christ by the power of the Spirit in the face of its particular context is the greatest challenge facing the missional congregation.

Niche Marketing Comes of Age

Because religion has become a product to be marketed, one aspect the missional congregation can begin to exploit is its ability to market its assets to a certain segment of the population's needs and desires. Although this aspect carries with it the dangers of homogenization and over-contextualization, it also provides an opportunity to meet specific people in specific situations with the gospel. The missional congregation is freed from having to water down its message to appeal to the widest audience; and it is free to minister to the needs of real people. Most importantly, the missional congregation can focus on the needs of people in a specific context, and it can bring the gospel to that context at the same time that it respects the integrity of that context. If that context is antithetical to the missional congregation and its Christian identity, it would appear that part of why God has put this congregation in that context is to witness to a different reality, but not at the expense of destroying that context, that is — in the terms I've used in this chapter — of undercontextualizing.

With so many Christian congregations in the major cities of this country, most missional congregations can seek to specialize their ministries and programs.[20] For example, almost all congregations offer worship of some kind. For a missional congregation that is seeking to make an impact in a community with difficult access to health care, why not start with a clinic as a worship site? For a congregation that is seeking to make an impact in a high-income, low-population area, why not choose a community center to worship in? Taking seriously that the God of relationship and incarnation creates and loves a context allows the missional congregation the freedom to take the context seriously and to minister to it accordingly.

As they reflect on how God, in Jesus of Nazareth, came into the world as the world needed God, missional congregations can draw strength to discern their own unique calling within a particular context. They can look at all the congregations in their contexts and ask, What can we offer that none of the others offer? Is God calling them to provide a better, higher-quality ministry (and thus one that is used more frequently and meeting more needs) than currently available in its context? In a world where most Christians can get a worship service without too much trouble, why should we believe that God calls missional congregations to offer another one? In a world in which the Son of God comes to engage our context, why should we assume that our particular context does not need to be engaged? Surveying the ecclesiastical landscape is an important part of a missional congregation's discernment of its context, and it can play a key role in its understanding of how God has called the congregation to make a difference in that culture and community.

The last component of a context takes place within the minds of the leaders. In order for the missional congregation to be effective in its context, its leaders must be aware of the mindset such work seems to demand. Perhaps the most important aspect of this component is a trust in God and a confidence in God's call. For example, Moses trusted God; but it is perhaps more important that, once he got his stick and his brother, he exhibited a confidence in God's call. We are never sure of God's motives; after all, God is a mystery. But we live in the confidence that God's call to both the leaders and the particular context is adequate for the missional congregation to flourish.

---

20. Note that I am not talking about specializing for certain kinds of people. Although it may be true that certain kinds of people prefer certain kinds of programs, I am suggesting that congregations focus on offering ministries and programs that might meet certain needs, regardless of which people might avail themselves of the ministry.

Perhaps it requires what Paul Ricoeur called, in a different context, a "second naiveté"?[21] Perhaps leaders must live as if the future is always to be revealed, knowing the heartbreak of yesterday and the joy of tomorrow? The mind of the leader is not the major link in the relationship between the missional congregation and its context, but it can go a long way toward binding them together. The leaders of a missional congregation are entrusted with bringing the gospel to a context. This requires them to be part of the context, yet, necessarily, not merely of the context. Leaders imagine not only how the gospel comforts, but also how it afflicts; how it brings change, yet continuity; how it tells the story of God without destroying the story of the community. Wolfhart Pannenberg's observation about mission, cited above, carries with it an understanding of apostolicity that is key to leaders of missional congregations. In Pannenberg's terms, the apostles keep the faith while they simultaneously understand that they are "sent" to new places to share that faith.[22] There is always a risk that they may lose the faith within the context (overcontextualization) or that they may destroy the context and ignore the faith (undercontextualization). But the apostle — the leader — lives on that boundary.

The Missional Congregation as Contextual

We recall that the congregation is to be influenced by its context in order to make inroads in reaching that context with a message that the context has not previously responded to. The point is not for the missional congregation to become like the context. It must be able to live with the context in a way that is mutually beneficial to itself and the context, at times supporting it, and perhaps at other times battling it. Understanding the key components of the context will help the missional congregation live out its calling.

Consider this quotation from the apostle Paul: "Welcome one another, therefore, just as Christ has welcomed you, for the glory of God. For I tell you that Christ has become a servant of the circumcised on behalf of the truth of God in order that he might confirm the promises given to the

21. Paul Ricoeur, *The Symbolism of Evil* (New York: Harper and Row, 1967), p. 347.
22. Pannenberg, "The Significance of Eschatology for an Understanding of the Apostolicity and Catholicity of the Church," p. 48.

patriarchs, and in order that the Gentiles might glorify God for his mercy" (Rom. 15:7-9). Notice how Paul has asked the Roman Christians to behave: everything is for the glory of God. Jesus has become a servant of the Jews on "behalf" of God (note the perichoretic implications). Why? So that the promise of God may be confirmed and, most importantly for a missional congregation, that the gentiles may glorify God.

Ultimately, that is what the mission of God in missional congregations is all about: the living and being of God's mercy for every person in every context. I argue that the best way to bring that message to every context is to encourage missional congregations to live in, with, and against their contexts so that message may be heard. In conveying the message of God's mercy to those who need it most, contextual congregations will not always be missional, but missional congregations will always be contextual.

CHAPTER 3

A Reformation Is a Terrible Thing to Waste: A Promising Theology for an Emerging Missional Church

Gary M. Simpson

> *For in Jesus Christ every one of God's promises is a "Yes." For this reason it is through him that we say the "Amen," to the glory of God.*
>
> 2 Corinthians 1:20

"A mind is a terrible thing to waste." So says the United Negro College Fund advertisement. My Grandma Klemm said it this way: "Waste not, want not." Now Grandma usually meant the food on our plate — "our daily bread," as she taught us to pray. Knowing Scripture as she did, she understood that Scripture also warned against waste. And not just the waste of our daily bread, which, as Luther taught her, meant our mind as well. Scripture pointedly warns against wasting Christ. Paul puts it poignantly: "I do not nullify the grace of God; for if justification comes through the law, then Christ died for nothing" (Gal. 2:21). If Christ were to die for nothing, what a waste! The ultimate waste!

The sixteenth-century Reformation decisively echoes that biblical warning. The Lutheran confessors, for instance, state this confessional caveat positively.[1] They do theology for the sake of church and world with

---

1. In this essay I, as a Lutheran theologian, will speak from within that particular stream of the Reformation tradition. I will use the terms "Reformation," "Reformation tradition," "Reformation confessors," "confessors," and others with various shades of particularity. At

the stated purpose to make Christ "necessary" rather than "useless."[2] Christ emphatically did not die for nothing. These Reformers took Paul's scriptural cue and inextricably linked making Christ necessary with a lively distinction between law and gospel, or — to follow the *Apology of the Augsburg Confession*'s more precise wording — the distinction between "law and promise." Famously, they brought this distinction to bear in their articulation of justification by faith alone.[3] For their fellow confessors ever since, justification by faith alone denotes "the hub" — as in hub of the wheel, as my teachers taught me way back in seminary — for critical theological reflection on Christian life and practice, indeed, reflection on all life and practice.

There are two ways to waste Christ. The church could miss, even distort, the promise *in* Christ; and the church could hoard to itself the promise *of* Christ for the world. Because of the sixteenth-century context, the Reformers majored in overcoming the *distorting* waste; increasingly today in North America, on the other hand, Christian churches are hearing the Holy Spirit's sure call to overcome the *hoarding* of the promise *of* Christ. At those times when our Reformation heritages have attended to the hoarding waste, it has too often come at the expense of contesting with equal vigor the distorting waste of Christ. Likewise, when our Reformation heritages attended to the distorting waste, that attention also has come at the expense of vigorously contesting the hoarding waste of Christ.

Let us not be naïve about North America today. Our market economy projects the most powerful and expansive culture ever assembled. Our consumptive culture of the commodification of all things is on the move, colonizing everything it in its path and stopping at little so far. How many of us can already cite frequent instances in which economic models

---

times, for instance, I'll use "Reformation heritage" to indicate commonalities between Luther and Calvin and others within the Reformed traditions; at other times, my use of "Reformation confessors," for instance, might indicate a more Lutheran perspective on things.

2. See *Apology of the Augsburg Confession*, Article IV.29-70, in *The Book of Concord: The Confessions of the Evangelical Lutheran Church,* ed. Robert Kolb and Timothy Wengert (Minneapolis: Fortress, 2000) [hereafter cited as *Apology*]. See Martin Luther's argument that St. Paul's overall "point" is "to make grace necessary" in *Bondage of the Will,* in *Luther and Erasmus: Free Will and Salvation,* Library of Christian Classics, vol. XVII, ed. G. Rupp (Philadelphia: Westminster, 1969), p. 300. On this same "necessitating Christ," see John Calvin, *Institutes of the Christian Religion,* Library of Christian Classics, ed. John McNeill (Philadelphia: Westminster, 1960), 3.13.1-4 [hereafter cited as Calvin].

3. *Apology,* IV.5; see also Calvin, 3.11.17-19.

of marketing have passed themselves off as the missional character of the church? Again, let us not be naïve about contemporary America. Our political state aims to impose its power through our military prowess wherever it serves the United States' global advantage. How many of us can already cite frequent instances in which such crusading models of power have passed themselves off as the dynamics of a missionary church among the nations?

The Reformation surely could be wasted, and that would be a terrible thing. Furthermore, this waste would come under cover of a professed good and a much ballyhooed benevolent intentionality. That is, it could come under the guise of proclaiming Christ worldwide. Only the promise *in* Christ, freshly rooted in the distinction between law and promise, firmly fastens and forever frees the missionary promise *of* Christ for the world. To put our theme more positively, the Reformation is a wonderful thing to proliferate. And that's the best way to disrupt either the market's or the state's colonizing of the missional character of the church. God calls the church today to a double major: to proliferate the promise *of* Christ to the world by promoting the promise *in* Christ. And vice versa: to promote the promise *in* Christ by proliferating the promise *of* Christ for the world. This is "promising theology," and it lives precisely for an emerging missional church that is called, centered, and sent to promote Christ for the world.[4]

In this chapter I will exploit the Reformation's hub insight for a theology of mission. My reflections will focus on five themes: mission as *promissio*, as *communicatio*, as *communio*, as *confessio*, and as *vocatio*.[5] In mission as *promissio*, I will dig deeper into justification by faith alone. In mission as *communicatio*, I will retrieve the Reformation's key insight regarding Jesus Christ, known as the communication of divine and human

---

4. "Promising theology" is an alternative to so-called "decision theology," on the one hand, and "sovereignty theology," which we will examine in the second section below, on the other. While "missional church" is catching the attention of some segments of American evangelicalism, American evangelicals seem too often to simply flip-flop back and forth between decision theology and sovereignty theology.

5. These themes surely do not exhaust what's needed. Reformation theology too often remains content with only the first and last, with *promissio* and *vocatio*, since these were the controversial issues for the Reformation's originating insights. But theological reflection neither began with the Reformation nor ended with it. Other worthy theological issues arise and, if ignored by Reformation reflection, could diminish the critical impact of Reformation insight.

attributes, the *communicatio idiomatum*. The *communicatio* overcomes a particularly "modern" sovereignty problem, which regularly creeps into the article of justification endangering the *promissio*. I will borrow a Christological metaphor from Dietrich Bonhoeffer's theology of the cross to make the point. In mission as *communio*, I will visit a turning point in twentieth-century missiology, the triune identity of God. We'll explore how *communio*, as our trinitarian category, fits snugly with the Reformation's *promissio* and *communicatio*, and how these three together innovate the emerging missional church. In this way, *communio* also initiates our ecclesiological reflections, which we will then intensify under mission as *confessio*. *Confessio* brings us to the question of public martyrological truth and to the horizon of world Christianity. We'll culminate our considerations with mission as *vocatio* by expanding this Reformation standby through a public theology of civil society for the emerging missional church. In these ways we shall find our five themes mutually influencing each other as true correlates.

Mission as *Promissio*

In the Reformation's doctrine of justification, the *sola fide*, by faith alone, has always been the "most embattled *sola* of all." Already at the Diet of Augsburg (1530), those confessors testified that "the logic of promise," of *promissio*, is the hermeneutical heart of the entire scriptures of the Old and New Testaments.[6] Faith alone justifies "based upon the nature of a promise," they emphasized. St. Paul provided them with concise formulations of the entire biblical teaching, of the entire Bible's chief truth claim. "For this reason it depends on faith, in order that the promise may rest on grace and

6. The phrase "most embattled *sola* of all" is Robert W. Bertram's in "Recent Lutheran Theologies on Justification by Faith: A Sampling," in H. George Anderson, T. Austin Murphy, and Joseph A. Burgess, eds., *Justification by Faith: Lutherans and Catholics in Dialogue VII* (Minneapolis: Augsburg, 1985), p. 252. There are, of course, many excellent discussions of justification by faith alone. Among the more incisive expositions that link faith and promise are: Robert W. Bertram, "'Faith Alone Justifies': Luther on *Iustitia Fidei*," in Anderson et al., *Justification by Faith*, pp. 172-84; see also Robert W. Jenson, "On Recognizing the Augsburg Confession," in Joseph A. Burgess, ed., *The Role of the Augsburg Confession: Catholic and Lutheran Views* (Philadelphia: Fortress, 1980), pp. 151-66; see also Christopher Morse, *The Logic of Promise in Moltmann's Theology* (Philadelphia: Fortress, 1979).

be guaranteed." Or again, "Scripture has consigned everyone under sin, so that, by faith in Jesus Christ, the promise might be given to those who believe."[7] Promise and faith go together like a hand and glove.

The Reformation proposes a linguistic innovation of Christian mission.[8] This innovation focuses on the public effects that God's promissory speaking has on the world's future for its redemption. Because communication always opens the future, the Reformation's basic confessional insight concerns how the church, Christ's missional body, speaks. And how does the Reformation propose the missional church to speak? It recommends speaking caringly.[9] Indeed, the church's sending Spirit authorizes this care.

And what's to care about? "Well, it all depends," we routinely say. Every worldly thing, of course, depends on meeting some condition; in fact, every tomorrow depends on some condition. Life is "conditional," thank God! The Reformation confessors saw that clearly. Furthermore, they saw that the dependability of all things — or not — itself depends on God's way of speaking according to conditions — or not. They urged the missional church to attend caringly to how it speaks in God's name.

Conditionality is the deep logic of law, "law" being the category the Reformation used to name everyday conditionality. Under the deep logic of law, in one way or another, life's possible futures exhibit an "if . . . , then . . ." conditional form. *If* you are this or that, or you do this or that, or you meet this or that condition, *then* you will be or have some resulting this or that. In the logic of promise, the promisor takes on the other's condition as the promisor's own, and thus opens up an unconditional, free future for the other. "Because I . . . , therefore you. . . ." Thus freedom is the deep logic of promise.[10] "For freedom Christ has set you free," Paul notes concisely. The "nature of a promise" constitutes the missional promise *in* Christ for the sake of the missional promise *of* Christ to the world. That's

---

7. *Apology*, IV.40-56, 84, citing Rom. 4:16 and Gal. 3:22, respectively.

8. See especially James Preus, *From Shadow to Promise: Old Testament Interpretation from Augustine to the Young Luther* (Cambridge, MA: Harvard University Press, 1969); see also Richard Lischer, "Preaching and the Rhetoric of Promise," *Word & World* 8 (Winter 1988): 66-79.

9. *Apology*, IV.188.

10. See Calvin, 3.11.17-19; see also *Apology*, IV.40-47, 185-88. For a well-known contemporary analysis, see Eric Gritsch and Robert Jenson, *Lutheranism: The Theological Movement and Its Confessional Writings* (Philadelphia: Fortress, 1976), pp. 2-11.

why Luther, for instance, raised up the "promising God" against the Babylonian captivity of the church in his era.[11]

By caring in this way, the church participates missionally in the Holy Spirit's promotion of Israel's Jesus as the world's Good News to the glory of the Son's Father. The Reformation exhorts the church to always tend to the difference between the Holy Spirit's speaking according to law and speaking according to promise. When you speak Christ Jesus to people, speak him in such a way that you communicate God's unconditional freeing promise into the living reality of the world and your hearers. In this way God truly calls into existence a newly trustworthy creation that is populated by a people of faith.

For the emerging missional church this means a critical revision of the still current mantra, *missio dei. Missio duplex dei*, the twofold mission of God, commends itself as more congruent with the Reformation's core confessional insight regarding law *and* promise. We'll explore this critical revision under our subsequent themes.

Mission as *Communicatio*

One biblical theologian has proposed "God's endangered promises" as the plot of the biblical story.[12] This raises the question about the conditions placed on every promise ever made. Every promise yields up its spirit when it meets some condition or another that limits that promise's lively future. Take the marriage promise as a case in point. Though it is divinely ordained to be the most endearing and thus the most enduring of promises, we know all too well how endangered this promise is. Even when marital promises outrun the usual slings and arrows, there is always that final "it depends": "Till death do us part" stylizes even the best-kept promises as conditional promises.

God's promises, likewise, travel dangerous terrain, and in the end they also come face to face with the condition that conditions all other conditions, namely, death — the death of sufferers, of sinners, even death

11. Martin Luther, *The Babylonian Captivity of the Church*, in the American edition of *Luther's Works* (St. Louis and Philadelphia, 1955-1986) [hereafter *LW*], 36:27, 60.

12. Nils Dahl, *Jesus the Christ: The Historical Origins of Christological Doctrine*, ed. Donald Juel (Minneapolis: Fortress, 1991), p. 76; see also Nils Dahl, *Studies in Paul* (Minneapolis: Augsburg, 1977), pp. 121-36.

on the cross. The Holy Spirit's raising of the crucified Son is the Father's own truth claim that this promise, made in Jesus' own body, is the world's singular unconditional promise, that is, a promise that surpasses every condition, every limit, every enemy. The promise of Jesus' cross involves the Son's taking on conditionality itself and all humans subject to life's conditions. Here conditionality meets its end. Here promising theology meets the cross and thereby meets its origin and consummation.

We noted earlier that the nature of a promise entails that the promisor take on the condition of the other. In Christian theology this "taking on" is known by the old Latin phrase *communicatio idiomatum*, the communication of properties, the sharing of what properly belongs to one with another, and vice versa.[13] Our shorthand will simply be the *communicatio*. Instead of engaging the doctrinal tradition regarding the *communicatio*, I will simply focus on a poignant moment in early twentieth-century theology that illustrates the significance of the *communicatio* for our new era of missional church: Dietrich Bonhoeffer's critique of Karl Barth's theology of sovereign lordship.

Bonhoeffer's 1930 critique was of Barth's concept of revelation. Barth introduced his understanding of "revelation" in his early dialecti-cal, or "crisis," theology in order to criticize and go beyond the liberal German theology and church life of nineteenth-century Protestantism. Barth indicted liberal Protestantism for reducing theology to anthropol-ogy and Christian faith to mere "religion."[14] He maintained that a singu-lar focus on divine revelation would reveal the bankruptcy of liberal anthropocentrism. Bonhoeffer agreed with this basic criticism, even though some of his own Berlin teachers, such as Reinhold Seeberg, Adolf von Harnack, and Karl Holl, were among the targets of Barth's criti-

---

13. Luther's discussion is particularly poignant in *On the Councils and the Church* (1539), *LW* 41:93-106.

14. In Barth's *The Epistle to the Romans* (1922) we find the "early" Barth, before his "change." For a critical overview of research into the development of "Barthian theology," see Bruce McCormack's careful study *Karl Barth's Critically Realistic Dialectical Theology: Its Genesis and Development 1909-1936* (Oxford: Clarendon Press, 1995), especially pp. vii-28. Bonhoeffer first read Barth in winter of 1924/25 and was already bringing Barth into his classroom discussions with Harnack. See Andreas Pangritz, *Karl Barth in the Theology of Dietrich Bonhoeffer* (Grand Rapids: Eerdmans, 2000), p. 15. Also see Eberhard Bethge, *Dietrich Bonhoeffer: A Biography*, rev. ed. (Minneapolis: Fortress, 2000), p. 67 [hereafter cited as Bethge, *Bonhoeffer*]. Pangritz offers rich resources for the Bonhoeffer-Barth connection, though I differ with his overall assessment.

cism.[15] Liberal theology had, as Bonhoeffer would say years later, "conceded to the world the right to determine Christ's place in the world." It had "compromised" with modernity's assumed optimism, progressivism, and superiority.[16] Still, Bonhoeffer did not find Barth's theology of revelation completely satisfying; nor did he find every basic insight of liberal theology totally bankrupt. Indeed, Bonhoeffer was quite dialectical: with insight, he upheld both a yes and a no to Barth, on the one hand, and to liberal Protestantism, on the other.

Barth framed "revelation" around the notion of God's absolute "freedom," and therefore the pure "contingency" of divine revelation.[17] He portrayed God's glorious, sovereign lordship as God's absolute free will to do anything God wants to do — to reveal God's self or not. Only in this way, said Barth, is God's revelation safe from being objectified, distorted, manipulated, exploited, and controlled by human pretensions. Encapsulating Barth, Bonhoeffer noted: "Revelation is an event that has its basis in the freedom of God." God's revelation is pure act, "with all the instability of a deed being done right now," said Bonhoeffer in his summary of Barth. "How could it be otherwise," mused Bonhoeffer, since, as sovereign, "God has sole control?"[18] This he referred to as Barth's "actualism."[19]

15. For instance, the famous 1923 controversy between Barth and Harnack is reprinted in James M. Robinson, ed., *The Beginnings of Dialectical Theology* (Richmond, VA: John Knox Press, 1968), pp. 163-87. Bonhoeffer was quite indebted to Holl's focus on Luther's doctrine of justification by faith alone. However, Holl's interpretation of Luther's theology "as a religion of conscience" left Holl vulnerable to liberal anthropocentrism. Holl's interpretation of Luther was defective, argues Bonhoeffer in his July 31, 1930, inaugural lecture at the University of Berlin, because Holl had "a remarkably scant estimation of Luther's Christology" (Dietrich Bonhoeffer, "Man in Contemporary Philosophy and Theology," in *No Rusty Swords: Letters, Lectures and Notes, 1928-1936*, from the *Collected Works of Dietrich Bonhoeffer*, vol. 1, ed. Edwin Robertson (New York: Harper & Row, 1965), p. 61.

16. Dietrich Bonhoeffer, *Letters and Papers from Prison*, enlarged ed., ed. Eberhard Bethge (New York: Touchstone, 1997), p. 327 [hereafter cited as *LPP*]; and Dietrich Bonhoeffer, *Ethics*, in *Dietrich Bonhoeffer Works*, vol. 6 (Minneapolis: Fortress Press, 2005), pp. 153-57.

17. Bonhoeffer noted that these notions go back pre-eminently to the nominalist philosophical theologies of Duns Scotus and William of Occam in the late 13th and early 14th centuries; see Dietrich Bonhoeffer, *Act and Being*, in *Dietrich Bonhoeffer Works*, vol. 2 (Minneapolis: Fortress Press, 1996), p. 85.

18. Bonhoeffer, *Act and Being*, pp. 82-83.

19. See Regin Prenter, "Dietrich Bonhoeffer and Karl Barth's Positivism of Revelation," in *World Come of Age*, ed. R. G. Smith (London: Collins, 1967), pp. 105-12.

Still, Bonhoeffer was not satisfied. A framework of Western modernism is "lurking here" in Barth, he noted. Like Immanuel Kant, Barth is out to limit human reason: that is, human reason is not in control; God is in control.[20] But, argued Bonhoeffer, limiting reason in this way, that is, by keeping God "at a distance," meant that Barth had surrendered true temporality. "It follows that, even though Barth readily uses temporal categories. . . his concept of act still should not be regarded as temporal. God's freedom and the act of faith are essentially supratemporal." Barth's attempt was "bound to fail," said Bonhoeffer, because for Barth "no historical moment is *capax infiniti*," capable of the infinite.[21]

Bonhoeffer countered Barth's formalistic-actualistic theology of revelation with an exposition of God's "substantial" freedom. "God freely chose to be bound to historical human beings and to be placed at the disposal of human beings. God is free not so much from human beings but for them. Christ is the word of God's freedom. God *is* present, that is, not in eternal nonobjectivity but — to put it quite provisionally for now — 'haveable,' graspable in the Word within the church."[22] Indeed, the crucified Jesus constitutes the very form of God's lordship for Bonhoeffer. This innovation in lordship merits closer attention in order for us to appreciate how truly new and truly good this crucified Jesus really is.

Bonhoeffer's 1930 intuitions and insights leaned determinedly toward a theology of the cross. They eventually led him to his now-famous prison confession of July 16, 1944 ("only the suffering God can help"),[23] not the typical omnipotent forms of divine lordship. In *Discipleship* (1937), Bonhoeffer uses a rich metaphor for this cruciform Christ: "God is a God

20. Bonhoeffer, *Act and Being*, p. 84.

21. Bonhoeffer, *Act and Being*, p. 84.

22. Bonhoeffer, *Act and Being*, pp. 90-91. He credited Luther with these crucial insights (*Act and Being*, pp. 116-17, 120-21) and drew from Luther's "That These Words of Christ, 'This is my Body,' etc., Still Stand Firm against the Fanatics" (1527) (*LW* 37:13-150). Here Luther emphasized the God who gets "handled" by humans. "It is the honor of our God, however, that, in giving the divine self for our sake in deepest condescension, entering into flesh and bread, into our mouth, heart and bowel and suffering for our sake, God be dishonorably handled, both on the altar and the cross." I've used the English translation of Bonhoeffer's transposition of Luther into modern German (*Act and Being*, p. 82, n. 1; see *LW* 37:72; *WA* 23:127). See Robert Bertram's understanding of the faith-side of "having" in "'Faith Alone Justifies.'"

23. Bonhoeffer, *LPP*, p. 361.

who bears."[24] He continues: "The Son of God bore our flesh. He therefore bore the cross. He bore all our sins and attained reconciliation by this bearing." Such bearing, Bonhoeffer argued, constitutes "that kind of Lord" who Jesus is, rather than some other kind of lordship.[25] With this metaphor, Bonhoeffer definitively tipped his critical Christology of lordship in a decisively cruciform direction.

Bonhoeffer saw clearly that Barth's concept of sovereign lordship distorts and thus wastes the *promissio,* the promise *in* Christ. Barth's lordship surreptitiously accommodated itself to the modern concept of the autonomous subject by using older nominalist means. By contrast, Bonhoeffer's puts the *promissio* into the center of his theology by placing it at the heart of his homiletical practice.[26] Finally, he portrayed the *communicatio* in everyday speech as the "bearing God" and thus as the true correlate of *promissio.* We turn now to the current critical retrieval of trinitarian theology and find there another true correlate of both *promissio* and *communicatio:* this trinitarian correlate is *communio.* In my account of *communio,* I will gather together what we have learned from *promissio* and *communicatio* for a missional theology of the church in the new era that the Holy Spirit is richly spreading out before us.

Mission as *Communio*

The sixteenth-century Reformation did not reflect in a sustained way on the doctrine of the Trinity. Reformation confessors and their papal interrogators all formally accepted the three ecumenical trinitarian creeds. Furthermore, both confessors and interrogators followed the Western, Augustinian tradition of trinitarian reflection, which we will review below.

24. Dietrich Bonhoeffer, *Discipleship,* in *Dietrich Bonhoeffer Works,* vol. 4 (Minneapolis: Fortress Press, 2001), p. 90.

25. Bonhoeffer, *Discipleship,* p. 85. In *Discipleship,* Bonhoeffer constantly uses the rhetorical metaphor of "bearing" rather than his more doctrinal category of "vicarious representative action" [*Stellvertretung*] or *communicatio idiomatum.* He uses *Stellvertretung* already in *Sanctorum Communio* (1927) and still uses it sparingly in *Discipleship* (e.g., p. 90). He uses *communicatio idiomatum* in *Christ the Center* (1933). Of course, "bearing" is a broadly based biblical metaphor. Luther, for instance, used it often in reference to "joyous exchange." In Luther's lecture on Gal. 3:13 he explicitly inquired "But what does it mean to 'bear'?" (*Lectures on Galatians* (1531/35), *LW,* 26:276-91).

26. Clyde Fant, *Dietrich Bonhoeffer: Worldly Preaching* (New York: Nelson, 1975).

Gradually, however, the new, modern Protestantism of eighteenth- and nineteenth-century Europe found Western trinitarian teaching to be no longer relevant to either the moral practice or the religious experience of the church in its day. Modernity's world was becoming ever more secular while also, curiously, continuing the Christendom habit.[27] As Immanuel Kant put it, "The doctrine of the Trinity, taken literally, has *no practical relevance at all.* . . . Whether we are to worship three or ten persons in the Deity makes no difference . . . no difference in rules of conduct."[28] Friedrich Schleiermacher, the father of modern liberal Protestantism, needed only a radically monotheistic mode of belief in order to ground the modern religious experience of absolute dependence. Thus Schleiermacher relegated the doctrine of the Trinity to the equivalence of an appendix in his path-breaking magnum opus, *The Christian Faith.*

Karl Barth, to his credit, resurrected trinitarian theology and placed it at the very beginning of his *Church Dogmatics.* From there, trinitarian reflection found its way into the theology of mission, particularly by way of the meeting in Willingen, Germany (1952), of the International Mission Council. In fact, through Willingen, Barth's trinitarian theology eventually became the heart and soul of the post–World War II theology of mission. *Missio Dei* is the concept that would eventually — not too long after Willingen — establish the basis for missional theology as well as for the inseparability of church and mission. This concept brought about a "Copernican revolution" in missiology.[29]

---

27. See Brian Gerrish, *The Old Protestantism and the New: Essays on the Reformation Heritage* (Chicago: University of Chicago Press, 1982); see also Gerrish, *Continuing the Reformation: Essays on Modern Religious Thought* (Chicago: University of Chicago Press, 1993).

28. Immanuel Kant, "The Conflict of the Faculties," in *Religion and Rational Theology: The Cambridge Edition of the Works of Immanuel Kant,* trans. and ed. Allen W. Wood and George Di Giovanni (Cambridge, UK: Cambridge University Press, 1996), p. 264. See my own more extensive analysis in Gary M. Simpson, "No Trinity No Mission: The Apostolic Difference of Revisioning the Trinity," *Word & World* 18 (Summer 1998): 264-71.

29. Craig Van Gelder, "How Missiology Can Help Inform the Conversation about the Missional Church in Context" (unpublished typescript), p. 9. See, especially, David Bosch, *Transforming Mission: Paradigm Shifts in Theology of Mission* (Maryknoll, NY: Orbis, 1991), pp. 389-93; see also Theo Sundermeier, "Theology of Mission," in Karl Mueller, Theo Sundermeier, Stephen Bevans, and Richard Bliese, eds., *Dictionary of Mission: Theology, History, Perspectives* (Maryknoll, NY: Orbis, 1997), p. 334. The Basel Mission director Karl Hartenstein was the one who incorporated Barth's trinitarian theology into the *missio Dei* concept and took it to the Willingen meeting. Missiologist Georg Vicedom, of Neuendettel-

The Willingen meeting stated the trinitarian basis of a theology of mission in this way: "The missionary movement of which we are a part has its source in the Triune God Himself."[30] An interim report from Willingen captured the church-and-mission significance of the trinitarian break-through this way: "All were agreed that 'mission' is essential to the nature of the Church and not something super-added to it."[31] Willingen's official report said: "There is no participation in Christ without participation in His mission to the world."[32] Put summarily:

> The classic doctrine of the *missio Dei* as God the Father sending the Son, and God the Father and the Son sending the Spirit was expanded to include yet another "movement": Father, Son, and Holy Spirit send-ing the church into the world. . . . Willingen's image of mission was mission as participating in the sending of God.[33]

Therefore, *missio Dei* means erasing the "and" in the phrase "church and mission." *Missio Dei* also means the end of "missions" in the plural: "The age of missions is at an end; the age of mission has begun."[34] Since Wil-lingen, *missio Dei* has achieved a kind of ecumenical consensus. More re-cently has come the trinitarian *missio Dei* breakthrough to "missional

---

sau, Bavaria, traces the *missio Dei* concept to Barth and, with insight, back to Augustine, the source of the Western trinitarian tradition (Vicedom, *The Mission of God: An Introduction to a Theology of Mission* [St. Louis: Concordia, 1965; originally published in 1958]). Vicedom was also the one who decisively promoted *missio Dei* as the breakthrough concept for a the-ology of mission (see Sundermeier et al., *Dictionary of Mission*; for Vicedom's role, see also Wilbert Shenk, "The Relevance of Messianic Missiology for Mission Today," in Wilbert Shenk, ed., *The Transfiguration of Mission: Biblical, Theological, and Historical Foundations* [Scottdale, PA: Herald, 1993], pp. 17-18). Norman Goodall, who edited the Willingen pro-ceedings, was not himself convinced that Willingen had made a breakthrough: "There did not finally emerge," he said, "the one inevitable word in which theological clarity and pro-phetic insight were manifestly conjoined. Nor did there appear the one new directive which might set the world mission of the Church on a surer and swifter road towards its fulfill-ment" (Norman Goodall, ed., *Missions under the Cross: Addresses delivered at the Enlarged Meeting of the Committee of the International Missionary Council at Willingen, in Germany, 1952; with Statements issued at the Meeting* [London: Edinburgh House Press, 1953], p. 14).

30. Goodall, *Missions under the Cross*, p. 189.
31. Goodall, *Missions under the Cross*, p. 244.
32. Goodall, *Missions under the Cross*, p. 190.
33. Bosch, *Transforming Mission*, p. 390.
34. Bosch, *Transforming Mission*, p. 391, here quoting Stephen Neill.

church," a term — and a reality — that itself needed nearly another half century after Willingen to emerge.

In the last quarter of the twentieth century we have witnessed the most widespread and fruitful critical re-engagement with trinitarian thinking perhaps since the time of Augustine. I cannot even begin to recap the richness. While the trinitarian significance of *missio Dei* has effectively permeated "missional church," the more recent trinitarian reflection has not yet reached, much less permeated, the emerging missional church. One figure at the Willingen meeting observed: "Any vital movement in theology ought to affect and be affected by the Church's world-wide evangelistic obedience, yet at this very point it was evident that much had yet to be done before some of the most distinctive theological insights of our time could contribute to the re-formulation of a 'theology of missions.'"[35] Shortly after Willingen, another figure lamented: "The harvest of missionary ideas from systematic theology has been extremely poor, partly because systematic theology has shown very little interest in the questions [about the missionary nature of the church]."[36] It would be an added tragedy if in our new era of mission we would waste the new trinitarian abundance, especially now that an increasing number of systematic theologians prayerfully hear the Holy Spirit's call rustling through the world of missional church. The emerging missional church will continue to flourish as it vigorously engages this new critical retrieval of trinitarian reflection. As this happens, we can anticipate another Copernican revolution.

I will now identify only six of the many fruits within this new trinitarian treasury that can help focus future interaction between missional church and theological reflection. First, modern Protestantism became moribund with respect to the Trinity in the context of an increasingly secularizing Christendom, which progressively privatized its faith and truth claims. This is no longer the case. Christendom habits continue to weaken, at least in the West, despite the dogged hope of some American evangelicals and fundamentalists to reinstate an American Christendom. The world's great religions, as well as the world's more local traditional religions, have today arrived in force. These religions are occupying the same turf, though surely with quite varied amounts of moral, social, economic,

---

35. Goodall, *Missions under the Cross*, p. 11.

36. Johannes Blauw, *The Missionary Nature of the Church* (New York: McGraw-Hill, 1962), p. 13.

political, cultural, and aspirational capital. Geographically we're all together now: *terra firma* is small, flat, fast, flexible, and reflexive. This context of multiplicity, fueled by modernity's many mobilities, makes trinitarian life lived on the level of missional congregations ever more necessary, interesting, and fruitful. No Trinity, no mission!

Second, Western Christianity has thought and lived its doctrine of God through a particular Western habit. It is time to reconsider an important aspect of Eastern Orthodoxy's trinitarian reflection. Karl Barth in Protestantism and Karl Rahner in Roman Catholicism both undertook their retrieval of the Trinity by refining the Western paradigm of thinking in a trinitarian way as it was forged by St. Augustine.[37] Augustine starts the doctrine of God by giving priority to the oneness of God and only subsequently considering what threeness would mean in reference to divine oneness.[38] Augustine's logic of beginning with divine oneness, which borrows powerfully from Neo-Platonic thought, has affinities going back to the Christological thinking embodied in the mid-second century, to the so-called Second Letter of Clement 1:1: "We must think about Jesus Christ as we do about God." First, you discover everything you can about deity generally, then support these findings with matching biblical references, and then fit Jesus the Son and the Holy Spirit as best you can into the generic deity framework. This line of theological logic appeared to the West to be the best antidote to ward off any return of the Arian heresy, which portrayed the Son as merely the firstborn of the one God's creatures and the Holy Spirit as an angelic figure. However, the Augustinian trajectory, followed and solidified by Thomas Aquinas, subtly but significantly shared in the basic theological logic that was followed by Sabellius and others known as modalistic monarchians.[39]

---

37. See Ted Peters's helpful recap of this twentieth-century retrieval of Trinity (*God as Trinity: Relationality and Temporality in Divine Life* (Louisville: Westminster/John Knox, 1993).

38. Augustine, *The Trinity,* trans. Stephen McKenna, in *The Fathers of the Church,* vol. 45 (Washington, DC: Catholic University of America Press, 1963). For the best and most comprehensive historical overview of the history of the doctrine of the Trinity available in English, see Edmund J. Fortman, *The Triune God: A Historical Study of the Doctrine of the Trinity* (Grand Rapids: Baker Book House, 1972).

39. Jürgen Moltmann, *The Trinity and the Kingdom: The Doctrine of God* (San Francisco: Harper & Row, 1981), pp. 16-20, 134-37; see Wolfhart Pannenberg's thorough analysis in *Systematic Theology* (Grand Rapids: Eerdmans, 1991), 1:280-99.

This monistic and monarchical logic of God begins with the divine monad, the one God, who subsequently appears as Father, as Son, and as Spirit. The three only come into being functionally in order to *reveal* to humans the divine monad and to express, transport, and execute sovereign power in the form of the Father as creator, the Son as redeemer, and the Spirit as sanctifier or sustainer. But among the world's religions, what deity worth its salt doesn't function powerfully in some way or another as creator, redeemer, sustainer? While Augustine and Aquinas avoid modalism in the severe sense, nevertheless they set in motion a modalistic, monarchian tendency and piety that remains deeply inscribed in Western Christianity to this very day. Is it any wonder that the sovereignty problematic that we exposed under *communicatio* shows up as a trinitarian correlate?

Barth and Rahner, each in his own way, take up this single subject logic of God, as it was recovered in the modern German idealism of Georg Hegel, in an attempt to counter other modern trends set in motion by moral and experiential monotheisms. What Barth and Rahner failed to see with sufficient clarity is that moral and experiential monotheisms are the logical outcome of the very Western pattern of the doctrine of God that they themselves also promoted. Unintentionally, to be sure, but true nevertheless, they handed over "a late triumph to the Sabellian modalism which the early church condemned."[40] Furthermore, as we saw in Bonhoeffer's critique of the early Barth, Barth and Rahner reverse modernity and the modern sovereign subject by locating sovereign subjectivity in God rather than in the human, but they do not *overcome* modern single-subject sovereignty. Might not their failure to recognize this be due to their own embeddedness within the still persistently pervasive situation of Christendom and modernity?

The third fruit in the new trinitarian treasury is a partial turn to the East, to the Eastern logic. Eastern Orthodoxy has long been wary of the West's modalistic tendencies. Several new trinitarians are exploring a logic for the Christian doctrine of God more in accord with the Eastern pattern set forth by Athanasius and the Cappadocian theologians — Basil of Caesarea, Gregory of Nazianzus, and Gregory of Nyssa. Remember, the Western pattern begins with divine oneness; the pattern that is more Eastern begins with the history of the relationships of the three persons as nar-

---

40. Moltmann, *The Trinity and the Kingdom*, p. 139; see also pp. 151-58. Pannenberg basically agrees with Moltmann's analysis regarding Barth and Rahner (*Systematic Theology*, 1:333-36).

rated in the biblical witness and subsequently attends to what these relationships in communion mean for divine unity.[41]

Our fourth fruit, then, is God's being as communion.[42] We've finally arrived at our third overall theme, *communio*. At the core of the Eastern logic of the doctrine of God lies the narrated history of the life, death, and resurrection of Jesus the Son in rich relationship with his Father and with the Holy Spirit, and the relationship of the Spirit with each of the others as well.[43] *Communio* highlights the nature and significance of the conspicuous reciprocal relationality of the Father and the Son. With *communio* we especially note the Father's dependence on the Son mediated in the history of Jesus Christ and him crucified, and raised by the Holy Spirit.[44] *Communio* also highlights the Holy Spirit's liberating reciprocity not only toward Jesus the Son but also toward the Father; thus both Father and Son also live dependently on the Holy Spirit.[45]

41. Along with Moltmann and Pannenberg, I include among the major new trinitarians Robert Jenson, Eberhard Jüngel, John Zizioulos, Catherine LaCugna, and Ted Peters, notwithstanding the significant differences among them. While the Eastern logic of the doctrine of God is fundamentally true to Scripture, a basic flaw still persists in the Eastern pattern, i.e., a patriarchal monarchy of the Father and correspondingly a certain "kind of subordination" of Jesus the Son. This flaw appears in John Zizioulas, *Being as Communion: Studies in Personhood and the Church* (Crestwood, NY: St. Vladimir's Seminary Press, 1985), p. 89. Critically engaging this crucial flaw lies beyond our scope here (see Pannenberg, *Systematic Theology*, 1:319-25, and Moltmann, *The Trinity and the Kingdom*, pp. 240-41).

42. This apt phrase is Zizioulas's in *Being as Communion*.

43. See David Fredrickson's important exegetical investigation of this trinitarian hermeneutical line of inquiry in "What Difference Does Jesus Make for God?" *Dialog* 37 (Spring 1998): 104-10. Pannenberg has undertaken the most thorough investigation of the nature and implications of the reciprocal dependence of the Father and the Son and especially the notion, largely undeveloped in the entire history of trinitarian theology, of the Father's dependence on the Son mediated in the history of Jesus (see Pannenberg, 1:259-336). Both Moltmann and Eberhard Jüngel bring the crucifixion itself into the very midst of divine identity more emphatically than does Pannenberg: Jürgen Moltmann, *The Crucified God: The Cross of Christ as the Foundation and Criticism of Christian Theology* (San Francisco: Harper, 1974); Eberhard Jüngel, "The Truth of Life," in *Creation, Christ and Culture*, ed. R. W. A. McKinney (Edinburgh: T&T Clark, 1976).

44. Robert Bertram takes up the perils and promise of the concept of "dependence" relative to divine things: Bertram, "Putting the Nature of God into Language: Naming the Trinity," in Carl Braaten, ed., *Our Naming of God: Problems and Prospects of God-Talk Today* (Minneapolis: Fortress, 1989), pp. 91-110.

45. See Robert Jenson, *Unbaptized God: The Basic Flaw in Ecumenical Theology* (Minneapolis: Fortress, 1992), pp. 137-39; see also Jenson, *Systematic Theology*, 1:158-61.

ITEM CHARGED

The dominant Western logic precludes *communio's* reciprocal relational dynamic. This rejection is the West's Neo-Platonic ballast still in play. Consequently, the Western church's modalism has often led it to worship the Father in the patriarchal and monarchical ways appropriate to a sovereign lord. Not surprisingly, the internal way of life of the Western church has been highly monarchical, patriarchal, and sovereignty-oriented. Likewise, externally, the mission of the Western church has too often readily adopted colonial sovereignty patterns. By not developing *communio's* reciprocal personhood, Western theology exhibited "a defect which plagues the Trinitarian theological language of both East and West, namely, that of seeing the relations among Father, Son, and Spirit exclusively as relations of origin."[46]

The doctrine of the "relations of origin" deals with the trinitarian sendings, sometimes called "derivations." Understandably, it is this "relations of origin" as sending that is taken up into the *missio Dei* concept that sprang from Willingen. But it is also this reductionism, from Augustine all the way through to Barth and Rahner, of trinitarian relationality to "relations of origin" that is problematical. This reductionism anchors Christendom's fixation on sovereignty with its constant tilt toward colonialist attitudes, practices, and ways of life. Theology of mission naturally is invested in sending, and it found in this trinitarian reductionism a deep ally. Still,

> [i]t is the chief residual paganism of the way in which the churches descended from the mission in Mediterranean antiquity have thought of God, that all the derivations run one way, from the Father through the Son to the Spirit: the Father begets the Son and the Son is begotten; the Father breathes the Spirit and the Spirit is breathed. All active-voice relations run from origin to goal; the relations from goal to origin are but their passive voice. Therein unbaptized Hellenism's celebration of beginning over ending, of persistence over openness, of security over freedom, maintains itself even within the doctrine of Trinity. The [pagan] God whose eternity is immunity to time lurks even within the church's vision of the God whose eternity is faithful adventure in and through time.[47]

46. Pannenberg, *Systematic Theology,* 1:319.

47. Jenson, *Unbaptized God,* p. 139. Joseph Cardinal Ratzinger, the new Pope Benedict XVI, also exhibits this same Western reductionism (see, especially, Miroslav Volf's analysis in *After Our Likeness: The Church as the Image of the Trinity* [Grand Rapids: Eerdmans, 1998]).

Trinitarian relationality, however, is richer than sending alone, and this richness is a treasury begging to be shared with emerging missional church life, practice, and reflection. The ancient Greek term *perichoresis* summarizes this rich *communio* relationality. Though it is an ancient term, "only in recent times" — in the new trinitarian treasury — has *perichoresis* "come to occupy a central position."[48] Historically, *perichoresis* meant whirl, rotation, or circulation, the dynamic of going from one to another, walking around, handing around a possession to be shared, such as a bottle of wine: encircling, embracing, enclosing.[49] It is the neighborly circulating and sharing of all things within a neighborhood, including sorrows and joys, fears and hopes, not to mention daily materiality.[50] The Old and New Testaments testify precisely to this *perichoretic communio* of the triune life that is God. Here we have "the dynamic and creative energy, the eternal and perpetual movement, the mutual and reciprocal permeation of each person with and in and through and by the other persons."[51]

A fifth fruit in the new trinitarian treasury is new ecclesial reflection under the theme of *communio* ecclesiology. At the moment this is highly fluid and contested theological turf and thus holds promise as a theological resource for the emerging missional church.[52] Furthermore, we dare not underestimate the reciprocal contribution that an emerging missional church might make to *communio* ecclesiology. Let the mutual influence increase. What is needed, for instance, in *communio* ecclesiology is the transformation of ecclesial power toward what I call "perichoretic power."

The emerging missional church could generate just such a social transformation of ecclesial leadership around the dynamics of perichoretic power. At present the emerging missional church appears still too interested and invested in leadership models largely generated within the

48. Leonardo Boff, *Trinity and Society* (Maryknoll, NY: Orbis, 1988), p. 136.

49. Jürgen Moltmann, "Perichoresis: An Old Magic Word for a New Trinitarian Theology," in *Trinity, Community, and Power,* ed. M. Douglas Meeks (Nashville: Kingswood Books, 2000), p. 113. See also Moltmann, *Trinity and Kingdom,* pp. 174-78; Catherine Mowry LaCugna, *God for Us: The Trinity and Christian Life* (San Francisco: Harper, 1991), pp. 270-278; William Placher, *Narratives of a Vulnerable God: Christ, Theology, and Scripture* (Louisville: Westminster John Knox, 1994), pp. 53-75.

50. See *perichoresis* in *A Greek-English Lexicon of the New Testament and Other Early Christian Literature,* ed. Frederick Danker (Chicago: University of Chicago Press, 2000).

51. LaCugna, *God for Us,* p. 271.

52. See Volf, *After Our Likeness;* see also Dennis M. Doyle, *Communio Ecclesiology: Vision and Versions* (Maryknoll, NY: Orbis Books, 2000).

economic marketplace of late capitalism. The one-way arrows of *missio Dei* sending have too often made the emerging missional church susceptible to, when not just plain defenseless against, hierarchical management models of ecclesial leadership. It's no wonder that certain missiologists worry that *missio Dei* has become "a Trojan horse through which the (unassimilated) 'American' vision was tethered into the well-guarded walls of the ecumenical theology of mission."[53] One of the new trinitarians, for instance, notes that *perichoresis* entails "neither leaders nor followers in the divine dance, only an eternal movement of reciprocal giving and receiving, giving again and receiving again."[54] Even though that formulation is not totally satisfying for ecclesial leadership, there is an intuition there that just begs to be developed into a real insight, and an insight that just can't wait to be transfigured into an eschatologically institutionalized way of life together as emerging missional church.[55]

The sixth fruit in the new trinitarian treasury is how coherent perichoretic *communio* is with both *promissio* and *communicatio*. It is surely no accident that, before *perichoresis* became a term of trinitarian reflection, it was the Greek Christological category that in the Latin West became interchangeable with *communicatio idiomatum*.[56] Perichoretic *communio* identifies an open roominess that is dense with mutual sharing within the triune life that's fit for all creation's finitude, frailty, failure, fault, and finery. It is the trinitarian signature of the "promising, bearing God," a fitting and forming mark for an emerging missional church.

---

53. Bosch, *Transforming Mission*, p. 392, quoting H. H. Rosin, *Missio Dei: An Examination of the Origin, Contents and Function of the Term in Protestant Missiological Discussion* (Leiden: Inter-university Institute of Missiological and Ecumenical Research, 1972), p. 26.

54. LaCugna, *God for Us*, p. 272.

55. Credit to George Cladis for making a first try through his Doctor of Ministry research at exploring *perichoresis* for church leadership (Cladis, *Leading the Team-Based Church: How Pastors and Church Staffs Can Grow Together into a Powerful Fellowship of Leaders* [San Francisco: Jossey-Bass, 1999]). Credit also to Stephen Rasmusson for a similarly inspired Doctor of Ministry thesis (Rasmusson, "Campus Peer Ministry in the Name of the Triune God: A Training Model Grounded in Trinitarian Theology" [St. Paul: Luther Seminary Library, Archival/Manuscript Material, 2003]).

56. Moltmann, "Perichoresis," pp. 113-14.

Mission as *Confessio*

Our fourth signature stroke of the emerging missional church is *confessio*. In our opening text, Paul utters his "Amen" to God's promissory "Yes" in Jesus within a martyrological setting. This "Amen" comes in the face of a "death sentence," when what's at stake is the public "testimony of our conscience," when what's called for is "frankness and sincerity." Similarly, Reformation confessors, whether at Augsburg or Westminster or Barmen or Birmingham's jail, recognize the martyrological context of *confessio*.[57] Precisely because churchly Christians have always and will always potentially face times for confession *(tempus confessionis)*, the emerging missional church entails *confessio*. Mission devoid of *confessio* is a seed with shallow roots confronting the withering sun of pluralism and relativism, as well as absolutism. *Confessio* concerns public truth in a world Christianity context. In order to promote *confessio* for the emerging missional church, we need a critical retrieval of post-Reformation history, necessarily too brief.

One unintended consequence of the Reformation was the jarring loose of decades of growing nationalism, German and otherwise. The Holy Roman Empire had long been the lid on the pressure cooker of medieval ethnic-political-military stirrings. The Reformation turned the burners up so high that eventually the pressure cooker exploded. Military battles fought along papal and evangelical lines filled the decades after Augsburg of 1530. Aspiring peacemakers signed numerous treatises. The Peace of Augsburg of 1555 famously and disastrously became the pattern: *cuius regio, eius religio* — whoever rules, his religion also rules. Predictably, the formula failed for various reasons.

In 1618 most of central and northern Europe broke out in a series of wars that lasted until 1648, when the Peace of Westphalia took effect. This series of wars, known best as the Thirty Years War, are also known as the Religious Wars, or the Confessional Wars. There, ironically, is our word *confessio*. For tragic reasons, confessing churches quit confessing — that is, quit making testable public arguments regarding truth — and became confessional churches bent more on bearing military arms for intramural crusading. The Confessional Wars were Christians killing Christians: Catholics were killing Lutherans; Lutherans were killing Catholics; Calvin-

---

57. See Robert W. Bertram, *A Time for Confessing* (Grand Rapids: Eerdmans, 2007).

ists were killing Catholics; Catholics were killing Calvinists. Christians were killing Christians for many reasons, but always along the lines of Christian doctrine. Europe was devastated. Historians have estimated that the population of the German territories alone went from thirty-eight million people in 1618 to eighteen million by 1648. This was Sarajevo during the 1990s writ large, and for three decades. No one emerged unscathed.

A powerful undertow swirled during and after these wars and produced one of the greatest social movements of all time. Gradually, momentum built within Europe for a new age, and the movement came armed with its own two-edged sword: the modern mandate. People from different walks of life summoned European Christianity with this mandate. Imagine the following:

> Listen up, Christians. Christianity has brought Western society to a grinding halt. More and more of us over the last decades are becoming enlightened about our European situation. It might have been the case for the last thousand years or so that Christianity and the church have been the public glue holding Western social life together. That is clearly no longer the case. The church and its faith are now the social dynamite bringing death and destruction on a massive scale.
>
> We insist, therefore, on the following:
>
> You can be religious, if you want — Catholic, Calvinist, Lutheran, Anabaptist, whatever. You can even believe in God, if you want. That's fine. Some of us do as well. But a new command we give you, a new and modern mandate: Keep your faith private! Keep it in your heart, between you and God. In your family, that's okay, too. You can even get together voluntarily with other like-minded Christians on Sunday mornings, for instance, and worship to your hearts' content. We only insist that you keep your faith out of public view, out of public places, and especially out of city hall.[58]

Generally speaking, Christians obeyed the mandate with a whispered "okay." The Enlightenment movement, armed with its modern mandate, drew a line in the sand and gradually and progressively divvied up the Western world according to this line. On one side of the line sits the private world, the domain where faith stands as authoritative. On the other side of the line is the public world. But what stands as authoritative there?

58. This narrative is my own.

That was the $1 trillion question. Every society needs some authorizing glue to hold it together; the Enlightenment folks never doubted that for a nanosecond. They had ruled out religion for sure, and they were very skeptical about ethnicity because it was quite often fused with religion. Thus the Enlightenment looked to what it considered the opposite of faith, namely, "sweet reason." Reason, purified especially of religion — if not of everything else! Reason alone, they reasoned, would provide the social glue that would hold the public world together.[59] Here we have the other side of modernity's two-edged sword. After all, for decades, even centuries, natural science reasoning had been claiming victory after explanatory victory in reference to the natural world. Why not extend the sharp edge of reason to the public, social world as well? Reason is fully competent to identify *the facts.* Soon John Locke became the Joe Friday of the modern project, postulating a public world based on "just the facts, ma'am." Such positivistic objective reasoning would do for the social world what it had already done for the natural world, that is, it would define truth. Technology, science's fraternal twin, would provide instrumental reasoning, and together they would constitute the final frontier of the great society, efficient control, and endless progress.

In addition to faith and church, Enlightenment reason sent other goods packing to the private side of an ever-widening divide between public and private: moral values, other mere opinions, and the domestic family of women and children. Enlightened people saw the public world as the "real world"; indeed, this real world was "a man's world," including, of course, the world of work.[60] Under the modern mandate, the private family, whatever else it might be, became principally instrumental for men's public world, "a haven in a heartless world."[61]

This devastating bifurcation of public and private still persists, though weakened somewhat, and mission as *confessio* remains an essential element of the emerging missional church. *Confessio* is the church's

---

59. See Gary M. Simpson, *Critical Social Theory: Prophetic Reason, Civil Society, and Christian Imagination* (Minneapolis: Fortress, 2002).

60. See Warner Brothers, *North Country* (2005), written by Michael Seitzman, and directed by Niki Caro.

61. Christopher Lasch's account of the family, *Haven in a Heartless World* (New York: Basic Books, 1977), remains flawed precisely because he does not account for the heartlessness of the family "haven" itself, leaving him unable to locate and access the moral resources that families themselves desperately need today.

public mode of life that is always ready for martyrological times of truth and testing. The Reformation confessors, already at Augsburg in 1530, clearly understood that *confessio* as a churchly mode of existence going back to its originating moments entails two irreplaceable traits, among some others: publicity (in the sense of full public accountability) and eschatological futurity (in the sense of desiring a future open for testing, correction, and confirmation).[62] *Confessio* goes right to the head of the line of open opportunities for an emerging missional church, especially in light of the martyrological situation of world Christianity and of the other religions.

Mission as *Vocatio*

We have focused on two aspects of trinitarian thinking. First, with the Willingen meeting, we have affirmed that God's own *sending* empowers and gives roots to the missional church. Second, we highlighted *communio* as God's being in, with, and for the emerging missional church in the world, and the perichoretic power of *communio* as true correlate of mission as *promissio* and *communicatio*. Mission as *vocatio* finds its roots in the trinitarian scope of God as creator of all things.[63]

As an old and familiar offertory prayer puts it, the emerging missional church dedicates itself "to the care and redemption of all that you [God] have made." *Vocatio* attends to Christian participation in the Triune God's care for the creation. God's care keeps sinful, predatory human creatures and demonic powers from going hog-wild, so to speak, but it doesn't cure sin or eliminate the demonic. *Vocatio* protects and promotes

---

62. See, especially, the preface to the *Apology of the Augsburg Confession*, in *The Book of Concord*, ed. Kolb and Wengert, pp. 107-9; see also pp. 635-40. Luther offers his most sustained analysis of *confessio*'s publicity in *Dr. Martin Luther's Warning to His Dear German People* (October 1530) in *LW* 47:11-54. See also Robert W. Bertram, "*Confessio*: Self-Defense Becomes Subversive," *Dialog* 26 (Summer 1987): 201-8. Certain "confessional" theologies quite consciously eschew publicity in the sense of full public and global accountability, arguing that Christian confessing can only, by its very nature, be a self-contained, internal affair, a self-referential intra-Christian language game (see Martin L. Cook, *The Open Circle: Confessional Method in Theology* [Minneapolis: Fortress, 1991]; see also Pannenberg, *Systematic Theology*, 1:1-188.

63. Regarding trinitarian "scope," see Bosch, *Transforming Mission*, pp. 391-92.

the world's flourishing without pretending to provide the world's salvation.[64] Luther Seminary's mission statement attends precisely to that difference: "Luther Seminary educates leaders for Christian communities called and sent by the Holy Spirit to witness to salvation through Jesus Christ and to serve in God's world." Here we can see the reason to revise *missio Dei* to be *missio duplex Dei*.

Reformation heritages have most often focused on the worldly vocations of individual Christians and how the church can equip and celebrate those vocations. That's laudable. Here, however, I wish to pay attention to the corporate public vocation of the emerging missional church and the location within the contemporary global situation for that public vocation. The location for this vocation is global civil society; the name for this vocation is public companion. God is up to something new in civil society, and it's time that an emerging missional church attends to this newness. What is God up to in and through civil society?

Civil society is that vast, spontaneously emergent, ever-dynamic plurality of networks, associations, institutions, and movements developed for the prevention and promotion of this, that, and the other thing.[65] Civil society refers to a sociological space, not to a society that behaves itself civilly — with civil speech and the like. Civility is welcome, even necessary, but civil society is not reducible to civility. Civil society has gradually emerged since the eighteenth century as a critical component of the overall architecture or landscape of Western civilization. It is now emerging increasingly in other great civilizations around the world, which may lead to

---

64. For a classic statement from Luther, see "Sermon on Eph. 4:1-6," in *What Luther Says,* ed. Edward Plass (St. Louis: Concordia Publishing House, 1959), 3:1323, no. 4251. See Edward Schroeder, "Laity in Ministry to the World: God's Secret Weapon for Reforming the Church and the World," *Currents in Theology and Mission* 21, no. 1 (Feb. 1994): 45-51; see also Marc Kolden, "Creation and Redemption; Ministry and Vocation," *Currents in Theology and Mission* 14 (Feb. 1987): 31-37; Kathryn Kleinhans, "The Work of a Christian: Vocation in Lutheran Perspective," *Word & World* 25 (Fall 2005): 394-402; Robert Benne, *Ordinary Saints: An Introduction to the Christian Life* (Philadelphia: Fortress, 1988). From a Reformed perspective, see Douglas Schuurman, *Vocation: Discerning Our Callings in Life* (Grand Rapids: Eerdmans, 2004).

65. For my more extensive interpretation of civil society, see Simpson, *Critical Social Theory,* pp. 101-22, 134-41. I explore biblical and theological frameworks for God in civil society and for the churchly vocation of public companion in Gary M. Simpson, Diane Kaufmann, and Raymond J. Bakke, *Living Out Our Callings in the Community,* ed. Frederick J. Gaiser (St. Paul: Centered Life Series, 2006), pp. 5-46.

a global civil society. A very basic sociological map will help us gain clarity and discern what God's up to in civil society.

We start our map (Figure 1) with the political state within Western experiences, remembering that within the West there will always remain important contextual differences from country to country.

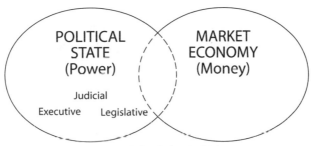

Figure 1. A Sociological Map

We can represent the political system as a giant sphere. Generally, there are three branches — executive, legislative, and judicial — though there are important national variations. The primary medium of the political system is power, administrative power. There is, in addition to the political state, another megasystem: the market economy. The medium of that megasystem is money. These are the two great systems that have come to dominate the landscapes of Western countries. The differentiations, autonomy, and overlap between and among these great systems vary from place to place and time to time; thus they are always empirical matters for inquiry and deliberative matters for interpretation and decision.

There is a third sphere, which sociologists call the lifeworld (see Figure 2 on p. 90). The lifeworld is where our personal lives unfold, where our values are formed, and where personal friendships develop. In the map represented here, the lifeworld appears flattened and squashed. Isn't that how we often feel about our personal lives and also about our personal values? The kinds of values that we have in the lifeworld of our families and friends do not seem to be nearly as strong or as vital or as determinative as do the two megasystems, with their respective media, that often drive and steer Western civilization and its values, virtues, and relationships. When this happens, and to the extent that this happens — again, this is always an empirical question — we experience the domination and colonization of

89

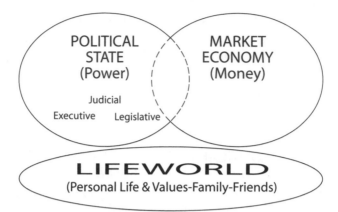

Figure 2. A Sociological Map

the lifeworld by the economy and the state. Lifeworld colonization generates and engenders injustices, diminished well-being, meaninglessness, suffering, oppression, and a host of seriously unpleasant things in various ways. In such contexts, civil society offers hopeful, emancipating possibilities for Western civilization, though there is no historical inevitability about civil society's emancipatory calling.

We can situate civil society on our map in the following way:

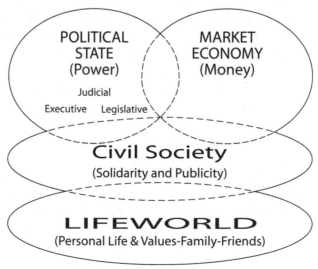

Figure 3. A Sociological Map

Figures 1 and 2 present a descriptive account accompanied by a critical aspect. Figure 3 flaunts, we might say, a normative hopefulness regarding civil society, which is held dear by civil society advocates. From here on I will exploit the normative aspects that do have empirical roots within existing Western experiences.[66]

The core medium of civil society is social solidarity, and we can imagine civil society's solidarity having two sides to it. These two sides correspond to the positioning that civil society has in reference to the everyday lifeworld, on the one hand, and the great systems of the state and the economy, on the other. We can call the side of civil society's solidarity that is turned toward the lifeworld the *sleuthing* aspect; and we can call the side of civil society's solidarity that is turned toward the state and the economy the *sluicing* aspect (Figure 4).

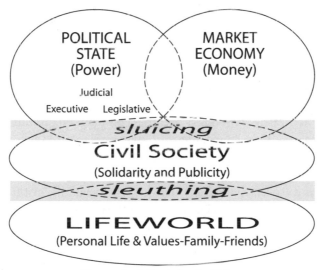

Figure 4. A Sociological Map

Sleuths, like their canine counterparts, always have their eyes, ears, and noses close to the ground. And thus it is with civil-society solidarity in its relationship to the everyday lifeworld. Civil society's teeming plurality of networks, associations, institutions, and movements for the prevention

66. For compelling international and cross-cultural research on civil society, see Center for Civil Society Studies, Johns Hopkins University, at http://www.jhu.edu/~ccss/.

and promotion of this, that, and the other thing regularly attune themselves like temperature sensors to how cultural, economic, and political problems, disruptions, and injustices resonate in the private arenas of everyday life as it really exists. As a sleuth, civil-society solidarity takes the form of research into the causative factors of, for instance, domestic violence. Civil-society organizations, networks, and movements identify, distill, and frame critical issues, and they give these critical issues a moral language and cultural energy. Often civil-society solidarity manifests itself through proposals, programs, and practices for moral and cultural formation within the lifeworld that alleviate, heal, liberate, and prevent problems, disruptions, and injustices.

Civil society also answers the vocation of solidarity with its sluicing side, which is turned toward the political state and the market economy. As a network of sluices with gates and canals connects uneven segments of a waterway, thereby facilitating the flow of goods across uneven sectors, so civil society regularly transforms and transmits its sleuthed critical intelligence, moral discourse, and cultural energy and practice about lifeworld problems into amplified forms of public opinion appropriate to the political and public spheres for democratic processing. By means of its sluice side, civil-society solidarity becomes a *political* public voice in a forthright way. More accurately, civil society becomes complex and multilingual political public voices that channel lifeworld dynamics toward the formation of political will and proposals to the political state for legislative, administrative, and judicial processing, decision-making, and implementation. Also in their sluicing aspect, civil-society networks, associations, institutions, and movements constantly and vigilantly assess the political state and its political processes. Civil society is thus the crucial sociological space for ongoing accountability all along the way. Civil society can also inform the market economy. At the present time, the sluicing processes related to the market economy remain less institutionalized and thereby less effective than those related to the constitutional nation-state. Civil society offers its critical, normative assets to the market economy with the goal of realizing corporate citizenship and responsibility for just and sustainable economies rooted in a more context-specific, stakeholder ethos. These public dynamics represent the *publicity* feature of civil society. Publicity as "making public" is the prime normative vocation of civil society. What God is up to here correlates with *confessio's* publicity, which we explored in the previous section. While the missional church's *confessio* makes God's redemption publicly available for testing and confirmation, the missional church's *vocatio* makes God's care publicly available for testing and confirmation.

Today an increasing number and variety of civil-society institutions need public companions who will encounter with them the moral meanings latent in the problems of contemporary life. There's a calling here. It's a risky vocation, of course, because the emerging missional church does not have a corner on the moral wisdom needed in many conflicted situations. As a public companion, the missional church becomes an encumbered community, encumbered with the predicaments of civil society and of its sleuthing and sluicing relationship with today's lifeworlds and mega-institutions. But the emerging missional church is no stranger to an encumbered life, to a life of bearing the cross.

In summary, consider certain marks that characterize the missional church's vocation as public companion: as such, the emerging missional church acknowledges a *conviction* that it participates in the Triune God's ongoing creative work; in civil society the missional church exhibits a *compassionate commitment* to other institutions and their predicaments; this commitment, in turn, yields a *critical* and *self-critical* — and thus fully communicative — procedure and practice of public engagement; finally, the emerging missional church, as public companion, participates with civil society to *create* and *strengthen* the fabrics that fashion a life-giving and life-accountable world.

I long to see how the promising, cruciform, Triune God will produce fruit through this interaction of an emerging missional church with mission as *promissio, communicatio, communio, confessio,* and *vocatio.* It is appropriate that we, those who stand with one foot still planted in a bygone era and the other poised to step into another, into a new era of mission, join that ancient evening prayer:

> Lord God, you have called your servants to ventures
>   of which we cannot see the ending,
>   by paths as yet untrodden, through perils unknown.
> Give us faith to go out with good courage,
>   not knowing where we go,
>   but only that your hand is leading us
>   and your love supporting us;
> through Jesus Christ our Lord, Amen.

CHAPTER 4

Ecclesiology and Leadership
for the Missional Church

Mark Lau Branson

God's grace — that is, God's initiatives throughout Scripture, God's love for the world, God's missional heart, God's great redeeming presence in Jesus Christ — is to be most clearly visible and tangible in faith communities. We have profound and rich texts from those biblical years: court records and prayers, narratives and sacred legislation, long poetic prophecies and festival liturgies, Gospel accounts, Epistles, and apocalyptic images. And I believe these texts should serve us just as they served their early recipients, as words that the Holy Breath uses to shape us as messianic communities.

It is this community-shaping labor of God that too often gets missed in our individualistic, positivist, pragmatic lives. We are prone to focus on personal activism or individual rights, on strategies and effective plans, on tasks, measurable outcomes, and credit. It's not that God's graces are not for individuals. Thomas Cahill, in *The Gifts of the Jews*,[1] shows how the Psalms teach about a countercultural God who is not just about tribes and their turf, but also about the human heart. Also, God does care about results, if by that we mean God's initiatives toward a full-orbed shalom and the identity and agency of those who use God's name. Individuals matter. Action matters. And, to use an organic metaphor, fruit matters. But in all of this, the front line, the focus, the mode is God's generative work of forming and nurturing worshiping communities, who by

1. Thomas Cahill, *The Gifts of the Jews* (New York: Anchor, 1998), pp. 198ff.

their nature are called and sent to participate in God's missional presence and actions.

In my participation in a church in Oakland, California, some time ago, we had begun to rethink the significance of our corporate life: How does personal discipleship relate to what we mean by the word "church"? As persons who were formed during late-modern consumerism, we recognized that we had been shaped by such priorities as individual choice, personal affectivity, and expectations (imaginations) that emphasized the pursuit of careers that should supply meaning and resources for our lives. We shared a growing conviction that these traits were being — or should be — questioned. In conversations, study, and prayer, we began a long journey of seeking alternatives. All of us who participated in that endeavor carry both wounds and joys from the journey.

All of our churches — indeed, all human communities — are shaped and sustained by hermeneutics: that is, the cohesion that makes possible human community, the energized glue that forms and deploys a people, is the generative cohesion of meanings.[2] We are formed, personally and corporately, as those around us (concurrently and historically) give us access to the world: the interpretive community gives meaning to, and makes real in particular ways, everything from the stars and clouds, to persons and places, to our days and years. A community's imagination, its stories and practices, its history and expectations — these are created and carried by words that interpret everything. We are constructed by and live our lives in and through language; not language as we have come to understand it as a tool, as positivism or as propaganda, but more like a "house of language."[3] Communities are formed and sustained — or not — by their hermeneutics.

2. I will use the word "hermeneutics" as a way to refer to what we do continually, often subconsciously: we interpret *everything* and we live inside our interpretations. By that I mean that we take a jumble of thoughts and experiences that exist in our minds and in our encounters with the world and we make meaning out of them. Our thoughts and experiences, any new perception or reasoning, are processed (always or almost always) through language. We have access to this process, internally and in conversation with others, mainly through words. So hermeneutics is the continual process of making the meanings in which we live.

3. The metaphor of language as a "house" has a lineage from Heidegger (who wrote that language is our "house of being") to Nietzsche (who called language a "prison-house") and into later linguistic theories. I will use it — less technically — to emphasize that we dwell inside a language, as a house provides setting and resources for life but can also restrict us.

In our Oakland church, our conversations revealed the limits of the "language house" we lived in. We brought into our newly common life our own concepts and experiences about "being church together." As we used words such as "church" and "salvation" and "mission," we began to create more space to live in. Our ideas and the texts we were reading began having a generative effect, as though we were remodeling our house. Without changes in language — the meanings of words, the give-and-take of conversation — we would have been stuck within the limits of the small, common ground constructed from what we brought into our first discussions. But within the ever-changing language of conversation and study, our imaginations and actions could change.

The Beatitudes as Hermeneutics

We all live and move and have our being in the dance of personal and communal experiences and interpretations. Because this interpretive work is socially constructed, shaped by traditions, narratives, and images, the language that we place alongside our lives gives us interpretive access to various definitions concerning blessings, hopes, fears, troubles, identity, and agency. It is within this framework that I propose that the Beatitudes give us access to reality, an access that we do not have without Jesus' presence and proclamation. Our vulnerability to the Beatitudes allows us to live into this reality of a Jewish, eschatological story as narrated by God. Or, in contrast, if we do not live in the house (or the interpretive framework) of the Beatitudes, we have limited access to God's reign as announced by Jesus. This is my beginning place for a gospel ecclesiology, by which I mean a missional ecclesiology, which is centered in the Good News of Jesus Christ.

Communities are often myopic, and their inadequate vision concerning what is real will leave them malformed. Faith communities that are unable to see and interpret themselves, their context, their traditional texts, and the presence and movement of the Holy Breath, assume shapes and practices that too often run counter to God's grace. The Moses of the Exodus worked on this with the murmurers; and the prophets spoke to the reality-denying communities of Israel and Judah. In the Beatitudes, Jesus provides access to reality — a hermeneutical entree — so that colonized Israel might be able to see and believe.

This takes place in the midst of a language house constructed by others. Rome had great plans for developing a globalized economy and bringing peace to its many subjects. It used indigenous leaders, significant military presence, taxation, and economic restructuring among its approaches to spread its wisdom and control. Many of Israel's leaders accepted that arrangement, thus creating a place for themselves. (These are like the "renegades" under Hellenist culture who are noted in 1 Maccabees.)[4] In this environment of globalization and accommodation, many Jewish leaders of Jesus' day claimed that this mix of Roman governance and continued temple practices was an arrangement blessed by God. It was pragmatic, it was workable according to their perspectives of reality, and, if all the people just stayed in their place, Pax Romana could continue.

The language house as provided by Rome would say, "Enter into Roman life, participate in the Herodian dynasty, and you will receive mercy, you can stay on the land, and you can be comforted and filled. Your reward can be now; you can avoid persecution; you can enter the Kingdom of Rome." And that is just what many of the Sanhedrin promoted. These words would shape a people in particular ways. The language indicated coherence between current arrangements and what some claimed that God was offering. So participants were encouraged to interpret a linkage between their leaders and God's mercy and grace in relation to provisions and rewards. But not everyone lived at ease in this house. If you avoided being formed by the words of official Israel, then you were likely formed by other texts, by other conversations.

Let's say that you are part of village life and are not quite sold on the current arrangements. Economics have been somewhat unpredictable because of globalization: Rome has worked toward some commodification in the Galilee fishing industry, and family farms are also being merged into larger operations, a necessary step for supporting Roman troops. And, though you can't say it too publicly, you do not have confidence in many of the priests appointed by Rome. You know the economic dislocation of the day, and that many are losing out to the Roman style of globalization. Many struggle with the temple compromises. You know that some have spoken out. You know that some have even taken up arms in rebellion. Many pray for a messiah. You meditate on the Psalms and Isaiah and Jere-

---

4. In agreeing with the 1 Maccabees perspectives on Roman oppression, I am not sympathetic with the violent counter-moves. Jeremiah and Jesus provide alternatives.

miah, and sometimes on the Maccabean narrative. Then disciples of this Jesus, along with others, gather around Jesus and hear these words:

> Blessed are the poor in spirit, for theirs is the kingdom of heaven.
> Blessed are those who mourn, for they will be comforted.
> Blessed are the meek, for they will inherit the earth. (Matt. 5:3-5)

Now what do you see? Whom do you see? What access to reality do you now have that you did not have until Jesus spoke these words? Let's say you are mourning about the current state of affairs in Israel. Voices around you work to change your political and theological outlook in order for you to decide that the current arrangement is great. But now Jesus announces another reality: those in mourning will receive comfort from God. This mourning is appropriate, and lamentations are appropriate because the situation calls for corporate sadness. But it doesn't end there, because God is involved: Jesus proclaims, "You will be comforted."

Or let's say you know God continues to bring about formation, but you are neither one to fight Rome nor to partner with them for a type of landownership. You are strong in your sense of God's presence and initiatives, but you have no need to "make it happen." And you hear Jesus say, "The meek will inherit the earth." Whether you are a subsistence farmer or a Jerusalem insider, the Beatitudes are earthshaking. Commentators and preachers have too often mistaken the Beatitudes for commands, or written them off as idealistic and naive, or relegated them to matters of internal disposition. But they are a lesson in communal sense-making, or hermeneutics. With this proclamation, and the fact that you are hearing it, Jesus is providing access to reality, access you have not had prior to the proclamation. In the language exchange, reality changes. In the proclamation, centered in the presence of Jesus, there is a reality that had not previously existed. A group of people — this circle of learners — are different and become named players, agents of an incipient interpretive community. Instead of "blessed are those who accommodate and acquire," Jesus says that God's blessing surrounds the poor and the meek. Rather than living as if the Sanhedrin and Roman globalization provide the truth, you now have an option. God's generative presence is available to those who mourn, those who are persecuted, those who hunger for righteousness.

There are other glimpses of the "Sermon on the Mount as Hermeneutics," where some have mistakenly sought pragmatic rules but where

Jesus offers a different reality. I do not, however, make the classical move that places the Sermon in the realm of attitudes;[5] nor do I just push for individuals to get a grip on God's reality, though that wouldn't hurt. Rather, I believe Jesus is forming an interpretive community that sees and receives the announced reign of God. The formation of such a community is necessary, or Jesus' actions and words will be misinterpreted. The parables, the miracles, the other teachings and practices — all serve to shape a learning community that is created within a new *house of language*. The Beatitudes uniquely offer us the gift of seeing and interpreting reality as God sees and interprets it, and that's the beginning place for the church. If one cannot enter this reality of the perspectives offered by Jesus, then the gospel is beyond reach.

Because of the presence of the reign of God in the presence of Jesus, there is a reality that is beyond the perceptions and interpretive capacities of the listeners. So Jesus begins by describing reality. The relationship between those shaped by Jesus and those shaped exclusively by other cultural forces is not merely a matter of values or doctrines. It is about hermeneutics (concerning what is real) and embodiment (practices).

Glen Stassen provides insights into the Sermon's structure by proposing fourteen triads.[6] Each triad names how historical Jewish piety interprets the tradition and specifies practices; then the triad notes how a "vicious cycle" develops that counters God's community-shaping salvation. So the earlier "eye for an eye" piety leads to violence and revenge, and alms-giving has led to hypocritical public displays. In each triad, Jesus offers practices that, rather than being idealistic and impractical, are grounded and doable: "turn the other cheek," "give your tunic and cloak to a thief," "pray for your enemies." If you live in the reality announced in the Beatitudes, then you can begin embracing such practices; but if Caesar and Herod are your interpreters, then you may believe that the Sanhedrin are the reliable leaders.

---

5. St Augustine (in *Our Lord's Sermon on the Mount;* available at www.newadvent.org/fathers/16011.htm [accessed Mar. 14, 2006]) taught that some behaviors called for in the Sermon on the Mount were impractical, but that the Christian is herein instructed concerning inner values and attitudes. See recent alternatives in Robert Guelich, *The Sermon on the Mount* (Waco, TX: Word, 1982) and Glen Stassen and David Gushee, *Kingdom Ethics* (Downers Grove, IL: InterVarsity, 2003).

6. Glen Stassen, "The Fourteen Triads of the Sermon on the Mount," *Journal of Biblical Literature* 122, no. 2 (2003): 267-308.

What Jesus offers is a story for us to enter, a story that counters Roman hegemony and Sanhedrin collusion — thus the requirement for repentance. Those who hear Jesus, those who witness his activities and have ears for his words, can enter the story of God's reign. The missional center of the new social entity is clarified by Jesus' dissolution of boundaries: wherever wealth or sins or holiness codes or other approaches to social isolation were formative, Jesus offered inclusive hospitality based only on whether hearers would entertain a turn from their previous story. Jesus sought out a shamed tax collector and a shamed adulterous woman.

In sending the twelve and the seventy-two, Jesus sought the social locations where the shalom of God's reign would be received. Even in the midst of the empire's dangerous military-trade routes, the twelve (and later the seventy-two) were to carefully interpret the setting to identify any welcome they could discern (Matt. 10; Luke 10). The reality provided in the Beatitudes, that is, the blessings prepared for the meek, the disenfranchised, and those who mourn, would help these missionaries interpret what they saw and what they heard. They were embodying the Jesus narrative in a set of practices: going, traveling light, avoiding conflict on the empire's roads, interpreting social realities, conversing, working alongside their hosts, sharing meals, announcing Jesus' initiatives, and regathering to interpret their experiences in conversation with Jesus.

During our early experimental years in the Oakland church, we were being shaped by several growing convictions.[7] As a United Methodist church, we had the denomination polity, but we did not have other early Wesleyan narratives, such as those of class leaders (lay pastors), covenanting groups, and those engaged with the working poor. We experimented with these stories and formed mission covenant groups that gathered around practices of covenant accountability and some specific missional engagement. Over the years, these mission covenant groups lived and worked and witnessed in public schools, through block parties, through public art, by building affordable housing, and in other tangible ways. Such activities allowed for friendships, for conversation, for invitation into homes and into church life. We also gathered every Wednesday evening for soup and Scripture. We usually worked through entire books of the Bible,

---

7. For a ten-year narrative concerning changes in the meanings and practices of this church, see Mark Lau Branson, "Forming Church, Forming Mission," *International Review of Mission* XCII, no. 365 (April 2003): 153-68.

but we continually found ourselves led back into wrestling with the Gospels and, more specifically, with the Sermon on the Mount.

We found that these practices changed how we read texts: we saw new meanings and we encountered new questions, and the text changed how we saw our daily lives. I especially remember a Wednesday evening, during perhaps the third time we had set aside several months to discuss the Sermon, when the questions turned on us. In reading Jesus' Sermon, we had often before that night asked: "What do we do with this? How do we apply these teachings." It all seemed distant. That night we heard the question, "What kind of people do we need to be for this text to make sense?" Over those next months, as we held before God our marriages, our money, our sorrows and sins, our neighbors and society, we found ourselves with new clarity and new energy.[8] The text interpreted us and beckoned us more deeply into its world. I have since then realized that this is consistent with Lesslie Newbigin's observation that the congregation is the hermeneutic of the gospel.[9] Thus, as a local church embraces the Beatitudes as hermeneutics, and as it lives into the narrative and its practice bundles, that church becomes the hermeneutic for others.

Church Formation

The primary narratives we have concerning how God takes new initiatives with his creation concern the formation of social entities that we often call "faith communities." From Abrahamic clan to a coalescing body of wandering former slaves, to a network of newly landed tribes, then a monarchy (united, divided, exiled, regrouped), Israel as the community-forming work of God is narrated through Jewish and Christian scriptures. God's new initiative in Jesus reinterprets that formation, brings power into those narratives, and announces a new era of God's reign that welcomes the world into a new covenant, into a new story. I believe that, by paying atten-

8. A notable new practice for us was extended group *lectio*. After significant times of study and discussion on the Sermon on the Mount, we gathered for four evenings in which we read the entire Sermon, followed that with silence, then gradually voiced what we were hearing as "words for us" as we sought the Spirit's promptings. This often clarified and made more specific how we were to enter the gospel narrative.

9. Lesslie Newbigin, *The Gospel in a Pluralist Society* (Grand Rapids: Eerdmans, 1989), p. 222.

tion to various aspects of God's initiatives and to how we are graced with narratives that give us access to that work, we can more faithfully participate in what we now call ecclesiology.

The reality authored by God, that is, the reign of God revealed in Jesus Christ, calls for the formation of churches with particular DNA. There are several essential aspects of ecclesiology, and they all commend specific attentiveness. In using the phrase "church formation," I am referring to the comprehensive work of God, with our participation, to shape the identity (being) and agency (doing) of a specific group of persons who are called and sent.[10] In order to better understand how we participate in God's grace, I will designate three aspects of this cooperative life as spiritual formation, congregational formation, and missional formation. Again, I use the word "formation" to note that these spheres of our corporate life deal with essential matters and how they are embodied. To create cohesion in the midst of these movements, I posit the centering characteristics and practices of worship and learning, with *praxis* as a description of our practice bundles.[11]

A Worshiping, Learning Community

Community

Meanings exist among specific persons; practices are embodied by groups. So if our discussion about ecclesiology deals with matters of meanings and practices, we are required to specify the social entity that is shaped by and gives shape to those meanings and practices. We need to ask: Where do the meanings and practices cohere? To what social entity do they apply? The development of concepts around the word "church" is not unambiguous. This is my thesis: meanings and practices are to cohere to a local on-the-ground church that is called and sent by God; and the word "church" in the

10. I am not sympathetic with modern efforts to fragment being from doing, especially those in which a person or group is encouraged to attend to their "being" because they have been attending too much to "doing." Jesus' words to Martha were not "Quit doing, start being"; rather, he acknowledged that Mary was doing something important other than cooking: she was listening. We would benefit from study and reflection on how particular activities shape us — our intellects, emotions, intuition, tendencies — but this is not a prompt to "be" instead of "do."

11. I will provide more on *praxis* below.

New Testament is primarily a reference to such local groups. There are other important related groups, such as mobile mission teams and regional networks.[12] However, I believe that these other concepts, including the humanly unidentifiable — thus invisible — existence of all true believers, are derivative.[13]

Standard reference works can provide extensive etymological resources, and I will note some highlights. The word *ekklēsía* was chosen often by the New Testament writers. The Septuagint uses *ekklēsía* and *synagōgé* for translating the Hebrew word *qâhâl* to indicate the summoning of people to assemble for war or administrative work or ritual.[14] Invisible social entities are generally not capable of those tasks. Like *qâhâl*, *ekklēsía* is in a word group concerning voice and call. In classic Greek literature, *ekklēsía* referred to the political assembly of urban citizens for decisions about laws, officials, policies, and judicial rulings.[15] In other words, these terms referred to an identifiable social group that gathered for the purposes of having specific influences on the larger local social environment. As post-Resurrection believers gathered, they chose neither *synagōgé* (except in James 2:2) nor *thíasos*,[16] both terms for cultic gatherings, but those with religious content differing from that of the Jesus movement.[17]

Word counts are inadequate for theological work, but some observations can be informative. Of the 114 occurrences of *ekklēsía* in the New Testament, through context or the use of the plural, the vast majority of usages indicate that the term refers to a local community of believers. Other terms and metaphors — body, house, building, family — also give weight to images of physical, local embodiment. Even when some supralocal uses appear, such as a regional network of churches or the expansion of the

12. Craig Van Gelder, *The Essence of the Church* (Grand Rapids: Baker, 2000), pp. 169ff.; see also Lesslie Newbigin, *Conversion and Context* (London: Church Missionary Society, 1978).

13. By "derivative" I mean that the regional networks and mobile mission teams (understood as visible and tangible) exist for the sake of the initial and ongoing formation of churches; and that without local churches the word "church" quickly becomes fundamentally altered and without its essential meanings even if one wanted to apply it to these other groups. However, I am not advancing congregationalism as a superior polity; interaction and accountability among churches is apparent in the New Testament and important today.

14. "Church," in *Dictionary of Paul and His Letters.*

15. "Church, synagogue," in *New International Dictionary of New Testament Theology.*

16. Worship and other cultic practices and beliefs mainly around Dionysos.

17. *Kaléō, ekklēsía,* in *Theological Dictionary of the New Testament,* abridged.

body metaphor in Ephesians and Colossians, my thesis holds: the intent of such usages is to bring meanings and practices to bear on the local group. Miroslav Volf says:

> The church nowhere exists "above the locally assembled congregations, but rather in, with, and beneath it." A congregation *is* the body of Christ in the particular locale in which it gathers together. . . . A particular denomination, the local churches in a cultural or political region, or the totality of local churches can be called "church" only in a secondary rather than a strictly theological sense.[18]

Barry Harvey's work is helpful in making links between eschatological identity (citizenship beyond the embodied time and place) and this local alternative *pólis*. Parallel to Roman civic gatherings, in which male landowners governed, ever mindful of "eternal" and idealized Rome, the congregations met to clarify identity and agency as citizens of God's reign; then they lived out those meanings in their context.[19] The "sent" nature of such *altera civitas* is important for our understanding. The "call" of *kaléō* and *klésis* (the word group for *ekklēsía*)[20] and the "vocation" in the Latin *vocare* speak to the identity and agency of churches as God's agents in the world. The call is corporate: we as churches are to be worthy of this calling (Eph. 4:1-4); it is a calling to specific corporate practices, a participation in God's initiatives in Christ Jesus for the sake of the world. This supports the phrase "called and sent" in current missional church discussions. My earlier comments on the centrality of hermeneutics finds emphasis here, in the implied "voice" that calls and the critical role that ecclesiastical leaders play in the proper working of their gifts that focus on the uses of words in the congregation (Eph. 4:11-16).

Therefore, I choose to reclaim the word "community" as central to ecclesiology. However, like other words, its popular usage is not especially helpful. Those of us in the "boomer" generation had to wrestle with meanings of humanness in the midst of corporations, computers, and commuting. So we developed relational concepts that were often based on nothing

---

18. Miroslav Volf, *After Our Likeness: The Church As the Image of the Trinity* (Grand Rapids: Eerdmans, 1997), p. 138. Volf is quoting Otto Weber.

19. Barry Harvey, *Another City: An Ecclesiological Primer for a Post-Christian World* (Harrisburg, PA: Trinity Press International, 1999), p. 22.

20. *Kaléō*, in *Theological Dictionary of the New Testament*, abridged.

more that affinity and affection. If we met someone, and shared some common interest, and "kind of liked" each other, we were instantly friends. On college campuses, including in Christian groups, we would speak of "community" with these emotional and fleeting traits. Lamentably, it happened that marriages often had no more substance than that supporting them. Then, as commodification became the *modus operandi* of churches, "community" (as affection and affinity) was packaged and marketed and sung in soft-rock tempo.

We need a conceptual framework for situating *community* in contemporary social life. This is not a new discussion; trajectories in the modern world have pushed philosophers and sociologists to engage these definitions because they go to the heart of humanness, our personal lives, and our lives together. Sociologists Talcott Parsons and Edward Shils have conceptualized a social triad of the individual living in relationship to society and culture.[21] "Society" is a system of structured relationships, embodied in micro-systems such as families, clubs, and neighborhoods; middle-sized systems such as clans, institutions, and cities; and macro-systems such as tribes and nations (and, for us, globalized entities). Jürgen Habermas emphasizes that societies are created "via the systemic interconnection of functionally specified domains of action."[22]

Parsons and Shils examined four dimensions of a society: social (the way a society defines, allocates, and uses social relationships); economic (the manner of defining, allocating, and using resources); political (the norms for defining, allocating, and using power); and legal (the structural approaches to individual and institutional legitimacy). For Parsons and Shils, "culture" is the patterned and interconnected system of ideas and beliefs, symbols and feelings, and values. Missiologist Paul Hiebert draws on this work and includes mental maps, symbols (especially language), worldviews, synchronicity, and diachronicity (somewhat similar to my own connection between meanings and practices).[23] As society has more

21. Talcott Parsons and Edward Shils, *Toward a General Theory of Action* (Boston: Harvard University Press, 1951).

22. Jürgen Habermas, *The Theory of Communicative Action,* vol. 2, trans. Thomas McCarthy (Boston: Beacon, 1987), p. 115. Habermas also works with the triad of culture, society, and personality (p. 138), but within a somewhat different framework.

23. Paul Hiebert, "The Gospel in Our Culture: Methods of Social and Cultural Analysis," in George Hunsberger and Craig Van Gelder, eds., *The Church Between Gospel and Culture: The Emerging Mission in North America* (Grand Rapids: Eerdmans, 1996), pp. 139-57.

to do with institutionalizing the means to serve the goals of large social entities, so smaller entities such as families and neighborhoods are important inasmuch as they serve the ends of the larger society. Culture embodies patterned meanings that are transmissible, and they may best be understood as ethnically or geographically based.

I believe that a fourth social entity, community, can add conceptual clarity to Parson and Shils's triad of person, culture, society. I am combining the common trait of proximity (the geographical concept of neighborhood) to what anthropologists A. L. Kroeber and Clyde Kluckhohn have developed in their collection of over 150 definitions of culture, in which a cluster of definitions emphasize the importance of patterned meanings and normative ways.[24] Josiah Royce, a philosopher in the American pragmatism tradition, said that the elements of memory, cooperation, and hope are essential for community.[25] Memory comes from a commonly held set of interpretations; cooperation requires that shared meanings are expressed in common; and hope arises from projecting the group, with its meanings, toward the future. Sociologist Robert Bellah and his coauthors emphasize how a "community of memory" retells its constitutive narrative in order to shape persons and the ongoing community. Some stories are exemplary, but there are also stories of suffering, not only suffering received but of suffering inflicted on others. In the context of such stories, members of the community participate in "practices of commitment," including "ritual, aesthetic, ethical — that define the community as a way of life." The shared memory also forms a set of meanings that helps turn the community to the future as a "community of hope."[26] Royce distinguishes between "a highly organized social life" of a society and this concept of "the life of the true community." He observes: "There is a strong mutual opposition between the social tendencies which secure cooperation on a vast scale, and the very conditions which so interest the individual in the common life of . . . commu-

---

24. A. L. Kroeber and Clyde Kluckhohn, *Culture: A Critical Review of Concepts and Definitions* (New York: Random House, 1952); I am combining elements from their "Groups C" and "E."

25. This is congruent with Paul Ricoeur's work on narrative and *mimesis* concerning human communities and hermeneutics. See, especially, *Time and Narrative,* vol. 1, trans. Kathleen McLaughlin and David Pellauer (Chicago: University of Chicago Press, 1984), Part 1.

26. Robert Bellah et al., *Habits of the Heart: Individualism and Commitment in American Life,* updated ed. (Berkeley, CA: University of California Press, 1996), pp. 153-54.

nity."[27] In other words, society and community often work against the shaping powers of the other.[28] We are all embedded in these overlapping spheres, caught by competing hermeneutics, leading to the phrase "community of interpreters," which Royce borrowed from Charles Peirce,[29] a designation concerning the priority of meanings:

> [Men and women]. . . form a community . . . when they not only cooperate, but accompany this cooperation with that ideal extension of the lives of individuals whereby each cooperating member says: "This activity which we perform together, this work of ours, its past, its future, its sequence, its order, its sense — all these enter into my life, and are the life of my own self writ large."[30]

In his exposition on the church, Cardinal Avery Dulles notes that Charles Cooley proposed a similar construct in his expansion of *gemeinschaft*. Dulles summarizes the characteristics of "primary groups": "face-to-face association, the unspecialized character of that association, relative permanence, the small number of persons involved, [and] the relative intimacy among the participants."[31] I believe these characteristics help with my definition of a community: a community is not a society; it is smaller, the shared meanings are more complex, its meanings and practices may or may not serve the purposes of the society, and individuals are covenanted into the community so that they project themselves fully into the meanings and practices.[32] In fact, Royce notes that struggle, that a loss of communal meanings occurs under the weight of the society: "It is the original

27. Josiah Royce, *The Problem of Christianity* (Chicago: University of Chicago Press, 1913; reprint, 1968), p. 262.

28. This is especially apparent in Jurgen Habermas's work on internal colonization; see *The Theory of Communicative Action*, vol. 2, pp. 332-73; see also Gary Simpson, *Critical Social Theory: Prophetic Reason, Civil Society, and Christian Imagination* (Minneapolis: Fortress, 2002), pp. 113-14.

29. Charles Peirce, *Charles S. Peirce: Selected Writings* (New York: Dover, 1958).

30. Royce, *The Problem of Christianity*, p. 263.

31. Avery Dulles, *Models of the Church*, expanded ed. (New York: Doubleday, 1987), p. 47. Dulles refers to C. H. Cooley, R. C. Angell, and L. J. Carr, *Introductory Sociology* (New York: Scribners, 1933), p. 55.

32. Over a period of time, participants develop tacit agreement, implicit or explicit, concerning some fabric of behaviors. This agreement or covenant is passed on as children are reared and newcomers are initiated. The basics of a covenant include founding stories (memories), required behaviors (cooperation), and a sense of direction (shared hopes).

sin of any highly developed civilization that it breeds cooperation at the expense of a loss of interest in community."[33] I am also making a distinction between community and culture. Community requires proximity for ongoing tasks of meaning-making and cooperative work, and, while adaptive, it has irreducible meanings and a porous border that allows persons and groups to enter the community, in words and actions, with what is an implicit or explicit covenant.[34] Persons of several cultures can be included as meanings and practices are negotiated by the interpretive community. And communities can connect across societal boundaries in order to understand the world and themselves, and cooperate in internal and external activities.

In our Oakland church, we were constantly aware that our social formation was in the context of an urban, late-modern consumer society, and in the midst of several ethnic groups of which we were composed. For example, we were trying to understand God's call to us to be church (a primary *vocation,* if we were reading Scripture correctly); but this call was in the context of the society's value on careers, a mobile workforce, and vocation as an individual's path to a meaningful life. We invested significant energy in discernment and in experiments that reinterpreted work as a subset of the church's vocation. We also found that matters of money needed attention, so families often decided to work on budgets together. Concerning ethnicity, we used cinema, literature, and field trips to stimulate conversations so that we could better understand the resources and challenges we brought from cultures. We frequently saw in the book of Acts and in Paul's letters the kinds of processes we had to engage in as we tried to understand what it means to be a faith community.

33. Royce, *The Problem of Christianity,* p. 252.

34. The size of the covenanting/core community probably correlates with Dunbar's number (approximately 150). I have seen such healthy churches plan ahead to plant new churches rather than to grow further as a congregation. I believe that cathedral churches (larger) have often played a significant role in networking and resourcing other churches, and they can do so today. They need to find ways to create multiple missional communities among their participants. In addition, smaller churches can have some flexibilities (concerning buildings and organizational structures); they also need networks for accountability and encouragement. In all cases, missional hospitality is a good measure of appropriate size. For psychological, sociological, and brain studies related to Dunbar's number, see R. I. M. Dunbar, "Co-evolution of Neocortex Size, Group Size and Language in Humans," *Behavioral and Brain Sciences* 16, no. 4 (1993): 681-735.

Worshiping

Worshiping is both adjective (character trait) and practice. Being a worshiping community is also a matter of hermeneutics and catechesis, which coheres with the Beatitudes discourse. In the Beatitudes, Jesus proclaims and invites: because the reign of God is present in Jesus, hearers can enter. That is, they can receive and respond to the reality available in the presence and words of Jesus. Similarly, worship is a church's centering access to God and the world as they really are. In worship we live into an interpretive act. Roman Catholic educator Thomas Groome says:

> By the grace of God's Holy Spirit, Christian liturgy is an intensified symbolic mediation of covenant and encounter between God and a Christian community in the Risen Christ; as such it is to symbolically express "in Spirit and truth" God's life in love to its community of participants and their life in faith to God, to empower people for God's reign in the world.[35]

Alexander Schmemann, coming from an Eastern Orthodox tradition, notes that Christian (and Jewish) worship implies a particular relationship with God and with the world.[36] In worship the meaning of the world is revealed: world as creation, our communion with God. Our participation with hands and ears and words and wine and bread and water and rhythm brings the sacramental nature of creation into our personal and corporate consciousness and practice. "[It] is this communion with God by means of 'matter' that reveals the true meaning of 'matter.'"[37] The world needs to be interpreted; its meaning is available to us as those who worship "God made flesh." In the particulars of this communal practice, we are reminded of the fact that we are "in the heavenlies," that is, we live at the cusp of God's redeeming initiatives.[38] "Worship is by definition and

35. Thomas Groome, *Sharing Faith: A Comprehensive Approach to Religious Education and Pastoral Ministry* (San Francisco: HarperSanFrancisco, 1991), p. 341; see also Patrick Keifert, *Welcoming the Stranger: A Public Theology of Worship and Evangelism* (Minneapolis: Fortress, 1992).

36. Alexander Schmemann, *For the Life of the World: Sacraments and Orthodoxy,* 2nd rev. and expanded ed. (Crestwood, NY: St. Vladimir's Seminary Press, 1973), p. 119.

37. Schmemann, *For the Life of the World,* p. 121.

38. This from interpretive work on Eph. 1–3 concerning Jesus and the churches he addresses being currently in the heavenlies.

act a reality with cosmic, historical, and eschatological dimensions. . . ."[39] Worship is at the core of our acknowledgment of who God is, what the world is, and who we are as called and sent.

Learning

So worship helps us learn that God is missional, that is, God enters the world and in love and grace God sends Jesus, the Holy Spirit, churches, even kings and asses into the world so that the world will know and be drawn to life and allegiance.[40] God's missional nature is expressed in the grace that draws us to worship — to submit to the centering revelation of communion and praise and sacraments and texts. In worship we are formed and transformed into a community of disciples. Churches are to have this discipleship character trait: we are to be learning communities. We are beckoned to learn of and from Jesus,[41] to be disciples and to make disciples and to attend to and follow the Holy Spirit. Learning is a communal activity, and God has made us interpreters together.

Charles Peirce and Josiah Royce emphasized the triadic nature of knowledge. William James had explained religious insight and knowledge as the interplay of percept and concept (with a bipolar reality between some experience and a person); but Royce claimed that this was inadequate. He called for a third element, providing a schema whereby a person perceived an experience and continued on with the interpretive work of explaining it to another person. In this theory of knowledge, reality was unavailable without the conversation; learning was always communal.[42] If we are to

---

39. Schmemann, *For the Life of the World*, p. 123.

40. I have been influenced by the last few decades' appearance of this theological insight concerning *missio Dei*. See, especially, David Bosch, *Transforming Mission: Paradigm Shifts in Theology of Mission* (Maryknoll, NY: Orbis, 1991); Lesslie Newbigin, *The Open Secret* (Grand Rapids: Eerdmans, 1978) and *Foolishness to the Greeks* (Grand Rapids: Eerdmans, 1986); Darrell Guder, ed., *Missional Church: A Vision for the Sending of the Church in North America* (Grand Rapids: Eerdmans, 1998). For a historical perspective with cultural awareness concerning our need to proceed beyond the hermeneutics and practices of Christendom, see Wilbert Shenk, *Write the Vision* (Harrisburg, PA: Trinity Press International, 1995).

41. Matt. 11:29.

42. Donald Gelpi, *Committed Worship: A Sacramental Theology for Converting Christians*, vol. 1 (Collegeville, MN: Liturgical Press, 1993), pp. x-xi. Gelpi agrees with Royce, against William James; see Josiah Royce, *The Sources of Religious Insight* (New York: Scribners, 1912).

know God and creation, we will be continual learners: that is, we will be a community of interpreters, shaped in the midst of language and practices.[43]

Learning is transformational because the community, including "strangers," gathers inside a story being written by God.[44] With numerous other communal narratives around us and in us, we repent or convert or are born again into the story of Israel and Jesus. Like the fellowship of the ring, we say "yes" and take off down the road in the heavenlies. We live in the world in such a way that, by knowing the Creator and Lord and Spirit, we also know the world as God's claim, and we know Jesus' redemption and the Spirit's company. So we have much to learn: sacred texts and worldly texts, stories of neighbors and enemies, narratives of nature and church. Reading these texts, entering into the triadic interplay of corporate study, we become communities of discernment, able to participate in God's story because it is revealed, sometimes clearly, sometimes *darkly.*

As we live into the story of the sending Trinity as a community of interpreters, we shape each other and we are shaped by a social imagery. Modern, functionalist approaches to vision, mission statements, or planning may create some important conversations, but they can also create straitjackets and thwart innovation and participation. There is a significant difference between corporate mantras and shared imagination, between church T-shirts and a courageous walk into missional innovation.[45] Any social entity lives into a matrix of meanings and practices that gel into images — organic, complex pictures of life-in-situation. Social imagery is a corporate, complex hermeneutic that a community has of itself: its past, present, and future. It is an interpretive imagery — cognitive, affective, conative — in which people live, giving them sanction, expectations, norms, and a sense of moral and metaphysical order.[46] A learning community has

---

43. Charles Taylor develops these critiques of individualism and delimited experiences in his *Varieties of Religion Today: William James Revisited* (Cambridge, MA: Harvard University Press, 2003).

44. Debra Dean Murphy proves to be a helpful guide on matters of Christian formation in *Teaching that Transforms: Worship as the Heart of Christian Education* (Grand Rapids: Brazos, 2004).

45. Slogans and multiple expressions can have their place, but churches need wisdom concerning real interpretive work and congruent embodiment.

46. Charles Taylor, *Modern Social Imaginaries* (Durham, NC: Duke University Press, 2004), pp. 23-25; see also Paul Ricoeur, *From Text to Action,* trans. Kathleen Blamey and John Thompson (Evanston, IL: Northwestern University Press, 1991), pp. 177ff.

such an imagery, and through the transforming grace of the Holy Spirit that imagery is shaped and reshaped as the local church discerns and moves in participation with God's initiatives. Because God's initiatives are also beyond the faith community, the church's borders are porous, and strangers are always entering into the learning, worshiping community.

Formation Triad

Churches, as worshiping, learning communities, while birthed and nurtured by the Holy Spirit, are also always shaped by the persons and social entities in their midst. Churches inherit traditions and images and languages and worldviews. Thus, to be churches of the gospel, of grace (by which I mean "God's generative initiatives"), they must reinterpret everything in light of God's reign as made present in Jesus. Church formation, that is, the shaping of particular people as a called and sent local church, is mainly a matter of receiving and attending and participating. In the midst of the promises of globalization, the images of the American Dream, the practices of commodification and consumerism, and the communication styles of marketing and propaganda, a church directs its attention to God's gifts and God's sending. Though there are a number of ways to parse this work, I will focus on congregational formation, spiritual formation, and missional formation.

By *congregational formation,* I mean the shaping of a specific, concrete Christian community. Perhaps the term "social formation" would be equally helpful: as participants we attend to our social life together; we pay attention to both the core and the periphery of our life as a covenant community. As I observed earlier, God has always been about shaping social entities for God's glory, so congregational formation is congruent with those narratives. The New Testament Epistles give us specific insights into early meanings and practices; the Gospels, partially because they were written later, give us additional texts that were intended, I believe, to shape the early churches by helping them enter more deeply into the Jesus narratives.

As communities initiated and continually shaped by the Holy Spirit, congregations are *people on the way.* They share a common memory (borrowed from texts and generated in their own common life), a common hope (both eschatological and as *chronos* imagery), and a present life of committed practices. They share relative intimacy, proximity, and permanence; and as those traits are reduced, there is often a sense that New Testament texts are somehow distant or irrelevant. A congregation's shaping takes place in the midst of societal and cultural and individual forces.[47] We are provided with numerous practices that allow us to participate in this shaping: worship, study, fellowship, service, prayer/discernment, generosity, and the equipping and deploying practices of the priesthood of all believers.[48] While there may be context-specific, temporal reasons for elements of homogeneity, the Pauline Epistles indicate intercultural and intergenerational norms.[49]

By *spiritual formation,* I mean corporate and personal attention to and participation in the initiatives (past, present, future) of God, including the generative and ongoing graces of the Holy Spirit. This last sentence also provides my definition of "spirituality," a concept that has numerous non-Christian meanings even in literature intended for Christians and churches. New Testament texts name specific Holy Spirit graces for congregations: gifts, fruit, wisdom, healing, hope, comfort, power, and ministry. As is true with our social life (congregational formation), our spiritual life requires that we pay attention and embody what God provides for us

47. For example, see Michael Budde, *The (Magic) Kingdom of God: Christianity and Global Culture Industries* (Boulder, CO: Westview, 1997); Rodney Clapp, *A Peculiar People: The Church as Culture in a Post-Christian Society* (Downers Grove: IL: InterVarsity, 1996) and *Border Crossings: Christian Trespasses on Popular Culture and Public Affairs* (Grand Rapids: Brazos, 2000).

48. On practices, see John Howard Yoder, *Body Politic: Five Practices of the Christian Community* (Nashville: Discipleship Resources, 1992); on narratives and rituals, see Herbert Anderson and Edward Foley, *Mighty Stories, Dangerous Rituals* (San Francisco: Jossey-Bass, 1998); on universal priesthood, see Hendrik Kraemer, *A Theology of the Laity* (Philadelphia: Westminster, 1958); John Howard Yoder, *The Fullness of Christ* (Elgin, IL: Brethren Press, 1987); Elton Trueblood, *The Company of the Committed* (New York: Harper & Row, 1961). A critical matter in contemporary discussions about the "ministry of the laity" is how difficult it is to understand the corporate nature of a missional membership in the U.S. society: see Branson, "Delayed-Disestablishment, the Emerging Church, and All God's People," www.fuller.edu/faculty/branson [cited Mar. 10, 2006].

49. On intercultural church life, see Curtiss DeYoung, *Coming Together: The Bible's Message in an Age of Diversity* (Valley Forge, PA: Judson, 1995) and Curtiss DeYoung et al., *United by Faith: The Multiracial Congregation as an Answer to the Problem of Race* (New York: Oxford University Press, 2003). On intergenerational congregational life, see John Westerhoff, III, *Will Our Children Have Faith?* rev. ed. (Toronto: Morehouse, 2000); Merton Strommen and Richard Hardel, *Passing on the Faith: A Radical New Model for Youth and Family Ministry* (Winona, MN: Saint Mary's Press, 2000).

even as we are in the midst of other shaping powers.[50] This spirituality is both corporate and personal in that all New Testament spirituality is congregation-based; that is, it is essentially engaged in God's initiatives of community formation as missional presence and outreach. Such spiritual formation is nurtured by worship, word, and mission; it is shaped in festivals, small groups, spiritual friendships, and families; it benefits from pastoral care and private disciplines. Among the traits of sanctification that are expressed in personal and corporate character, faithfulness, discernment, and missional engagement are the individual and corporate capacities for being an interpretive community attuned to God's Word and the immediate initiatives of the Holy Spirit.

By *missional formation,* I mean to indicate the local church's identity and agency in its encounter with the people and powers of the immediate context as well as in the larger world. As is true concerning a church's social and spiritual formation, this is God's initiative, and it is rooted in God's profound and abiding love. Missional formation is grounded in and defined by *missio Dei.* As an interpretive community, living in the midst of peoples and cultures and societies, a congregation discerns the shape of gospel life (the Holy Spirit's presence and initiatives) in a given place. This discernment is rooted in the biblical texts and takes shape in the interplay with historical and contemporary church materials and our own autobiographies. These are placed in conversation with the cultural and societal texts of the church's time and place, matters of ethnicity, migration, wars, famines, nations, economics, and media. A church does this kind of interpretive work with a network of nearby churches and in contact with the worldwide body of Christ. Congregational life is to be both centrifugal and centripetal — both incarnational and attractional.[51] The church as a hermeneutic of the gospel is salt, light, and a city on a hill: the church loves, does good, seeks justice, brings healing, celebrates, proclaims the gospel, and invites.

Our congregational, missional life is lived "in the heavenlies" (Eph.

50. See Philip Kenneson, *Life on the Vine: Cultivating the Fruit of the Spirit in Christian Community* (Downers Grove, IL: InterVarsity, 1999).

51. Some contemporary discussions speak of "incarnational" to emphasize an ecclesiology in which a congregation is dispersed into its environment, and "attractional" to emphasize an ecclesiology that draws others into its life. These definitions are problematic: I do not see these adjectives as either conceptually polar or as a choice. See Shenk, *Write the Vision,* pp. 45-48.

1–3): that is, there is an ongoing encounter between God's reign and all facets of creation, the substance and powers of the cosmos. At this cusp are the churches of God, missional congregations as God's primary agents for God's reign. As we receive the reign of God, we are continually transformed into the likeness of Christ; most notably, we are sent to live at that cusp. This is why *praxis,* while a framework that is helpful for all three aspects of church formation, is especially revealing concerning the missional formation of a congregation.

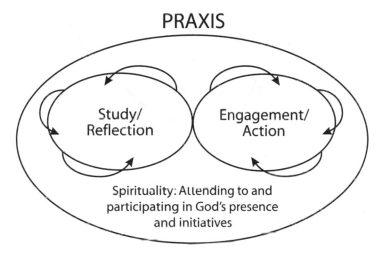

PRAXIS

Study/Reflection

Engagement/Action

Spirituality: Attending to and participating in God's presence and initiatives

Congregational Praxis

These three aspects of church formation must be nurtured in ways that make them mutually reinforcing and mutually interpreting. There is not a choice to major in only one; the three are interdependent. This work, as an ongoing transformational initiative of the Holy Spirit with a congregation, requires personal and corporate *praxis.* This term, rooted in Aristotle's concept of the interaction of theory and practice in the realm of ethics and politics, is often confused with practice. Critical theory has challenged the positivist sequence of theory-to-practice, a fragmented framework that posits pure theory leading to instrumentalist application. Paulo Freire posits a required "rhythm between action and reflection."[52] In expanding on

52. See Paulo Freire, *Education for Critical Consciousness* (New York: Seabury, 1974), pp. 100-101. While conceptually different, Freire's work is consistent with Aristotle's empha-

this, and using missional formation as a heuristic subject, I believe a local congregation engages a set of practices for "study/reflection" and a set of practices for "engagement/action."[53]

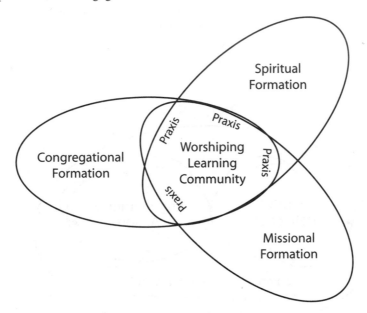

Hermeneutics is an ongoing work: the congregation as a whole, its many small subgroups and individuals, are interpreting and being interpreted as a learning community in mission. In study/reflection we are changed as the Holy Spirit leads the community, shaping our meanings and practices as we deal with texts and each other. During engagement/action we are transformed as we participate in the Holy Spirit's generative work among neighbors in the world. Then we are different as we come back to study/reflection. Thus we hear each other differently, we are engaged by texts differently, and we continue to be transformed. *Praxis* is this whole, this mutually transforming and changing set of practices and meanings. A church, in its identity and agency, is thus called and sent, formed and trans-

---

sis that *praxis* includes the true ends/meanings in an action. My emphasis is that *praxis* is a way of life that allows the texts of our past, our current experiences, and the substance of our eschatological hope to be brought to bear, by the work of the Holy Spirit, in our ongoing church life.

53. See Thomas Groome, *Sharing Faith*.

formed. A church is both reconciled and an agent of reconciliation.[54] We can only know the meaning of "church" in this concrete specificity.

Further, *praxis* is what makes conversion possible. Churches, and the people in the church, are converted into Christlikeness. Don Gelpi, a Jesuit, in connecting worship and conversion, posits five facets of conversion. Working within the Royce trajectory of American pragmatism and the functional specialties of Bernard Lonergan,[55] Gelpi gives a secular definition of conversion that refers to the change from irresponsibility to responsibility, and that includes accountability, in which humans "acknowledge a duty to render an account of the motives and consequences of their decisions to someone or to some community of persons."[56] Gelpi expands on five areas of conversion, and he describes adult Christians as those who can account for initial and ongoing conversion in all five areas: religious, affective, intellectual, moral, and sociopolitical. I believe that the local congregation is another sphere that needs specific attention, because in our Protestant environment many people would understand "religious" conversion as individualistic, something that is less likely in Gelpi's Roman Catholic context.[57] Therefore, parallel with the other initial and ongoing conversions, adult Christians need to be transformed from irresponsible to responsible practices in covenant life with a local church.

I believe that this definition of conversion and these five spheres can also apply to a church as a whole; the local congregation is called to move from irresponsible to responsible practices. The New Testament texts — Epistles and Gospels — show how the *praxis* rhythm of disciples and churches was expected to deepen the maturity, the transformation, of these new God-breathed social entities and their individual participants. So the heuristic focus on missional formation also sets the *praxis* norm for spiritual and congregational formation. There is continual movement between study/reflection and engagement/action in our lives with God and with each other. This is ecclesiology: a house of meanings and a bundle of practices that are given by God and that shape us on God's behalf for the sake of the world.

---

54. 2 Cor. 5:16-21.

55. Bernard Lonergan, *Method in Theology,* 2nd ed. (Toronto: University of Toronto Press, 1973, 1990), pp. 134ff.

56. Gelpi, *Committed Worship,* p. 19.

57. I made this case in a doctoral paper, and Gelpi concurred with the need for such an expansion on his work in many U.S. contexts.

Leading Congregations

Modernity and its institutions have shaped us and our understandings of congregational leadership with a mix of management theory, therapeutic models, and media/marketing that builds on earlier paradigms of scholarship and rhetoric. These are all efforts at "contextualization," that risky work of interchange between congregations and the sociocultural meanings and practices of an environment.[58] What I am pleading for is greater competence in hermeneutics. To be converted in Gelpi's framework would mean that congregations and their leaders become more responsible and skilled at interpreting the epistemologies, the motives, and the consequences of specific leadership models and emphases.[59] The leadership of any specific faith community will of necessity be nuanced by its context; so, rather than detailing a job description, I will limit myself to spheres of leadership that are congruent with the emphasis on hermeneutics and the *praxis* of church formation. Leadership needs to be plural, and it needs to be skilled in the work of interpretive, relational, and implemental perceptions and practices.[60]

Interpretive Leadership

Spirit-led interpretive leadership concerns the work of shaping "communities of interpreters" by forming churches that learn how to deal with texts in

58. See David Fitch, *The Great Giveaway: Reclaiming the Mission of the Church from Big Business, Parachurch Organizations, Psychotherapy, Consumer Capitalism, and Other Modern Maladies* (Grand Rapids: Baker, 2005); Brian Walsh and Sylvia Keesmaat, *Colossians Remixed: Subverting the Empire* (Downers Grove, IL: InterVarsity, 2004); Phil Kenneson and James Street, *Selling Out the Church: The Dangers of Church Marketing* (Eugene, OR: Wipf and Stock, 2003). In addition, Shane Hipps provides a thoughtful exposition on the impact of various forms of media in *The Hidden Power of Electronic Culture: How Media Shapes Faith, the Gospel, and Church* (Grand Rapids: Zondervan, 2006).

59. By "epistemologies," I am referring to the background knowledge, assumptions, and theoretical frameworks within which persons and cultures live. Habermas calls this "pretheoretical knowledge," and interpretive leadership brings clarity to what is often fragmented and unconscious (Habermas, *Communicative Action*, vol. 2, p. 153). See also Alan Roxburgh, *The Sky Is Falling: Leaders Lost in Transition* (Eagle, ID: ACI, 2005), pp. 87-98.

60. Mark Lau Branson, "Forming God's People," *Congregations* 29 (Winter 2003): 22-26; available at www.alban.org/ShowArticle.asp?ID=147 [accessed Mar. 14, 2006].

such a way that they participate more fully in God's initiatives.[61] I am using the term "texts" in its broader meaning, which includes inscribed materials but also experiences and perceptions and oral events — anything that can be interpreted. Craig Van Gelder observes that the visible church is at the intersection of biblical, historical, and contextual realities, with the Holy Spirit's ongoing initiatives serving as a fourth "text" to be interpreted.[62] How, for example, do congregational leaders initiate and nurture conversations about Leviticus and Jeremiah and Luke, placed alongside Calvin or Wesley, with attention to contemporary globalization and the American empire? As Groome notes, "the hermeneute steps into the back and forth between interpretation and explanation, between 'meant' and 'meaning.'"[63] This is a conversation into which interpretive leaders invite congregants.

Ronald Heifetz and Marty Linsky, both of the Kennedy School of Government at Harvard University, require that leaders "get on the balcony." Their analogy is of a dance floor, with constantly changing configurations, participants, pace, and space. Leaders face observational challenges about the situation itself, but also the difficult challenge of seeing themselves as players:

> Achieving a balcony perspective means taking yourself out of the dance, in your mind, even if only for a moment. The only way you can gain both a clearer view of reality and some perspective on the bigger picture is by distancing yourself from the fray. Otherwise, you are likely to misperceive the situation and make the wrong diagnosis, leading you to misguided decisions about whether and how to intervene.[64]

A major task, in the Heifetz-Linsky framework, is for leaders to discern whether they are dealing with technical or adaptive challenges. Technical challenges, while requiring significant leadership skills, are within the general realm of an organization's competencies. Adaptive challenges are beyond the current knowledge, competencies, and regularized activities of the organization. Adaptive leaders are able to mobilize the whole organiza-

---

61. Thomas Groome, *Christian Religious Education: Sharing Our Story and Vision* (San Francisco: Harper & Row, 1980), p. 25 (drawing on Gadamer).

62. Van Gelder, *Essence of the Church*, pp. 39ff.

63. Groome, *Sharing Faith*, p. 224.

64. Ronald Heifetz and Marty Linsky, *Leadership on the Line: Staying Alive through the Dangers of Leading* (Boston: Harvard Business School Press, 2000), p. 53.

tion toward change in culture, perspectives, and learning, so that effective interpretive leadership sets up the related tasks that reshape activities and relationships.[65]

Jürgen Habermas posits that one's lifeworld (or worldview, including culture, language, and other preconscious assumptions about "the way things are") is available for consideration in "world concepts,"[66] in which communication must function with integrity. Habermas specifies these three worlds as objective, subjective, and social.[67] The triadic understanding of knowledge from Peirce serves well here: our "communicative competence" (Habermas's term) is dependent on the interpretive work that we do in communicating about something, and there are recognizable standards for the adequacy of the communication aligned with the "something" we are discussing. In the object world, where description and validity claims are important, Habermas uses the standard of *truth* (with basically a correspondence definition) with the goal of creating a body of shared knowledge about states of affairs. In the subjective world, in which communication is expressive and affective, honesty is the measure and trust can be fostered. In the social world, in which humans form and reform ways of living together (such as regulations and intentions), a priority for love and justice allows appropriate norms to be shaped. Interpretive leaders can shape environments, questions, topics, and input that serve such competencies.[68]

Church groups can easily begin and end with "oughts," but they fail to deepen the conversation to embrace subjective and objective narratives and

---

65. In addition to the Heifetz-Linsky book, see also Ronald Heifetz, *Leadership Without Easy Answers* (Cambridge, MA: Harvard University Press, 1994).

66. A lifeworld is a socially constructed set of meanings and behaviors within which a social group lives, communicates, and acts. It is a taken-for-granted "background" for everything. But a group has access to the lifeworld through problematizing (or making conscious in conversation). This is the basis for Habermas's delineating of three worlds, each with its own conceptual framework and requirements for communication. See also Simpson, *Critical Social Theory*, pp. 87ff.

67. Jürgen Habermas, *Communicative Action*, vol. 2, pp. 119-21. Habermas works explicitly to improve our skills within late modernity; he counters frameworks by positing a postmodern shift.

68. Habermas's theory gives access to matters of legitimation, such as the assumptions and epistemologies behind conflicts that exist between a culture or community and the society in which it lives. This can be helpful for churches seeking a way forward on meanings, identity, and imagination. See Habermas, *Communicative Action*, pp. 113-97, and Simpson, *Critical Social Theory*, pp. 131-45.

other materials. Or conversations can begin and end with subjective expressions, avoiding any (implicit or explicit) covenant or theological claims. Conversations about money in our Oakland church were prompted when we considered tithing as a norm for covenant members. (This would be Habermas's social world: requiring that we seek to be just and appropriate.) Overall, this was considered a faithful step; but as the covenant groups met, we often had confessions as we struggled with the norm. We decided to have members write a "money autobiography," then speak as they chose about how they would answer a set of questions concerning the best and worst memories of money during phases of their lives. The exercise also asked for a person's candid assessment of his or her current relationship with money. (This pushed us on Habermas's subjective world, which requires honesty.)

In several groups, and between some families, this led to specific tasks, such as tracking income and expenses, creating and evaluating personal and family budgets, and experimenting with some shared property (appliances, cars, tools, and the like). (Habermas's object world and his call for truth are about these matters of discovering and describing observable states of affairs.) The combination of honesty, truth, and appropriate norms provides a thicker access to our life together, giving us multiple approaches to reality and communication. Interpretive leadership requires this kind of comprehensive work.

Relational Leadership

Relational leadership concerns how social construction works generatively to form new muscles and synapses so that we are healed and loved and grouped and partnered as the body of Christ. As we are working toward increased fluency within the congregational house of language, that fluency and any resulting characteristics require human connections. Congregational leaders help weave new relational networks within the church and with neighbors; they form new connections across old boundaries, modeling and creating new contexts for speaking and listening, and for experimenting with synergism. This is a work that follows the lead of the Holy Spirit and needs the Spirit's power. Love, reconciliation, and missional partnering are all based on the Son's relationship with the Father, which is then promoted in the church by the Spirit.

Relational leaders often need to bring forward the resources of conflict resolution and healing. They nourish the social imagery about who is with whom, who has a voice, and how personal and corporate character is formed. Networks of families and single people become the corporate youth ministers of a congregation; seniors and children learn to converse and serve together; newcomers and pillars of the church share meals and stories, and thus ethnic and economic boundaries are crossed. This work of leaders is based in the interpretive work of discernment: How do we connect with the Holy Spirit's initiatives in the world, and what kind of people is God making us into? It is notable that Paul's Epistles give a significant amount of attention to relational matters: how we treat each other and how we express God's grace in our relationships. The assumption is that our environments and histories have already had a major influence, so relational leaders, ever aware of the context and its powers, find and nourish the resources that make for love. This work is especially relevant to congregational formation and missional formation; and both of these are interactive with spiritual formation (our discernment of and participation in God's initiatives).

Implemental Leadership

Implemental leadership attends to structures, activities, resources, and responsibilities in order to give meanings and relationships the necessary avenues for embodiment, equipping, expression, organization, and endurance.[69] We inherit structures; members bring in structures from work and community; our society assumes (sanctions) certain structures. The work of implemental leaders is to shape and reshape activities and structures to be more coherent and consistent with generative meanings and relationships.

Leaders can implement interpretive work in Bible studies, sermon planning, numerous settings for dialogue, ways to locate and disperse printed resources and other media, means for intentional catechesis, and continual engagement with people and powers of the local context and beyond. If studies and sermons and small groups all pull participants in different directions, the formation of communal meanings is fragmented.

---

69. On polity and governance, see Van Gelder, *Essence of the Church*, pp. 172ff.

If meanings and activities of mission or worship are shared only in a small group, and separated from the overall life of the congregation, coherence is impossible. Critical matters concerning cultures and other on-the-ground circumstances exist here. Implementation, like the work on meanings and relationships, is always local, even as it benefits from larger and broader associations.

In a Presbyterian (USA) church that I attended, I observed that decades-long relationships existed, but there also seemed to be some ongoing intimacy among members. I asked an elderly member: "Are you ever in each other's homes for meals or social gatherings — other than scheduled meetings?" He replied, "No. We used to do that, but we haven't for awhile." A couple of weeks later he saw me at church. "You know," he began, "We were in each other's homes back when our kids were younger. Not so much now." Then again, a couple of weeks later, he approached me and said: "You know, we were in each other's homes for meals until the church started the monthly potluck lunch." A commendable intention to initiate a serving relationship through a regular shared meal may have resulted in relational losses. I doubt that those who started up the monthly potlucks were aware of the consequences. Implemental leadership needs to attend with care to a congregation's structures, activities, and behaviors; it needs to analyze the systems and connections and be observant when it introduces experiments and changes.

Cohesion and Dispersion

Plural leadership, in which a local church recognizes and nurtures the Holy Spirit's numerous gifts and prompts, makes more likely the priesthood of all believers. Leadership is usually circumstantial, arising in a situation, funded and guided as appropriate. Expectations need to be constantly clarified; the cohesion is largely set through the interpretive activities. Sometimes experiments need to be sequenced or delayed, and members need to join in (submit to) the activities and leadership of others even as new ways may be arising. Congregational leaders play a large role in sanctioning and modeling, prompting and encouraging, participating in risks, and continually making explicit the meanings, relationships, and operations. Sometimes congregational leaders function in formal, identifiable groups; at other times there are temporary groups that set in motion certain experiments, introduce practices, or provide monitoring, evaluation, or imagination during transitions.

Heifetz's distinction between technical and adaptive leadership is important.[70] Churches need excellent technical leadership to shape a church's identity and agency when challenges and activities are within existing capacities. *Technical* matters still require learning and change and decisions and experiments, but much is knowable: circumstances, basic direction, resources, and forms of evaluation. *Adaptive* matters concern the challenges we face for which much is unknown: we do not adequately know the circumstances, direction, means, resources, or goals. This is harrowing for those who treasure predictability and control. Not only does adaptive change require that leaders bring others along into an indefinable and unpredictable future, but it also means that we as leaders, and those we lead, will become something else: our identity and agency will change in the midst of the movements.

Churches are not served well by functionalist approaches to leadership in which different interpretive work, relational work, and implemental work are separated. Some group of leaders in a congregation needs to give ongoing attention to the cohesion of leadership spheres and the various aspects of church formation.[71] Sermons and budgets and youth and loving our neighbors must not be merely separate departments or committees that are tangentially related under an IRS nonprofit letter. This knitting together of people and meanings and activities — the cohesion and consistency — is the generative work of the Holy Breath, who provides for leaders who constantly spread the capacities for identity and agency throughout the congregation.

Churches and the Trinity

James McClendon, in emphasizing the "flesh-and-blood local congregation" that "echoes in its present life Jesus' prayer," also cautions against in-

---

70. Heifetz, *Leadership Without Easy Answers*, pp. 73ff.

71. In our Oakland church we observed that our mission covenant groups, which adopted basic Wesleyan disciplines plus a specific missional outreach, tended to be healthy and engaged if we could identify three specific leadership roles, paralleling the spheres of leadership noted here: mission prophet (interpretive), mission administrator (implementation), and class leader (a Wesleyan term for someone doing pastoral work, attending to relationships and spiritual formation).

strumental understandings of the congregation.[72] This is a concern I have also tried to address in my positing various aspects of church formation. These are not first a set of functions; rather, these are narratives of God into which we are led by the Holy Spirit. The Trinity, understood as *perichoresis*, helps us understand how we in a church indwell each other and dwell together in the flow of love, mutuality, intimacy, and submission.[73] We are given some insights into the life of the Trinity in passages about the Father and the Son, their mutual indwelling, and how in seeing Jesus we see the Father. Further, the Son follows the Spirit, and the Spirit is "the Spirit of the Lord" and "the Lord is the Spirit." There is inclusion, unity, and cohesion; but there is also differentiation, identity, and plurality. Our life together is to have correspondence with their life together.

The interior life of the Trinity grounds its sending nature and activity, and defines it as essential.[74] As the Father sends the Son, as the Son does the Father's business, as the Spirit leads the Son, as Jesus breathes the Spirit into the disciples, as Son and Father send the Spirit, churches learn the essence of our identity and agency. Our *esse*, as congregations and as the worldwide church, is social/relational, spiritual, and missional. This is our vocation, our salvation, our glory — in and for the glory of God.

72. James McClendon, Jr., *Systematic Theology: Doctrine* (Nashville: Abingdon, 1994), p. 328; the reference is to Jesus' prayer in John 17.

73. Perhaps initiated by Pseudo-Cyril; see Colin Gunton, *The One, the Three, and the Many* (Cambridge, UK: Cambridge University Press, 1993), pp. 163ff., 214ff.; see also Volf, *After Our Likeness*, pp. 208ff.

74. Van Gelder grounds his ecclesiology in the being-ness, social reality, and roles of the Trinity.

SECTION II

Introduction

These next four chapters provide the reader with case-study examples of how to think about the missional church from the perspective of a particular church tradition within a particular context. Thinking about the missional church in relation to a variety of church traditions and cultures is instructive for understanding both what is common to all the traditions and what is unique to each of these missional churches in context.

In the first chapter, Terri Martinson Elton provides an overview of the historical development of the United States and the Protestant denominations that developed within this context. She proposes a fourfold lens for framing the development of both: discovery, democracy, equality, and diversity. The key issue Elton addresses concerns how to reframe Protestant denominations from a missional perspective. Questions she explores include: To what extent is it helpful to use a denominational understanding of the church in our time? How is the emerging postmodern condition changing the face of the denominational church? What insights does a missional church perspective bring for reclaiming a denominational understanding of the church by inviting a rethinking of its identity?

Joon Ho Lee's chapter brings the reader into the context of Korea and the denomination there known as the General Assembly of the Presbyterian Church in Korea (GAPCK). Lee introduces the reader to the historical development of mission activity and the rapid growth of the church in Korea, both of which are fairly recent in origin. Drawing on the unique contextual understanding of Korean culture through the lenses of love, suffering, and patience, this case study develops an argument for a missional understanding of the church in this unique context. Questions that Lee explores include: To what extend did Western mission practices and forms of the church both contribute to and hinder the development of the church in Korea, especially the Presbyterian Church? How can one explain the rapid growth of the church in all of Korea up to the 1950s, and in South Korea since that time, yet also account for the recent plateau that the church has experienced? What resources are available within Korean culture that a missional church understanding can use in reframing the identity and purpose of the GAPCK?

Mary Sue Dehmlow Dreier's chapter introduces the reader to the challenges facing the Evangelical Lutheran Church in America (ELCA). This denomination was formed from several predecessor bodies in 1987; and those bodies themselves had been the result of numerous historical mergers. Although Lutherans have been hesitant to view themselves as a mainline denomination, this essay shows how this faith tradition was dramatically shaped and reshaped by the historical developments of the American story. Noting the diverse theological perspectives that are now confronting this denomination, and the crisis that many feel the church is experiencing because of them, Dehmlow Dreier offers an alternative way of framing a path forward in the midst of this diversity — a missional church perspective. This perspective is grounded in a proposal that seeks to develop a communally discerned and theologically framed understanding of this denomination, and then applying that understanding to the particular issues confronting the ELCA.

James Tzu-Kao Chai's chapter introduces the reader to the nation of Taiwan and the Southern Baptist Church within this unique context. Chai provides a helpful overview of the historical introduction of foreign missions into this context and the development of the church that followed. He notes especially the importance of the formative period following World War II, when the Nationalist party in China was displaced by the Communist party and fled to Taiwan. Scores of missionaries who had worked in China joined this relocation, including significant numbers of Southern Baptists, who then proceeded to introduce this denomination into Taiwan. The questions Lee explores include: How does one account for the very small percentage of the Taiwanese population (under 3 percent) that has become Christian? What are the implications of trying to transition a denomination from being led primarily by Western personnel to one that is led by indigenous leadership? How well do the Western practices of church life that were introduced by missionaries serve the life of the church within this context, and how might a missional church perspective offer fresh insights for re-envisioning and recontextualizing this denomination?

CHAPTER 5

Corps of Discovery: A Twenty-First-Century Contextual Missiology for the Denominational Church in the United States

Terri Martinson Elton

Introduction

On May 14th, 1804, the Corps of Discovery set sail up the Missouri River with forty-seven men under the direction of Meriwether Lewis and William Clark.[1] The object of their mission was to find a "northwest passage" to the Pacific Ocean.[2] On September 23rd, 1806,[3] twenty-eight months after setting sail, the corps returned, having crossed more than 8,000 miles of frontier only to report that they had not accomplished their mission.[4] It was true that they had not discovered a continuous waterway all the way to the Pacific, but Lewis and Clark had accomplished so much more. They were the first to chart maps of this territory; they discovered thousands of new plants and animals; and they found their way through previously unknown terrain, something no "United States citizen had ever done before. [E]very American living or traveling west of the Mississippi River today goes in the footsteps of Lewis and Clark."[5] As a result of this mission, the

1. *National Geographic Lewis and Clark: Great Journey West* (2002) DVD.
2. Stephen E. Ambrose, *Lewis and Clark: Voyage of Discovery* (National Geographic Society, 1998), p. 2.
3. *National Geographic Lewis and Clark: Great Journey West* (2002) DVD.
4. Ambrose, *Lewis and Clark*, pp. 229, 234.
5. Ambrose, *Lewis and Clark*, p. 231. I will use "American" in this essay to describe the people living in the United States. I realize that American can also refer to people living in Central or South America; but many of the sources I refer to are writers from the United

United States' focal point changed: it shifted from the East toward the West, and a new ideology emerged.[6] It is not clear what drove Lewis or Clark, but with their quest they set a new course that redirected the future of a people.

At the time of this 200th anniversary of Lewis and Clark's historic Corps of Discovery, it may be appropriate to form a new "corps of discovery" and set out on another mission — a mission that seeks new opportunities for sharing the gospel in the United States during the twenty-first century. It is perhaps time for leaders of the twenty-first-century church to heed God's call and participate in God's mission so that the denominational church may discover a contextual missiology for a new era.[7]

The church of the twenty-first century can learn from the trailblazing adventures of past leaders as it prepares to move forward at a new moment in time. In an effort to prepare for such an adventure, I will look back in this chapter into American history, unearthing things we have learned in the political setting of the United States and from the history of denominationalism within the American Protestant church. I hope to stir the reader's imagination about the future of denominationalism, particu-

---

States who use this term to describe themselves. Periodically, I will use "America" to refer to the geographic region of the United States. This, too, picks up on the reference writers use in describing their own land.

6. Ambrose, *Lewis and Clark*, p. 26.

7. Hereafter, I will use "church" (with a lowercase "c") as a shortened version of the denominational church in the United States. While I will lay out the evolution of the denominational church later in this essay, I will offer a brief definition here. "Demonination," as a word, was used in the early years of the United States as a way for the Christian church to speak of the multiple expressions of Christianity in a neutral and unifying way. It referred to the group being discussed as but one member of a larger entity. "Denominationalism" was used as the opposite of sectarianism. Many church historians took up "denominational theory" as a way to study the unique evolution of the Christian church in the United States. While denominationalism has sociological elements to it, it also has theological ones, for within denominationalism there exists a theology of the church, or ecclesiology. This embedded ecclesiology is the primary angle of denominationalism that I will use in this essay. It is important to note that, in the early years, denominationalism primarily referred to the Protestant church. More recently it has come to encompass Catholics and Jews as well. This essay, however, will focus primarily on the Protestant development of denominationalism. For more on denominationalism, see Sydney E. Ahlstrom, *A Religious History of the American People* (New Haven, CT: Yale University Press, 1972), pp. 381-82; Winthrop S. Hudson, *Religion in America: An Historical Account of the Development of American Religious Life*, 4th ed. (New York: Macmillan, 1987), pp. 80-81; Russell E. Richey, ed., *Denominationalism* (Nashville: Abingdon, 1977), pp. 9-15, 19-42.

larly about developing a missional ecclesiology for the denominational church in a postmodern age.

The Landscape of the United States

Setting the Political Scene

Each year millions of tourists drive across South Dakota prairies through farms, ranches, and tourist spots for the sole purpose of pausing at a significant piece of U.S. history. Mount Rushmore, a tribute to four influential presidents, is a lens into the heart of the United States: George Washington, Thomas Jefferson, Abraham Lincoln, and Theodore Roosevelt highlight crucial sources of the DNA of the nation they served.

Thomas Jefferson, who was vice president for one term and president for two, shaped the United States in its founding years — before it was a democratic republic — as much as when he was in office. He was known for his writing ability and thus was asked to draft a document that articulated the desires of the nation's early leaders. In a time when wealthy landlords ran society, and when opportunities were not available for all people, he called for "life, liberty and the pursuit of happiness." In an age when equality was not practiced, he wrote that "all men are created equal," and in doing so, "foresaw a United States with a democratic, representative government — one that placed much responsibility on the individual and relied little on strong central control."[8] Thus Jefferson's writings gave birth to the Declaration of Independence, and the road to democracy began. It is almost impossible to imagine how radical these ideals were at the time, and equally hard to imagine the United States without such a foundation.

However, putting these ideals forward in writing was not enough to build a country. People needed to move these ideals into reality. And people did! George Washington, recognized for his military success, rose up among the passionate Founding Fathers as the one who would help give form to this new society. Moving from the chair of the Constitutional Convention to serve as the first president of the United States, Washington helped establish a democratic, representative governing system. The cor-

8. Robert G. Athearn, *American Heritage Illustrated History of the United States: A New Nation,* vol. 4 (New York: Choice Publishing, Inc., 1989), p. 291.

nerstone was laid: the United States was a new nation operating within a new framework. Just as the poetic words of Jefferson continue to call for freedom, the mall in front of the Washington Monument embodies the democratic ideals Washington believed in: it continues to be the location for demonstrations, protests, and rallies.[9]

The establishment of the United States was not all smooth sailing: the country that strove for equality, liberty, and unity had many heavy seas to navigate. In fact, "[i]n the middle of the 19th century . . . many people in America saw the northern and southern halves of the country as being so different that they might as well have been two different worlds."[10] A nation that was divided and still practicing slavery was the situation Abraham Lincoln stepped into. On January 1, 1863, the Emancipation Proclamation went into effect, though it did not immediately end slavery — or the Civil War. But it did become a turning point in the nation's history, once again embedding the principles of the Founding Fathers into a new generation of Americans. In his Gettysburg Address, Lincoln "eloquently outlined his general hope for the outcome of the war," and called the nation back to its core principles.[11] On April 9, 1865, the news of Lee's surrender signaled the end of the war, but, "[l]ess than a week later, on April 14, the entire country was stunned by the news that Abraham Lincoln had been shot by an assassin."[12] Lincoln's primary work, however, was completed. He had done what some considered impossible: by the end of his life as president, he had laid the foundations for freeing the slaves, and the United States had remained a union.

As the American nation moved into the twentieth century, it needed a new style and focus of leadership. Theodore Roosevelt "realized that in the new century America would have to assume more responsibility, expand its reach and interests, reject its nineteenth-century role of isolationism, and take up its twentieth-century burden of leadership" (Ambrose, p. 80). And with Roosevelt's lead, the new century was marked with a new style of leadership. Theodore Roosevelt's "greatness lay in preparing America to become a world power" (p. 78). Roosevelt moved America to

9. Stephen Ambrose, *To America: Personal Reflections of an Historian* (New York: Simon and Schuster, 2002), p. 13.

10. Rachel Filene Seidman, *The Civil War: A History in Documents* (New York: Oxford University Press, 2001), p. 13.

11. Seidman, *Civil War*, pp. 156-57.

12. Seidman, *Civil War*, p. 142.

an offensive posture as he prepared the country for world conflict, demonstrated that the United States was a strong and independent force to its allies and foes, and had the foresight to preserve large sections of the country. In fact, one hundred years after Lewis and Clark first passed through the land known today as Yellowstone Park, Roosevelt made it a national park, preserving it and entrusting it to future generations (Ambrose, pp. 79, 91). Roosevelt picked up on the themes already established in the nation and optimistically looked to the future.

Living Out the Proclamation

Democracy and equality were more easily proclaimed than lived: the ideals set out by the United States at its inception still challenge its people more than two centuries later. The freeing of the slaves, waves of immigrants, women's right to vote, and the civil rights movement — all of these, individually, tested these notions and challenged the United States to add yet another core principle to its DNA: diversity.

Immigration has been a constant throughout the history of the United States, and it can provide great insight into the reality behind this core principle. Witnessed over the centuries along the country's borders, at its shores, and in its airports, immigration has been a part of the rich heritage that has blessed the United States. The land of the free has welcomed, sheltered, and provided opportunities for people from many countries and has created a mosaic of people seeking refuge, religious and economic opportunity, and the opportunity to be reunited with family members.[13]

In fact, the United States is a land of immigrants. Immigrants "are our parents, grandparents, teachers, friends, doctors, lawyers, sports heroes, actors, cooks, waiters, baby-sitters, merchants, and yes, even our politicians."[14] No other country is known as a country of immigrants as the United States is. The colorful diversity that these many immigrant groups have brought to America can be seen in the neighborhoods of urban centers but also in small rural towns, in the Northeast of the United

---

13. Barbara Brooks Kimmel and Alan M. Lubiner, *Immigration Made Simple: An Easy-to-Read Guide to the U.S. Immigration Process*, 6th ed. rev. (Chester, NJ: Next Decade, 2003), p. ix.

14. Kimmel and Lubiner, *Immigration Made Simple*, p. x.

States, in the Midwest, in the South, and on the West Coast. Immigrants have been numerous and diverse: the earliest were primarily from Europe, but other waves have come from Asia and Africa, as well as from Mexico and the Caribbean.

Throughout history, immigration "continually brought transfusions of new blood and energy and ways of thinking that kept the United States in flux." President John F. Kennedy said that immigration was "the secret of America," for it was a nation of "people with the fresh memory of old traditions who dared to explore new frontiers."[15] The flow of immigrants reminds U.S. citizens that this nation does not belong to one race, creed, or ethnic group. Rather, it is a nation of diverse people, from different homelands, sharing one country based on a set of ideals they strive to keep alive with each new challenge and opportunity.

The DNA of the United States

What is the DNA of the United States? *Discovery, democracy, equality,* and *diversity* — four virtues that have been born, tested, and challenged in this country and still stand strong today. Lewis and Clark were men of *discovery.* Unsuccessful in finding a new waterway, they discovered much more and demonstrated for future generations that courage and mission are powerful resources. They showed courage as they left their known resources and vehicles behind and sought a new destination. But they also learned that, in order to survive in unknown territory, they had to engage the wisdom of those already familiar with it.

Washington, Jefferson, Lincoln, and Roosevelt were significant leaders who moved *democracy* and *equality* from concepts into reality. Each played a role in helping the people of the United States believe that a democratic government, for the people and by the people, was worth the fight. The American people would need to be reminded again and again of what it means to be a democracy, but each time the people would accept the challenge. Equality has been a difficult principle to embody. Perhaps the Founding Fathers did not realize, or could not even imagine, what true equality in the United States would mean. Yet they envisioned

15. *Immigrants: The New Americans,* Our American Century series (Alexandria, VA: Time-Life Books, 1999), p. 20.

and proclaimed it, and over time it has become the foundation on which future generations would wrestle with the issues of their day. "Liberty and justice for all" has become more than a line embedded in the Pledge of Allegiance; it has become a challenge for the American people to turn into a reality.

Diversity, as seen in the waves of immigrants throughout United States history, has only just begun. This mosaic nation continues to change, adapt, and change again as waves of immigrants continue to arrive. As second- and third-generation immigrants assimilate into their new country, cultural differences fade, allowing people to forget that members of their own family were once foreigners who were welcomed to this soil. Celebrating and sustaining this virtue of diversity will demand a continual reminder that it is a significant part of the nation's character.

The Landscape of the Denominational Christian Church

Implanted in the United States landscape is yet another story, one that parallels and draws from the political story and one that continues — yet departs from — the existing Christian story. The denominational church was planted in this soil of *discovery, democracy, equality,* and *diversity.* In the second part of this chapter I will unearth the state of the church by exploring different stages of denominationalism in the United States. In each stage I will seek to articulate the adhesive principle, highlight important events, and note the prevailing structure.[16]

16. Robert Bruce Mullin and Russell E. Richey, eds., *Reimaging Denominationalism* (New York: Oxford University Press, 1994), pp. 77-93. I recognize the modern temptation to oversimplify complex and diverse realities by creating neat, all-encompassing categories. This typology could certainly be used for such purposes, and any use flirts with the dangers of such reductions. Acknowledging that this typology does not acknowledge all the historical elements of the denominational church, this essay uses this typology in a general way so as to serve as a snapshot of the history of the denominational church in the United States. It is my premise that, in order to deconstruct the current reality of denominations, it is necessary to have a handle on its historical evolution. This history, then, serves as another contextual lens with which to view the denominational church. Having named the shortcomings, I move forward hoping that this history both informs and criticizes the denominational church's current moment in history.

Stage One: Ethnic Voluntarism, the Separation of Church and State, the Great Awakening, and the Emergence of Denominations

In *The Lively Experiment,* Sidney Mead says that the church in the United States is both a continuation of the European state church and a new experiment.[17] The freedom that the Founding Fathers exercised was not only political; it was also religious. While some colonists tried to establish religious uniformity enforced by the state, it was clear that this approach was not going to work. Hence, religious freedom and the separation of church and state prevailed, and suddenly choice was a word connected with religion. "The form of church life that resulted . . . depended on the voluntary support of a committed laity."[18] The church's success required that people attend local congregations, and that gave congregations increased power.

The result of this new voluntary state of affairs was the formation of denominations, and the denominational church. While denominations have primarily English roots, that is, in the Glorious Revolution (1688-1689) and the Toleration Act (1689) in England, the principle of separation of church and state that was developed by Roger Williams's community in the United States provided new soil in which these ideas could grow.[19] Thus denominations are the direct result of a free religious society in which many churches could coexist, as like-minded churches organized into distinct organizations.[20] This emerging reality created the backdrop for the first stage of denominations, known as ethnic voluntarism, an eighteenth-century phenomenon that was essentially a continuation of the logic of the Toleration Act.

In this stage, denominations tended to honor ethnic boundaries: this is known as the adhesive principle. Denominations here functioned pri-

17. Sidney Mead, *The Lively Experiment: The Shaping of Christianity in America* (New York: Harper and Row Publishers), p. x.

18. Ahlstrom, *American People,* p. 382.

19. Information on the Glorious Revolution is available at www.britannica.com/eb/article-9072799. A copy of the Toleration Act is available at www.agh-attorneys.com/4_act_of_toleration_1689.htm [both accessed Oct. 1, 2005].

20. Mullin and Richey, *Reimaging,* pp. 75-76. Russell Richey puts it this way: "Denominationalism presents the denomination as a voluntaristic ecclesial body. It . . . presupposes a condition of legal or de facto toleration and religious freedom. . . . It is . . . a movement or body understanding itself to be legitimate and self-sufficient, a proper 'church' . . . a body that concedes the authenticity of other churches even as it claims its own . . . with intentions and the capacity for self-perpetuation."

marily as extensions of European state church bodies planted in a new frontier. Their basic structure was that they were associations formed out of struggles. These associations usually understood "themselves as under the authority of some home country judicatory," yet they "found themselves to be quasi-independent and forced by the sheer distance to resolve problems, adjudicate moral and theological disputes, and identify, train, and authenticate leadership" (Mullin and Richey, p. 79).

During this period, the most influential force alongside the church was the Enlightenment. Missiologist David Bosch believes that no single factor has had a greater influence on the church than the Enlightenment. The Enlightenment era had its beginnings in the seventeenth century and quickly became the established worldview.[21] Knowledge and science would become the rule of the day. Faith in God was seen primarily as a private thing, though theology was viewed as a science, and "God's kingdom became increasingly aligned with the culture and civilization of the West" (Bosch, p. 271). This "enlightened" view led to the idea that the United States had a divine role in God's providence (the footings of the idea that would become known as *manifest destiny),* an ideal that would drive its mission, shape its attitude toward the world, and impact the church's view of world missions.[22]

"Although religion played a profound role in motivating settlement in North America, by the early eighteenth century many observers were

---

21. David Bosch, *Transforming Mission: Paradigm Shifts in Theology of Mission* (Maryknoll, NY: Orbis Books, 1991), pp. 262-67. David Bosch identifies seven factors of the Enlightenment: "age of *reason,* operated with a *subject-object scheme,* the *elimination of purpose* from science and the introduction of direct causality as the clue to the understanding of reality, its belief in *progress, scientific knowledge was factual, value-free and neutral, all problems were in principle solvable,* and regarded people as *emancipated, autonomous individuals."* See also Ahlstrom, *American People,* pp. 357-58.

22. Michael T. Lubragge says: "Americans used Manifest Destiny as their proclamation of superiority and insisted that their conquests merely fulfilled the divine mission that man is impelled by forces beyond human control." He continues: "To some, the Manifest Destiny Doctrine was based on the idea that America had a divine providence. It had a future that was destined by God to expand its borders, with no limit to area or country. . . . For example, the idea that the Puritan notion of establishing a 'city on a hill' was eventually secularized into Manifest Destiny — a sort of materialistic, religious, utopian destiny." http://odur.let.rug.nl/ ~usa/E/manifest/manif3.htm. See also http://en.wikipedia.org/wiki/Manifest_Destiny for a history/origin and http://www.mtholyoke.edu/acad/intrel/osulliva.htm for John L. O'Sullivan's historic article on Manifest Destiny in 1839 [all accessed Oct. 1, 2005].

beginning to detect a severe deterioration in the quality of spiritual life."[23] But all that changed by the middle of the eighteenth century, when "a wave of religious revivalism swept through the British colonies in North America" (Findling and Thackeray, p. 6). The Great Awakening of the 1730s-1760s birthed a pietistic spirit that would come to characterize much of American religious life. This Awakening was widespread and involved people across denominational lines. "People everywhere were caught up in the movement, and its influence was spread by innumerable local pastors, passing itinerants, and lay exhorters."[24] The Awakening played an important role in forming a national consciousness, and it embedded a renewed spiritual life and mission spirit in the church,[25] which became the catalyst for interdenominational and intercolonial activities.[26] People got on board, enthusiasm spread, a movement was created, and in many ways the unifying factor of denominations was born.

Stage Two: Purposive Missionary Associations: Christianizing America, Divine Purpose, and Mission Societies

As the country expanded, a need for the church to reach out to the expanding frontier developed; thus denominations became active in missionary and evangelistic activities that led to the second stage, the purposive missionary association.[27] Denominations began viewing the entire country as their mission field, beginning the slow process of breaking down the ethnic enclaves and moving "towards the building of a Christian America" Territory, ethnic groups, piety, and regions influenced the makeup of denominations, but not as much as the unifying idea that God had blessed the United States in giving it a divine purpose, an ideal that served as the cohesive principle (Mullin and Richey, p. 81).

23. John E. Findling and Frank W. Thackeray, eds., *Events That Changed America in the Eighteenth Century* (Westport, CT: Greenwood Press, 1998), p. 7.

24. Hudson, *Religion in America*, p. 75.

25. Stephen B. Bevans and Roger P. Schroeder, *Constants in Context: A Theology of Mission for Today* (Maryknoll, NY: Orbis Books, 2004), p. 210; Ahlstrom, *American People*, p. 289. "By the end of the nineteenth century more missionaries were being sent from the USA than from any other country, which is a testimony to missionary enthusiasm especially among Congregationalists, Presbyterians, and Baptists."

26. Ahlstrom, *American People*, p. 29.

27. Ahlstrom, *American People*, p. 77.

During this stage, national denominational structures became more formal in an effort to keep up with the growing needs of the expanding nation. Many adopted the form of the voluntary mission society, which was one of the strategic enterprises born during the late eighteenth and early nineteenth centuries, as independent agencies formed outside the church for the purpose of mission.[28] Mission societies were created throughout Europe and North America and became the "Protestant archetype."[29] Voluntary mission societies and the ideology of divine purpose not only fueled missions in North America but also were the force behind sending missionaries around the world. This stage created an outward, optimistic posture for the church in the United States.

Stage Three: Churchly Denominationalism: Definition, Doctrine, and Immigration

After the Civil War, denominations saw the rise of a churchly style (Mullin and Richey, p. 77). This stage was marked by the "old insiders," those who tended to be shaped by the views of the established churches of Europe, pushing against the revivalistic spirit that had overtaken the church on the frontier in the previous stage. These "old insiders" responded with an increased confessionalism, a focus on tradition, a claim for the importance of "one's own ecclesial identity," and a defining of themselves over against the nonliturgical movements. The expansive push of the previous stage now turned inward for reorganization. Continuing the common drive for a Christian nation, denominations put great effort into youth and men's organizations, improving Sunday school literature, erecting church build-

28. Bevans and Schroeder, *Constants in Context*, p. 210. William Carey (1792) is credited as the founding father of this kind of organization: he was sent from England to India, not by a church body or magistrate, but by a group of individuals who banded together apart from the established church for the purpose of missions.

29. Bevans and Schroeder, *Constants in Context*, p. 212. List of Societies: London Missionary Society (1795), Scottish Missionary Society (1796), Netherlands Missionary Society (1797), Church Missionary Society (1799), British and Foreign Missionary Society (1804), American Board of Commissioners for Foreign Missions (1810), American Baptist Foreign Mission Society (1814), Basel Mission (1816), Wesleyan Methodist Missionary Society (1817-1818), Danish Missionary Society (1821), Berlin Missionary Society (1824), Rhenish Missionary Society (1828), Swedish Missionary Society (1835), and the North German Missionary Society (1836), to mention a few.

ings, and enhancing congregational life. In addition, each denomination worked to enhance their issues of polity, governance, and structures for mission (Mullin and Richey, pp. 82-84).

The most influential outside event during this period was the Civil War. As the country struggled to remain united, the issue of slavery found its way into the church. While slavery was not the cause for the divisions between denominations, it exacerbated the differences that were already present. In fact, "slavery exposed important ecclesiastical issues and . . . after the divisions, if not before, each of the sectional churches found it important to construe its purposes in theological and ecclesiastical terms" (Mullin and Richey, p. 83).

To the unifying purpose of Christianizing America, another practical purpose was added: the need to address immigrants. "In America the immigrants had to begin anew, individually and in groups, to achieve their aspirations for culture and well-being. Religious institutions, therefore, often became a more vital factor than they had ever been before." Immigration both influenced the landscape of the United States and shaped the church. During the colonial period, three denominational bodies (Congregationalists, Anglicans, and Presbyterians — all with British backgrounds)[30] made up 80 percent of Americans claiming any church affiliation. However, that drastically changed during the nineteenth century.[31]

> In 1926, by which time 40 percent of the population claimed a religious relationship, Roman Catholics were the largest single group (18,605,000), while the next three largest denominations — Baptists (8,011,000), Methodist (7,764,000), and Lutheran (3,226,000) — accounted for 59 percent of the Protestants. (Ahlstrom, p. 517)

Immigration greatly influenced the churches that thrived; that is, the church affiliation that immigrants brought with them dramatically shaped the denominational profile of the American church during this stage.

---

30. Ahlstrom, *American People,* p. 517.
31. Ahlstrom, *American People,* p. 517.

Stage Four: Corporate Organization: World Conferences, Ecumenism, and Corporate Structures

In the late nineteenth and early twentieth centuries, denominations added another layer to their polity: organizational structures influenced by the emerging discipline of organizational theory. This corporate view was the fourth stage of denominationalism, and it began with a deepened, internal focus on structure, which, over time, resulted in a more instrumental view of the church (Mullin and Richey, p. 85). Bureaucracy, organizational grammar, and professionalism were some of the byproducts of this stage. For example, national agencies with staffs became commonplace; denominations now included national, regional, and local expressions; and clear expectations for clergy were established. All of these were the evolutionary precursors of denominations becoming top-down regulatory systems, what would emerge in the fifth stage.

Significant outside influence during this stage came from a series of world mission conferences. In 1910, participants from over 160 boards or agencies came together with optimism for world missions. The focus was not on doctrine or polity but on consultation, cooperation, and mission strategy for evangelizing the world.[32] The Edinburgh World Missionary Conference "is often considered the high point of this nineteenth-century ecumenical mission movement" (Bevans and Schroeder, pp. 208-9), marking a new day for the international church. It was the culmination of a series of international events that would eventually both draw the international ecumenical church together and divide it.

The International Missionary Council (IMC), formed in 1921 in the aftermath of Edinburgh, led the international missionary conversation for the next four decades. Of the seven IMC gatherings, the 1952 Willingen meeting was the most important: it resulted in the eventual formulation of the *missio Dei* concept.[33] This concept changed the church identity from being the sender in missions to the entity being sent, turning existing missionary practices upside down.[34] In 1961, the IMC merged with the World

---

32. Bevans and Schroeder, *Constants in Context,* p. 220.

33. Bosch, *Transforming Mission,* p. 370.

34. Bosch, *Transforming Mission,* p. 370. Lesslie Newbigin, in a pamphlet published soon after the convention, summarized the consensus with three points: "the church is the mission," "the home base is everywhere," and "mission in partnership."

Council of Churches (WCC)[35] and became the Commission on World Mission and Evangelism (CWME), which would set forth the idea that "God's mission was not geographically bound; rather, one should talk of 'mission on six continents'" (Bevans and Schroeder, p. 260).

The Roman Catholic Church burst forth with a renewed missionary posture in 1962 with the Second Vatican Council's *Ad Gentes,* proclaiming that the church is "missionary by its very nature."[36] Under Pope John XXIII's leadership, the Roman Catholic Church set in motion major changes that would not only shake up the world of that church body but also influence the entire international religious scene. "[T]he church began to 'read the signs of the times' and to acknowledge the movement of God's Spirit outside the Catholic Church" (Bevans and Schroeder, p. 243), which opened the door to dialogue between Roman Catholics and Protestants in new and significant ways. As a result, a broader ecumenical conversation commenced.

By this stage, the adhesive principle of denominations was fading, but two themes remained. First, denominations were full-fledged organizational systems with defined processes, roles, and techniques imported from the corporate world. The result of this reality was that the mission of the church was now deeply embedded in a formal organizational structure. Second, the modern ecumenical movement was finding some cohesion among many denominations. While a good number of these efforts emerged from the need for cooperation both at home and abroad, the by-product was new opportunities for dialogue and the beginnings of imagining a broader view of God's mission.

Stage Five: Post-Denominationalism Confessionalism — Regulation, Pluralism, and a Turn

The fifth stage began in the late 1960s and early 1970s when denominations started to become full regulatory agencies. The professional, bureaucratic, and organizational structures that began in the previous stage had now become commonplace. Yet they were unable to provide the de-

35. Bevans and Schroeder, *Constants in Context,* p. 243. The WCC was formed in 1948 by bringing two streams of international work together: the Life and Work movement and the Faith and Order movement.

36. Bevans and Schroeder, *Constants in Context,* p. 7. See www.ewtn.com/library/COUNCILS/v2miss.htm for the full document [accessed Oct. 7, 2005].

sired cohesion that was required to address the new diversity being experienced. Russell Richey says: "Denominations have lost or are losing long-familiar adhesive and dynamic principles and are groping, often desperately, for tactics that work and unite" (Mullin and Richey, p. 87). The notion of a Christian nation that earlier denominational leaders dreamed about was not to be, because the United States was well on its way to becoming a pluralistic society. At the same time, however, there was a rising effort among conservative Christians to reclaim a moral foundation for the country. During this time, Robert Wuthnow notes, denominations "split badly and fairly cleanly into theologically conservative and liberal camps."[37] Christian unity would not occur across the country — or even within Christian churches themselves.

Without a clear, cohesive purpose, denominations grabbed for control by developing themselves into regulatory agencies, and they sought to win converts by establishing new mechanisms through consulting, marketing, and offering grants. But these efforts, while offering some short-term wins, did not produce the long-lasting results that were needed. "The top-down, imposed, common denominational grammar [began] to erode." And, as a result, church members began to shop *among* denominations to find a church home. This required denominations to refocus their efforts on establishing their own unique identity, which called for denominational loyalty and refined church polity (Mullin and Richey, pp. 88-90).

Outside the church, "the advent of new social movements opposing the Vietnam War, imperialism, racism, sexism, and capitalist societies" were visible signs of an emerging stirring that was taking place.[38] Just as the dream of the United States truly becoming a Christian nation within a framework of civil religion was fading, so were the hopes of the "enlightened" beginning to weaken. Sociology, philosophy, the arts, literature, and science all experienced the first tremors that would soon question many of their basic ideals.[39] While no one could clearly articulate what was going on, something was in the air and many were beginning to feel a turn coming.

37. In Mullin and Richey, *Reimaging,* pp. 87, 88.
38. Steven Best and Douglas Kellner, *The Postmodern Turn* (New York: Guilford Press, 1997), p. 4.
39. Craig Van Gelder, "Mission in the Emerging Postmodern Condition," in *Church Between Gospel and Culture: The Emerging Mission in North America* (Grand Rapids: Eerdmans, 1996), pp. 113-38.

Stage Six: What's Next?

Russell Richey notes that each stage of denominationalism "partook of organizational materials of its day," and "[e]ach type or style functioned with a distinctive vision of American society and of Protestant responsibility therein." It is true that the typology of previous stages did not die out as the next stage surfaced; thus, in some denominations, many of the historical frames were — and still are — operating concurrently. Yet these typological stages highlight the cohesive factors during each stage, and they reflect the church's needs at that point in history (Mullin and Richey, p. 77).

Currently, denominations are in a state of flux. The organizational structures created in stage four and the regulatory agencies of stage five are no longer affordable or sufficient for the twenty-first-century church mission. Some are pessimistic about the future of denominations and have proclaimed their imminent death, while others are optimistic and have witnessed pockets of vitality and innovation. While opinions vary on the future status of denominations, one thing everyone agrees on is that denominations are in a stage of transition.[40] Transition is not something new for denominations; but, in order to move through this transition effectively, they have to address some key questions: "What is the mission of the church in the twenty-first century?" "What is the role of denominations in the future?" These are questions that I will take up in the final section of this chapter.

The Future of Denominationalism in a Postmodern Age

Imagine, if you will, this absurd scene: you are on a weeklong backpacking trip with a group of colleagues, hiking through beautiful forests and along trails in a national park. Everyone is enjoying the scenery, the fresh air, the peace and quiet, and the chance to reflect on oneself in God's wondrous creation. On the fourth day the leader of your recreational expedition, for the first time, pauses in the trail and appears uncertain. Looking around in several directions, he takes off his hat, scratches his head, digs through his

---

40. David A. Roozen and James R. Neiman, eds., *Church, Identity, and Change: Theology and Denominational Structures in Unsettled Times* (Grand Rapids: Eerdmans, 2005), pp. 1-4.

fanny pack and pulls out a map with many folds. He scrutinizes the details of the map, glancing up now and then to survey the scene ahead of your party.

This ritual continues for a few minutes. Members of the party begin to murmur to each other, quietly at first. Before long, though, one of the group steps out of line, walks up to the deliberating trail guide, and bends down over the map with him. A few seconds later, she jumps to her feet and exclaims, "This will never get us where we are headed! It's a map of downtown Kansas City!"[41]

Some of us have felt this way about the church in recent times: the church seems to be living in a new time, a time when the terrain often doesn't match the map. More pertinently, perhaps, what maps are churches using today? Are these maps providing the needed direction? What about tomorrow? And what has come of this turn? The church, using a Thomas Kuhn concept, is in the midst of a *paradigm shift.*[42]

As I have observed above, denominations are also in a state of flux. To attend to this flux, we need to address both form and function. The first task has to do with defining the work of the church (the cohesive principle), and the second asks what form this work will take (leadership and structure).[43] In addition, the church needs to recognize its current location (context). Hence there are four elements that are key ingredients for understanding the future of the church and for developing a twenty-first-century ecclesiology: cohesive principle, context, leadership, and structure. I will discuss these elements in this final section.

Cohesive Principle: What's the Mission?

In a time when the center has been called into question, it's time to ask: What is the mission of the twenty-first-century church? What will be its cohesive principle? Any adequate answer will have to begin with a strong

41. George B. Thompson, Jr., "Leadership for Congregational Vitality: Paradigmatic Explorations in Open Systems Organizational Culture Theory," *Journal of Religious Leadership* 2, no. 1 (Spring 2003): 53.

42. Thomas S. Kuhn, *The Structure of Scientific Revolutions,* 2nd ed. (Chicago: University of Chicago Press, 1970).

43. Roozen and Nieman, *Church, Identity, and Change,* p. 12. These are two lenses used in this study of eight denominations.

biblical and theological base. Recognizing that the church is the one being sent rather than the sender means viewing the church as missionary by its very nature and requires the church to have a missional theology. The missional theology that I suggest here, while very brief, will address three primary areas: view of God, view of the church, and view of the gospel.

View of God

"The Church in North America has an obstacle to overcome if it is to get past its impoverished missional imagination," says Gary Simpson. "That obstacle is its inadequate view of God."[44] The church's doctrine of God matters, and it matters because a person's view of God influences her view of herself in relationship to God, others, and the world. It matters because a person's understanding of God's mission will impact his understanding of the church's mission.

As I have suggested above, the *missio Dei* is the core to understanding missional theology. The trinitarian view of God found in *missio Dei* has two main impulses. The first impulse is a sending one: "God the Father sending the Son, and God the Father and the Son sending the Spirit [is] expanded to include yet another 'movement': Father, Son, and Holy Spirit sending the church into the world."[45] The second impulse is its communal nature: "In confessing that God is, we encounter God's existence as a trinity — a tri-unity, a social community of three persons within the Godhead."[46] This sending, communal God works in and through community; and with this doctrine of God, not only is the church's mission God's mission, but here God acts as the primary agent in mission, the church as secondary. This means that God has been, is, and will be active in the world. We, as God's church, simply must seek to participate in God's mission in the world.

---

44. Gary M. Simpson, "No Trinity, No Mission: The Apostolic Difference of Revisioning the Trinity," *Word and World* 18 (Summer 1998): 264.

45. Bosch, *Transforming Mission,* p. 390.

46. Craig Van Gelder, *The Essence of the Church: A Community Created by the Spirit* (Grand Rapids: Baker, 2000), p. 96. For a full development, see Catherine Mowry LaCugna, *God for Us: The Trinity and Christian Life* (New York: HarperSanFrancisco, 1973), and John Zizioulas, *Being as Communion* (Crestwood, NY: St. Vladimir's Seminary Press, 1985).

View of the Church

What, then, is the view of the church? George Hunsberger says, "It is the church's mission to represent the reign of God."[47] The church is not the reign of God, but "presents it as its community (koinonia), its servant (diakonia), and its messenger (kerygma)." Or, to use Lesslie Newbigin's language, the church is the "sign, instrument, and foretaste" of God's reign.[48] Craig Van Gelder adds that the church's "very existence demonstrates that [God's] redemptive reign has already begun. Its very presence invites the world to watch, listen, examine, and consider accepting God's reign as a superior way of living."[49] Hence, the church bears witness to a different way of life, one that is shaped, modeled, and influenced by God. The church lives within the now and the not yet, the tangible pointing to the intangible, the embodiment of the messenger's message, a witness to the gospel. Bearing witness "is not about program and method. It is about openly inviting others into the community of new humanity so they can experience the grace of God."[50]

View of the Gospel

If the church is to bear witness to the gospel, then what exactly is the gospel? The gospel is brought into the world through the person of Jesus Christ. This was God's breaking into the world incarnationally. God, as the active agent in mission, took the form of a human and came to earth. It is the work of the church to continue to live out the gospel in its time in history. Douglas John Hall appeals for the gospel's active, surprising nature. He argues that the gospel is always good news "because it engages, takes on and does battle with the bad news, offering another alternative, another vision of what could be, another way into the future." So how is the gospel taking on the bad news? How is it that Christ's coming into the world offers us a new future today? If the church can engage the issues of its day with "a responsive Word that really addresses and engages context, that Word will be

---

47. George Hunsberger, "The Newbigin Gauntlet," in *The Church Between Gospel and Culture,* ed. Hunsberger and Craig Van Gelder (Grand Rapids: Eerdmans, 1996), pp. 15-16.

48. Lesslie Newbigin, *The Open Secret: An Introduction to the Theology of Mission,* rev. ed. (Grand Rapids: Eerdmans, 1995), p. 110.

49. Van Gelder, *Essence of the Church,* p. 100.

50. Van Gelder, *Essence of the Church,* p. 153.

gospel."[51] This is a missional understanding of gospel: gospel as missionary activity, initiated first by God, incarnational, embodied and located in a time and place, and which offers people an alternative way, a new future.

So what's the mission? The mission is that a communal, sending God calls and sends the church to be a witness to the reign of God, proclaiming and living this good news incarnationally. This is the church's reason for being; this is the center to which the church clings, for God has called the church to join in this mission of redeeming and transforming the world. God so loved the world that God sent Jesus to love the world, and now God sends the church. It is the church's mission to participate in God's mission, constantly seeking ways of bearing witness to this in-breaking of grace that has been bestowed upon it.

Context: Postmodernism

Cultural anthropology reminds us that context matters, for all culture is influenced and shaped by its context, both historically and geographically.[52] Hence, the church's context matters. Today a new contextual challenge has surfaced, and once again the church needs leaders to scout out new ways.

"It appears that postmodernism increasingly represents the cultural air that we breathe,"[53] says Van Gelder. The modern world that emerged out of the Enlightenment era was the foundation on which ideologies of the past centuries were built. It shaped the worldview for hundreds of years, it is the ground on which U.S. institutions were built, and it is the paradigm within which the church has operated. And now this foundation is being called into question. Stanley Grenz warns: "The shift from the familiar territory of modernity to the uncharted terrain of postmodernity has grave implications for those who seek to live as Christ's disciples in the new context."[54] Postmodernism is the single greatest influence on the context of the United States and the church today. But what is postmodernism?

51. Douglas John Hall, "What Is Theology?" *Crosscurrents* (Summer 2003): 177, 179.

52. For more on cultural anthropology and context, see Kathryn Tanner, *Theories of Culture: A New Agenda for Theology* (Minneapolis: Fortress Press, 1997), pp. 25-58.

53. Van Gelder, "Postmodernism and Evangelicals: A Unique Missiological Challenge at the Beginning of the Twenty-first Century," *Missiology* 30, no. 4 (Oct. 2002): 493.

54. Stanley J. Grenz, *A Primer on Postmodernism* (Grand Rapids: Eerdmans, 1996), p. 162.

The tremors that were noticed in the 1960s and 1970s have come to be known as "the postmodern turn."[55] By the 1980s the roots of this turn were firmly planted in popular culture, and the move from the fringe to the mainstream was complete: postmodernity was born (Grenz, p. 17). While various definitions are given for postmodernism, at its core postmodernism "represents a rejection of the Enlightenment project and the foundational assumptions upon which it was built," and instead the lifting up and celebrating of local, particular, and diverse lines of thinking and expression (Grenz, p. 5).

While many in the United States would not describe themselves as pure-bred postmoderns, postmodern ideals have already infiltrated the world in which they find themselves. For example, the personal computer and the worldwide web have opened up a whole host of new possibilities. These new realities allow for information to be accessible to people regardless of status or education; they create new venues of expression for professionals and amateurs alike; and they thrive on broad and diverse clientele and facilitate global networking. But the computer is not the only place one is exposed to this new world. Literature, theater, television, and film have introduced postmodernity into popular culture, juxtaposing ideas, images, and concepts that play with, clash, or confuse the reader/viewer. These efforts seek to raise questions, dislodge presuppositions, and challenge in ways that *moderns* would never have thought possible. The mere presence of postmodern discourse has forced most disciplines into new territory.

George Cladis has identified some postmodern characteristics that have an impact on church leadership.[56] These characteristics push the church to rethink its modus operandi. Critiquing church organizational structures and leadership qualities, Cladis calls the church to become more like an organism with flattened accountability systems and larger networks, while also providing opportunities for personal investment. Cladis believes vision, values, trust, meaning, and innovation will replace status, credentials, and bureaucracy. Cladis's boldest statements are his pro-

---

55. Best and Kellner, *Postmodern Turn*, p. viii.

56. George Cladis, *Leading the Team-Based Church: How Pastors and Church Staffs Can Grow Together into a Powerful Fellowship of Leaders* (San Francisco: Jossey-Bass, 1999), p. 18. Cladis approaches these postmodern times with optimism, seeing this as a time offering "wonderful new opportunities for the Church of Jesus Christ to be reformed and renewed along biblical lines."

nouncements that "Christendom is over in America"and that the "mainline church domination has ended" (Cladis, pp. 19-27).

If church leadership is to meet the challenges of postmodernity, something different must emerge. The landscape in which the church was planted and flourished has now changed. Van Gelder concurs: "We are living in a new day in America. The shifts in the cultural context have presented a new challenge for the churches to address America as a mission field."[57] As the church addresses its mission field, it must do so with a different form of church. Organizations that will thrive within postmodernity must be living systems attentive to interdependence, vision, innovation, and meaning-making. While it is true that the modern world is still alive in places throughout the country, it is also true that the old ways will not serve the world of the future. Thomas Kuhn might be a prophetic voice for the church today. He says that

> . . . the emergence of new theories is generally preceded by a period of pronounced professional insecurity. As one might expect, that insecurity is generated by . . . persistent failure. . . . Failure of existing rules is the prelude for new ones.[58]

Perhaps this is just such a time. Perhaps leaders are using maps that describe terrain different from their location; perhaps they need a new passageway. Context is both broad (i.e., historical) and particular (i.e., geographical): whereas postmodernism is the broad, historical context, context also applies specifically to one's geography. This means that the church must take its specific context seriously. This will require national, regional, and local attention, the study of changing surroundings, and the continual pondering of one's engagement of the gospel within one's unique situation.

Leadership: Missionaries Empowered by the Spirit

It should come as no surprise that leadership in this emerging context may look different from the way it did in the past. In fact, first-generation postmodern leaders already look different. One need only visit one of the

57. Hunsberger, *Church Between Gospel and Culture*, p. 68.
58. Kuhn, *Structure*, pp. 67-68.

hundreds of postmodern ministries that have sprung up across the United States to see the evidence.[59] Yet some common characteristics are surfacing: one characteristic of leaders in postmodern ministries is that they are missionaries. Postmodern leaders seek to engage their particular contexts with the good news of the gospel. They know their unique context through study and immersion; they know the language; and they are using any available resources to create missionary encounters. These encounters may result in forming faith communities, but they also may not do that. They may be ministries at skating parks, coffeeshops, or virtual communities that live solely on the Internet. While forms may vary, the core of each ministry is the common desire to effectively speak the gospel to its particular context. Postmodern missionary leaders demonstrate characteristics similar to those of Lewis and Clark as they explore postmodernity's new terrain and draw wisdom from the natives. These leaders will be called to discover the unique characteristics of this time and place in history, including engaging with those who are immersed in it.

If the first characteristic of a postmodern leader is to be a missionary, then who might these missionaries be? These missionaries are clergy and laity; they are people on the fringes and people steeped in the church; and they are professionals as well as novices from various socioeconomic and ethnic backgrounds. No one category defines them. But more than any category or status, authenticity seems central. As Cladis makes clear, postmodern people want leaders who are genuine, those who care little about educational background, titles, or positions (Cladis, p. 21). This reorientation both threatens current leadership structures and can provide new opportunities for leadership among the laity, just as mission societies provided those opportunities in the past. Therefore, future church leadership can grow to include a broader mix of people: the theologically trained and untrained, clergy and laity (with the line between them becoming blurred), a wider range of ethnicities, and the list could go on. This emerging phenomenon invites leadership models to become more decentralized and to allow for grass-roots leadership models to surface. Thus, the second characteristic is diverse leadership using decentralized leadership models.

The second characteristic leads to a third: similar to the blurring of

---

59. One great example of this diverse leadership is *The Church in Emerging Culture: Five Perspectives* (Grand Rapids: Zondervan, 2003), written by the leading postmodern church leaders and edited by Leonard Sweet. Their profiles are quite diverse.

lines within leadership, there exists a blurring of lines between the church and the world. In his book *Boundary Leaders,* Gary Gunderson articulates the stirring that he perceives taking place within people of faith. Faithful followers of Jesus are finding ways of living their faith in all areas of their lives. No longer does the church need to be the only place for ministry, because, as its people become apostolic and engage in God's mission, they are finding ways of living their faith wherever they are. Centered Life, an initiative of Luther Seminary in St. Paul, actually works with church leadership to create this spirit within congregations.[60] This apostolic nature marks the third characteristic of leadership.

In a missional church within a postmodern context, the source of power need not come from one's denomination or one's place in a structure. Rather, it needs to come from God. A church seeking power from God continually strives to maintain a connection with God and is alive in the Spirit. Ben Campbell Johnson and Glenn McDonald imagine such a church as being "a community of the Real Presence, the embodiment of the risen and living Lord, the community infused with transcendence, and the witness to the coming kingdom." Leadership in such a church allows it to be an organism that is shaped and molded by Christ.[61] In such situations, the church exercises leadership when it seeks to live out God's mission in the world, specifically God's unique mission for each church, in that church's time in history and in its particular location. With power resting in God's hands and not the hands of humans, leadership can be freed to proclaim and live out God's good news. When people rely on the premise that God has been faithful in the past and will continue to be faithful in the future, this final characteristic of postmodern leadership recognizes God as the source of power.

Structure: Open, Networking System

Having defined the mission, the context, and the key characteristics of leadership in the emerging postmodern context, I now want to step out even further and suggest a polity for a missional ecclesiology. Two things

60. See www.centeredlife.org.

61. Ben Campbell Johnson and Glenn McDonald, *Imagining a Church in the Spirit: A Task for Mainline Congregations* (Grand Rapids: Eerdmans, 1999), pp. 12, 117.

are worth noting here. First of all, the current ecclesiastical structures of denominations have been influenced as much by the political landscape in which they emerged as by the theological underpinnings of each denomination. To varying degrees, each denominational polity has been shaped by the state and federal governments in which it lives.[62] Therefore, what has become commonplace for many within the church needs to be deconstructed. This deconstruction is beyond the realm of this essay, but it is important to be aware of this reality and how particular ideologies of power have found their way into church structures. Second, it is important to note what a missional ecclesiology is and is not.

> A missional ecclesiology will always include organizational forms, but one should not see these as the church. Organizations need to serve, not to determine, the nature of the church with its duality of being both divine and human. They also need to serve the ministry of the church in all of its diverse functions.[63]

A missional ecclesiology in a postmodern context needs to reflect the organic nature of the emerging context. Here the new sciences can shed some light. Margaret Wheatley, in her study of new sciences in search of leadership lessons, has discovered that order can be found in a chaotic world, and nonequilibrium is actually healthy for a living entity.[64] In addition, self-organizing systems demonstrate their viability and resilience in their great capacity to adapt and create structures that fit the moment.[65] In such a system, "stability comes from a deepening center, a clarity about who it is," not a lack of chaos or a well-defined structure (Wheatley, p. 83). In a world that is fluid and flexible, control cannot provide stability within organizations. In fact, the opposite is true. Wheatley notes that "all life lives off-balance in a world that is open to change" (Wheatley, p. 89).

---

62. See Roozen and Nieman, *Church, Identity, and Change*, pp. 12-14, for a broad overview of this notion.

63. Darrell L. Guder, ed., *Missional Church: A Vision for the Sending of the Church in North America* (Grand Rapids: Eerdmans, 1998), pp. 71-72.

64. Margaret J. Wheatley, *Leadership and the New Science: Discovering Order in a Chaotic World,* 2nd rev. and enl. ed. (San Francisco: Berrett-Koehler Publishers, 1999), pp. 75-78, 85. "A living system changes in order to preserve itself."

65. Wheatley, *Leadership and the New Science*, pp. 82, 89. In fact, "[w]hen leaders strive for equilibrium and stability by imposing control, constricting people's freedom and inhibiting local change, they only create the conditions that threaten the organization's survival."

Therefore, any organizational form in a fluid, shifting environment will need to have the characteristics of a self-organizing system, open to change and centered on a clear purpose in order to survive. Immigration serves as a great example of how this fluidity has played out within the United States, for as immigration has interacted with the changing environment, structures have been transformed.

However, any proposed structure for the church not only needs to fit within the emerging postmodern context but also needs to participate in God's mission, drawing from biblical and historical resources. In *The Essence of the Church*, Van Gelder unpacks church structure by looking at the word *ecclesia* and its three uses in the New Testament. One use refers to the *local* gathering or congregation: "A congregation is an *ecclesia*, a called out assembly for the purpose of being the people of God in a particular place." The second use refers to a cluster of congregations in a general *region:* this is the concept behind the development of synods or regions within a denomination. The third use refers to the church *catholic,* identifying the universal visible church. The function of the local expression is articulated in many ways throughout the Bible, as are the attributes of the universal visible church. But the function of the second usage is less explicit. Van Gelder describes one key dimension of the second function as being "mobile missional structures" that exist beyond local congregations for the purpose of intertwining, coordinating, and expanding ministry. These structures do not all look alike: some are apostolic leaders sent out to congregations, others are mobile teams sent out or created for resourcing purposes, and others are simply at-large leaders.[66]

A missional polity needs all three elements and functions. To be missional, the local congregation must think theologically and sociologically about its context as it engages it with the gospel message. In a postmodern context, congregations will have a heightened role, for they are the closest to their particular setting and have the greatest potential for having an impact on it. Pairing congregations with the realities of new scientific theories and treating congregations as living systems could unleash the enormous potential that congregations have to regulate themselves if and when they are centered on a clear purpose.

"Mobile missional structures" also need to be in place. But what if these structures weren't actually structures at all, but loosely connected

---

66. Van Gelder, *Essence of the Church,* pp. 163-72.

networks instead? Paul Martinson says: "Rather than centralized bureaucracies, we need dispersed networks that fit the communication realities of our day." Using missionary agencies as a model, he suggests that mobile missionary structures could "serve to consult, inform, inspire, and connect" particular ministries, "letting the energy of local communities of faith take shape in any number of ways [and] in many manners of configuration."[67] Sharon Henderson Callahan integrated her own research with Boleman and Deal's frames[68] and Wheatley's new science, and she found that "new church leaders will attend to the relationships and gifts of humans (human resource), build networks to defy the notion of scarcity with the promise of shared abundance (political) and celebrate the reality of our shared grounding in Christ (symbolic)."[69] Judicatories, missionary agencies, and parachurch organizations are necessary in a missional ecclesiology, but they are intended to be supportive of local congregations. They are to be mobile missional structures that function as connective tissue, binding local congregations with the church's overall mission. Together, local congregations and mobile missional structures are to strive for, and to uphold the principles of, becoming one catholic church, the final element of the church.

A New Ecclesiology: Postmodern Denominationalism, a Missional Movement

"Why is it that some ideas or behaviors or products start epidemics and others don't?" This is the core question that has stimulated the explorations of Malcolm Gladwell in his book *The Tipping Point*. Gladwell wonders: "What can we do to deliberately start and control positive epidemics of our own?"[70] An epidemic is a movement that spreads rampantly, almost

---

67. Paul Varo Martinson, "Social Capital and the New Missionary Pragmatics," *Word and World* 18, no. 2 (Spring 1998): 158-59. For an already existing postmodern example, see www.emergentvillage.org.

68. Lee G. Bolman and Terrence E. Deal, *Reframing Organizations: Artistry, Choice, and Leadership*, 3rd ed. (San Francisco: Jossey-Bass, 2003).

69. Sharon Henderson Callahan, "Shifting Images of Church Invite New Leadership," *Journal of Religious Leadership* 1, no. 1 (Spring 2002): 78-79.

70. Malcolm Gladwell, *The Tipping Point: How Little Things Can Make a Big Difference* (New York: Little, Brown and Company, 2000), p. 14.

out of control, throughout society. What if the church could learn about and create such a movement?

Gladwell believes that there are three rules that make sense of epidemics: the Law of the Few, the Stickiness Factor, and the Power of Context. The Law of the Few refers to the fact that epidemics are "driven by the efforts of a handful of exceptional people." "The Stickiness Factor says that there are specific ways of making a contagious message memorable." The Power of Context recognizes that "[e]ven the smallest and subtlest and most unexpected of factors can affect the way we act," and "human beings are a lot more sensitive to their environment than they may seem" (Gladwell, pp. 21-29). Behind these rules lies an important belief that sudden change can (and does) happen. "We are all, at heart, gradualists. . . . But the world of the Tipping Point is a place where the unexpected becomes expected, where radical change is a possibility" (Gladwell, pp. 13-14). Using this frame of reference and these simple rules, we may be able to create positive epidemics or movements.

What if denominations in a postmodern age were about creating positive epidemics, epidemics similar to the Great Awakenings in early U.S. history — which moved across denominations and the country? The future work of denominations could be to fan the flames of a Christian movement, to suggest that radical change is possible, to ignite contagious behavior, to rely on and invest in a few critical individuals, and to tend to contexts. This move would focus on investing in a dynamic future, and it would require leaving many of the present vehicles behind. It would be a movement that sought to be aligned with the *missio Dei* and to be guided by the Spirit. With this loosely established missional center, individual denominations could live into this reality from their own theological frameworks with the particulars unique to their tradition, knowing that the mystery of God is broad enough and the current postmodern context diverse enough to embrace and welcome such a plethora of Christian expressions. National efforts could challenge the church missionally, recognizing again that the United States is a mission field and constantly pushing for a bigger vision of God's activity in the world. Local efforts could challenge the church communally, keeping it real and authentic as it lives into a new era of apostolic leadership. Put another way, the current postmodern context and the current denominational stage call for the pendulum to swing, from denominations being tightly run, inward-focused organizations to being mission-driven organisms that seek their vitality locally, nationally, and globally.

It is important to remember that the church's particular mission lives in tension with the greater culture. As the church seeks to create a Christian movement, it needs to find touch points from within the context in which it lives for bringing forth the good news. As the church seeks to be the sign, instrument, and foretaste of the reign of God, it lives within a dynamic paradox of being in the world but not of the world. Could the DNA of the United States offer points at which the church could address anew the current situation? Could the church set out to reframe the virtues of discovery, democracy, equality, and diversity into defining principles for living out God's kingdom here on earth?[71] Could church leaders today learn from leaders of the past about the necessity of exploring new paths and setting up new ways of being a people? Is there, once again, the need to listen to the emerging voices and offer a prophetic word, while operating from an offensive, rather than defensive, position? The dynamics of the postmodern American context provide both challenges and opportunities for the church as it rewrites its maps for participation in God's mission, rather than trying to Christianize America as its primary compass.

What, then, has emerged? A missional ecclesiology centered in a missional theology organized as a network of congregations that operate as self-organizing systems, led by missionary leaders empowered by the Spirit to create a Christian movement in a postmodern context. Missional theology becomes the church's driving force. Apostolic leaders who understand the importance of context are sent out with the good news of the gospel, blurring the lines between church and the world. The church values the various gifts and passions each person brings into the ministry of a particular location, and its leaders earn the right to be heard in their given context by being genuine and authentic.

Each ministry is part of a larger fluid network that, from the outside, might seem chaotic, but that is held together with a clear center allowing it to ebb and flow as needed. Networking begins locally but soon expands,

---

71. Framed within the political setting of the U.S., these virtues are not directly connected with God's kingdom. Yet it seems that each provides rich soil from which to grow new Christian missionary practices. One quick cut might look something like this: discovery = God's creative way of connecting and loving God's people. God makes God's self new all throughout the Bible; democracy and equality = God's kingdom turns upside down the power structures of society and throws open the doors of the kingdom to people that society has rejected (children, women, and slaves, to name a few); and diversity = God chose particular people with various experiences to be witnesses to the transformational power of God's message in their lives. This is but a foretaste of the kingdom of heaven.

eventually reaching to the far ends of the earth. The glue within these networks is the commitment to consciously strive toward unity and uphold the overarching attributes of the whole Christian church.

While individual churches or denominations could tend to this work on their own, it seems that there is an opening in history where denominations across the board are asking similar questions and wrestling with similar issues. Such timing is not often available and invites denominations to emphasize what they have in common — their missional drive — rather than emphasizing their differences. Perhaps this common calling can provide a foundation that is deeper than the civic religion that has emerged in the United States and can unite the denominational church at a more significant level, the level of bringing the Good News of God into a world filled with bad news. It is a fact that, as the church lives within the commingling of the modern and the postmodern, forgiveness and grace are attributes the church must not forget.[72] The church must keep in mind that its goal is not theological consensus; rather, its goal is Christians journeying together, grappling with what it means to live a life of discipleship in their day. A shift in paradigms will not happen overnight, and not everyone will make the leap at the same time. For just as it took the church almost a century to wrestle with the issue of slavery, so it might take the better part of a generation to fully make this shift.[73] But there will be moments when small, subterranean efforts will reach Gladwell's "tipping point," and the bulk of society will experience a paradigm shift. It is my prayer that the church will have the foresight to stand on the front edge of this postmodern turn rather than becoming an obstacle to change, for there is an emerging world that needs to hear the Good News of the gospel.

Conclusion

I have in this chapter sought to revive a spirit of discovery within the denominational church in the United States. I have done so by describing the landscape at various times in history, by articulating the DNA through which the country has lived, fought, and emerged, and by reminding the denominational church of its continuity within historical Christianity and

---

72. Van Gelder, "Postmodernism and Evangelicals," p. 495.
73. Tanner, *Theories of Culture*, pp. 141, 171-75.

challenging it to develop a new contextual missiology. Ultimately, the calling of the church is complicated and exciting, straightforward yet complex. Moving the church into the twenty-first century might seem as crazy as Lewis and Clark sailing up the Missouri River in search of the Pacific Ocean. Yet, if the church engages in this postmodern adventure, people for years to come may marvel at the beautiful landscape there is to discover. For Lewis and Clark, it only took a few leaders with a clear mission, determination, and a willingness to venture forth. Will you join the twenty-first-century church's Corps of Discovery and help create a Christian movement within the postmodern context?

CHAPTER 6

The Possibility of Transforming the General Assembly of the Presbyterian Church in Korea (GAPCK) into a Missional Church

Joon Ho Lee

Introduction

> Arirang Arirang Arariyo
> Walking over the hill of Arirang, you left me behind.
> You will get foot trouble before you reach one mile.
>
> Arirang Arirang Arariyo
> Walking over the hill of Arirang, the sorrows in my heart
> are as many as the stars in the sky.

"Arirang," whose literal meaning is "my beloved man," is the most famous Korean folk song. From ancient times to the present, Koreans have sung it across the Korean peninsula and throughout the world. "Arirang" is representative of a contextualization that encapsulates, at a deep level, the mentality and emotions of all Korean people over time and in all contexts. "Arirang" is about love and its ramifications, including its conflicts, sufferings, and pains. Despite his lover's plea, the beloved man departs, and after that she sings "Arirang" with a lingering love-hate in her heart, waiting for the return of the beloved. Why have Koreans loved to sing "Arirang," and what have they been waiting for when they sing this song?

The three themes in "Arirang" are love, suffering, and patience. These themes represent a hermeneutical code for understanding the life of Korean people, as well as serving as a contact point for Korean people to engage with Christianity. The gospel seeped into the life of Korean people riding the tune of "Arirang." When Christianity made its way into the peninsula, the Korean Christians turned "Arirang" into a Song of Songs to Jesus, whose love is unchanging and who would never leave the beloved. But in our time, the resonance of this love song to Jesus is fading in Korea. Has the Korean church experienced a midlife crisis? If so, how can the gospel once again penetrate the hearts and minds of Koreans with a new "Arirang"? In order to renew a love for Jesus, what should the church be and do? The issue for the church is not primarily about growth, but about restoration — restoration in its fullest sense. Getting at this restoration will require church leaders to reflect on the understanding of church. That is the focus of this chapter: the possibility of transforming the Korean church into a missional church. I will investigate this question in the following way: first, I will briefly introduce the history of Korea and the socioreligious situation of Korea; then I will trace the church's history in Korea and try to assess the key strategies that were applied in the process of missions coming to Korea; finally, I will review the theology, ecclesiology, and church polities that currently exist in the General Assembly of the Presbyterian Church in Korea (GAPCK) and discuss possible changes in the GAPCK in order to develop a contextual missiology in the context of Korean society.

Defining the Context of Korea

The Historical Setting before the Twentieth Century

For our purposes, we can divide the history of Korea into two eras: the time before the introduction of Christianity and the time following it. Koreans believe that Korea was founded by Dan-gun in 2333 BCE and was called the Old Choson. Several kingdoms and small city-states succeeded the Old Choson. The three major kingdoms were Koguryo (37 BCE–668 CE), Paekche (18 BCE–660 CE), and Shilla (57 BCE–935 CE). Ever since Shilla, which unified the peninsula in 668, Korea has been ruled by a single government and has maintained its political independence along with its cultural and ethnic identity and integrity in spite of frequent foreign invasions. Stephen Neill expresses the situation of Korea as follows:

Sandwiched between Japan and China, it does not belong to either of them. It has its own mysterious language, which is not akin to either Chinese or Japanese. Its people, extraordinarily tough and sturdy, have learned from both, but have retained their own individual character.[1]

The kingdom of Koryeo (Korea) was founded in 918 and replaced Shilla in the year 936; this kingdom lasted until 1392. During that period, Buddhism flourished, which resulted in the prevalence of Buddhist culture in the art and architecture of Korea. Taoism and Feng-shui theories were popular as well.[2] The early rulers of the Choson dynasty (1392-1910) replaced Buddhism with Confucianism as the sovereign ideology because they wished to oppose the dominant influence of Buddhism. Thus, Confucian ethics and values came to dominate the social structure and behavioral code for the five centuries of that dynasty. During the reign of King Sejong, the fourth monarch of the Choson, scholars of the royal academy invented the Korean alphabet, *Han-gul,* a highly scientific, simple, and effective system of writing (1443). Later in Korean history, *Han-gul* significantly contributed to the spread of Christianity and helped it to take root in Korea.

Until the late eighteenth century, Korea remained "a hermit kingdom": it adamantly opposed Western demands to open its doors until it finally made a trade treaty with the United States in 1882. After that, the Korean peninsula became the arena of competition among Western powers. However, Japan soon stepped into the power vacuum that existed in Korea as a result of its opening to the West, and that nation eventually annexed the entire country in 1910.

1. Stephen Neill, *A History of Christian Missions* (London: Penguin Books, 1986), p. 290.

2. Feng-shui theory, meaning literally "wind and water," is a part of the ancient Chinese philosophy of nature that explains the fortune of humans, who live dependently on the earth, in terms of the relationship between the two according to Taoism. Because they believe that geographical features (topography) determine the fortune of human beings, the fortune of humans will not change if geographical features are not changed. Feng-shui superstition is still prevalent in the life of Korean people.

The Historical Setting during the Twentieth Century

Korea's 1882 treaty with the United States allowed Western missionaries to freely enter the country for missions work, and Christianity sprouted in Korea during the twentieth century despite the country's experiencing a great deal of political upheaval. That period of upheaval began when the Japanese implemented policies that would assimilate Koreans into Japanese culture. The new strictures did not allow Koreans to speak their own language or to learn their history. During this period, Koreans fought relentlessly for freedom from Japanese rule. When Japan surrendered to Allied forces in August 1945, Korea finally received independence. Yet no sooner had the nation celebrated the joy of independence than it experienced the pain of national division. On August 15, 1948, the government of the Republic of Korea was inaugurated in the South, while a Communist regime was set up in the North under Kim Il Sung, a Stalinist who wielded absolute power.

On June 25, 1950, the Korean War broke out and lasted until 1953. The war left the entire land devastated: millions of people were either killed or became homeless and separated from their families. Reunification became, and remains, the long-cherished but elusive goal of all Koreans living on both sides of the vigilantly guarded Military Demarcation Line. Since the war, South Korea has made continual efforts to oppose military dictatorships and to establish democracy. The relentless efforts are evident in the continual democratic movements, such as the 4.19 Student Movement in 1960, the 5.18 Kwang-ju Democratization Movement in 1980, and the 6.10 Movement in 1987. In 1992, South Korea finally established a true democratic government and entered a new chapter in its history.

Political-Economic Setting

Liberation from the Japanese occupation did not bring the independence for which Koreans had fought so hard. Rather, it was the beginning of an ideological conflict in a divided country. After Japan surrendered on August 15, 1945, the peninsula came under divided rule: the USSR governed the northern part of Korea, while the United States governed the southern part. And the ideological differences between northern and southern Korea have intensified since 1945. Anti-Communism was the priority of national policy in South Korea, and the partition intensified conflicts in the peninsula and threatened the welfare of the entire country.

During Japan's thirty-five years of colonial rule (1910-1945), that nation ruthlessly exploited Korea's economic resources, and the Korean economy was further devastated during the Korean War (1950-1953). But over the last quarter century, South Korea has achieved an incredible record of economic growth and integration into the high-tech and global world economy. This is widely referred to as "the economic miracle on the Han River." "The key to success was the adoption of an outward-looking development strategy that reflected Korea's insufficient natural resources, its limited domestic market, and its abundant, well-educated, and industrious manpower."[3]

Sociocultural Setting

One of the cultural and philosophical ideals of Korea is known as "Respect the heaven and love the people" *(Kyung-Chun-Ae-In).* Although the ideology of *Kyung-Chun-Ae-In* is similar to the biblical idea of "loving God and loving one's neighbors" (Mark 12:31-32), the fundamental nature of *Kyung-Chun-Ae-In* practiced in Korea is "Loyalty and Filial Piety" *(Choong-Hyo).* The Korean society that was built on these ideologies has an odd distinction. First of all, it centers on family and kinship and an exaggerated emphasis on honoring parents that found expression in ancestral worship. Second, it is an authoritarian part of the ideology that later evolved into a patriarchal and male chauvinistic authoritarianism. Third, the authoritarian nature of the culture begot the prestige culture, or what is known as the "shame culture." Such a culture places more importance on saving face and keeping up with appearances, reputation, and prestige than on pursuing rational and practical benefits for the people. Although I have portrayed *Choong-Hyo* thought here in a somewhat negative light, it is the soil in which Korean Christianity took root, and its features have undeniably had an influence on shaping the character of Christianity in Korea.

Recent industrialization, urbanization, and massive migration, how-

3. *Facts about Korea,* rev. ed. (Seoul, Korea: Korean Overseas Information Service, 1993), p. 50.

ever, have resulted in a movement away from lineage- and neighborhood-based social relationships toward relationships based on function, from authoritarianism to anti-authoritarianism, and from a shame culture to a rational culture.[4] Thus we can say that one distinctive of the present Korean culture is conflict and confrontation between the old and new generations, and this also often results in confusion. There is a clear conflict between traditional Confucian culture and Western materialistic culture, and this radical shift in values from the old to the new generation has resulted in uncertainty. The identity confusion of Korea as a society is intimately tied to an identity confusion within the Korean church.

Religious Setting

The traditional culture and thought of Korea are closely related to three major religions: Shamanism, Buddhism, and Confucianism.[5] These religions have played an important role in the country's social and cultural development and have greatly influenced Korean Christianity. Shamanism, which consists of spirit worship and nature worship, is Korea's oldest belief. The shaman is an intermediary between humans and the spiritual world and is thought to be able to help avert bad luck, cure sickness by exorcising evil spirits, and propitiate local gods. This system of belief persists in Korea today in many ways. "[Confucianism and Buddhism] did not result in the abandonment of shamanistic beliefs and practices. They assimilated elements of shamanistic faith and coexisted peacefully. Shamanism has remained an underlying religion of the Korean people as well as a vital aspect of their culture."[6]

A second religion, Confucianism, was introduced into Korea from China in 3-4 BCE. Yi Song-gye, the founder of the Choson Dynasty, adopted Confucian teachings as the guiding principles for ruling the nation. Although Confucianism is no longer the ruling ideology, its place in contemporary Korean society is deeply rooted and broadly influential. It

4. Choong Soon Kim, "Korea," in *Encyclopedia of World Cultures,* vol. V: *East and Southeast Asia,* ed. Paul Hockings (Boston: G. K. Hall & Co., 1993), p. 147.

5. The statistics according to CIA reports: no affiliation 46%, Christian 26%, Buddhist 26%, Confucianist 1%, and other 1%. The World Fact Book by CIA. http://www.cia.gov/cia/publications/factbook/geos/kn.html [accessed Nov. 15, 2004].

6. *Facts about Korea,* p. 132.

remains a fundamental part of Korean society: it shapes the moral system, the way of life, and the laws.

A third religion, Buddhism, was introduced from China in the Three Kingdom period (372-527 CE). From the beginning, Buddhism was welcomed by the aristocratic, or ruling, class and became rooted deeply in Korean society because it embraced traditional religions such as Shamanism. Buddhism is "a highly disciplined philosophical religion which stresses personal salvation through the renunciation of worldly desires, thus avoiding rebirth in the endless cycle of reincarnations, and bringing about the absorption of the soul of the enlightenment into Nirvana."[7] Buddhism produced a magnificent boom in the arts and in temple architecture.

Finally, Christianity was introduced into Korea approximately 200 years ago, and it spread rapidly in a relatively short time. From the beginning of its introduction into Korea, Christianity had a leading influence in many aspects of Korean society, including education, medicine, politics, and ideology. However, it did not construct a Christian culture in the same way that Confucianism or Buddhism produced distinctive cultures that had wide societal impact.

Describing the Church's History and the History of Missions: Historical Development of the Church in Korea

The Beginning of Catholicism (1592-1800) and Its Sufferings (1801-1871)

There is no record of any Christian missionaries coming to Korea before the middle of the eighteenth century. Although contact with the Roman Catholic Church goes as far back as 1592, it was not until the latter part of the eighteenth century that *Silhak* scholars were first introduced to Catholicism.[8] *Silhak* scholars who were studying abroad were attracted to Catholic literature because of their hopes of learning about Western civilization. Seung-Hun Lee, upon his return from China in 1784, brought back

7. *Facts about Korea*, p. 132.
8. *Silhak* means "practical learning," which is a Korean philosophical reform movement under the later Choson dynasty (17th-19th centuries).

books and articles on Christian doctrine and distributed this Christian literature among the *Shilhak* scholars.[9]

Catholic churches were established in Korea after Lee's return, but for over a hundred years these churches went through severe persecutions (in 1801, 1815, 1827, 1839, 1846, and 1866-1867). During these recurrent persecutions, about ten thousand Catholic believers were martyred.[10] Yet, despite the severe persecution, Catholic churches spread throughout the Korean peninsula. However, the Catholic Church in Korea never fully recovered from the brutal persecutions; in its place, the Korean Protestant Church was established and prospered on the spilled blood of Catholic Christians.

The Beginning of the Protestant Church (1884-1895)

It was during the period of 1884-1895 that official Protestant missionaries became active in Korea. These missionaries could freely engage in their missionary effort because Korea had made its trade treaty with foreign countries, beginning with the United States in 1882. But the history of the Korean Protestant mission goes back some years before the arrival of the first official missionaries: it began with Bible translation works in Japan and China. Korean merchants, including Ung-Chan Lee and Sang-Yoon Suh, met John Ross, a Scottish Presbyterian missionary to China, and his brother-in-law, John McIntyre, in 1879. Lee and Suh were baptized by Ross and McIntyre, and the two helped these missionaries translate portions of the Bible into Korean.

Suh returned to Korea with his brother, Kyung-Jo Suh, one of the first native Presbyterian ordained ministers. In 1884 they established the *Sorai church,* the first Protestant Church in Korea. In Japan, Soo-Jung Lee, a Korean who was studying the modernization of Japan, was introduced to a Japanese Christian named Tsuda Sen. Lee became a Christian by reading a Bible written in Chinese characters that Sen had given him, and he was baptized. He started the Korean immigrant church in Japan and began to translate the Bible into Korean. When Henry G. Apenzeller (Methodist) and Horace G. Underwood (Presbyterian) came to Korea as the first foreign missionaries who were ordained Protestant ministers, they brought

---

9. Samuel Hugh Moffett, *A History of Christianity in Asia,* vol. II: *1500-1900* (Maryknoll, NY: Orbis Books, 2005), p. 309.

10. Horace G. Underwood, "Christianity in Korea," *Missiology* 22, no. 1 (1994): 67.

with them Lee's translation of the Bible. Underwood and Appenzeller arrived in Korea together on Easter Sunday, April 5, 1885. After that, missionaries from several mission bodies began to arrive in Korea.

The Expansion of the Protestant Churches (1896-1910)

The Korean churches began to develop structures and institutions between 1896 and 1910. They built seminaries, established presbyteries (1907), and organized the General Assembly (1912). Most significantly, the Great Revival Movement happened in Korea in 1907, and that movement was certainly the main element that made the Korean church exuberant and contributed to its exceptional growth. The origins of the movement can be traced to a prayer meeting held in Wonsan in Korea in 1903. R. A. Hardie, a medical doctor and Methodist missionary, read Luke 11:13 (". . . how much more will your Father in heaven give the Holy Spirit to those who ask Him") and was overwhelmed by the strong movement of the Holy Spirit in making him realize his sins. He could not but share his experience with his missionary colleagues and with his Korean congregation. His honest confession of his sins had a strong impact on the audience.

The Korean congregation eagerly yearned for the same Holy Spirit. Through Bible studies and prayer meetings, the Holy Spirit burst into flame at the conference in Wonsan. Similar revival movements took place in Seoul in 1906; and the movement reached its climax at the great revival in Pyungyang in January 1907.[11] The movement was not restricted to adult Christians; it quickly spread to children and students, and schools were often closed for several weeks at a time. In addition, most stores in Pyungyang were closed because of the Bible conference and the revival movement. Elements of this movement spread to the entire nation.

The Church under the Japanese Colonialism (1910-1945)

The Korean Christian church entered a new era when the Japanese annexed Korea in 1910. The period 1910-1945 represents a dark age in Korean

11. Young Hoon Lee, "Korean Pentecost: The Great Revival of 1907," *Asian Journal of Pentecostal Studies* 4, no. 1 (Jan. 2001): 76-77.

church history: it was stained with the blood of martyrs in the still-infant Korean church. The Japanese government noted the prominent role of Christians as leaders and organizers of the independence movement, and they also recognized the link between Christianity and Korean nationalism. Because of that link, they burned numerous churches and subjected hundreds of Christians to imprisonment, torture, and martyrdom. One of the Japanization policies demanded that Korean believers attend shrine worship of Japan's Shintoism, and authorities ordered all schools and churches to participate in Shinto shrine ceremonies. This put the Korean church in a very difficult situation: it led to the severe persecution of those many Christians who refused to comply because of their faith. Under the brutal policies of the Japanization of the Korean church, most of the foreign missionaries left Korea, and the Japanese authorities harassed those who remained. During this period, three thousand Christian leaders were imprisoned, and more than fifty of them were martyred. Yet, despite the persistent oppression and persecutions under the Japanese regime, Korean Christian churches amazingly continued to experience a steady growth.

Liberation and Ordeal (1945-1960)

The Korean church faced another sort of trial between 1945 and 1960 with the division of the church between North and South Korea. Before the liberation, North Korea had been the center of Christianity in Korea. After the liberation in 1945, and the division of the nation into two countries, the communist government began to suppress the churches in the North. During the Korean War, as Christians in North Korea began to face this harsh reality, millions of them fled to South Korea.[12]

After the liberation from Japanese rule, the church in South Korea faced two issues: the fact that some Christians had been complicit with the Japanese colonial regime, and the introduction of liberal theology into the country. A split in the Presbyterian denomination, based on the first issue, came during this period. In 1952, the *Koshin* Group left the church, drawing a hard line against anyone who had attended a shrine ritual during the

---

12. G. Thompson Brown, "Korea," in *A Dictionary of Asian Christianity*, ed. Scott W. Sunquist (Grand Rapids: Eerdmans, 2001), p. 448.

Japanese colonial rule. In 1953, the issue of the inerrancy of Scripture over against liberal theology caused a group called *Hanshin,* which was in support of liberal theology, to form the Presbyterian Church in the Republic of Korea (PCRK) under the leadership of Kim Jae-Joon. In 1959, the remaining Presbyterian group was divided over the issue of involvement in the World Council of Churches (WCC): *Tonghap* supported joining the WCC, and *Haptong* (GAPCK) opposed joining it.

The Conversion Boom (1961-1990)

In the three decades between 1961 and 1990, the Korean church experienced enormous growth. During this time Korean society was also in political turmoil and underwent rapid economic growth, which had an impact on the growing Korean churches. James Huntley Grayson says: "The 1960s stood at the threshold of the period of Korea's rapid urbanization and industrialization, and was also the time when the idea of 'Church Growth' became the theme for the evangelization of the nation."[13] In the 1960s the church reached out to people who were oppressed, such as prostitutes and new industrial laborers. As the Korean economy was burgeoning, the issue of the industrial labor force came to the fore as one of the most important areas of evangelization work.

Accordingly, churches established industrial chaplaincies among the workers within factories. In addition, with military service mandatory for men in South Korea, the role of the chaplains' corps in the armed forces became equally important. Many soldiers converted to Christianity during their military service. Furthermore, the churches began to send cross-cultural missionaries to Japan, Bolivia, Pakistan, and other places in the world.[14] In the 1970s, when President Park proclaimed the *Yushin* constitution, he was confronted with a nationwide protest. Some churches stood in the center of the political movement that called for the restoration of democracy and social justice, especially for the industrial workers. During this movement, many Christians were imprisoned and tortured. This process saw the emergence of *Minjung theology,* which dealt with *minjung* (the

13. James Huntley Grayson, "Korea," in *The Encyclopedia of Protestantism,* vol. 2, ed. Hans J. Hillerbrand (New York: Routledge, 2004), p. 1039.
14. Grayson, "Korea," p. 1039.

people) and *Han*.[15] Despite all of this societal chaos, the Korean church continued to double its congregational membership every fifteen or twenty years.

The Stagnation of Church Growth and the Transforming Period (1991-)

The period from 1991 to the present might be called a time of disorientation in preparation for reorientation. As the military dictatorship ended and a democratic government came into power, the force of the theological opposition between the progressive and conservative factions grew weaker. Within a society undergoing rapid changes in various aspects, the church now faces a need to define its identity in newly contextualized terms. Stuck in the midst of this identity crisis, Korean churches have experienced stagnation in both membership and attendance. Many megachurches have come onto the scene, but they are not necessarily healthy, nor have they necessarily had a positive impact on society. A major Presbyterian church reported a decrease of 1.8 percent in membership in 1998.[16] One positive result of this period is that Korean churches have become increasingly active in foreign missions. The number of Korean missionaries increased from 93 in 1979 to 1,645 in 1990, to 8,103 in 2000, to 13,000 in 2004. These missionaries are serving in 164 different countries.[17]

Strategies Applied to Mission in Korea

Early missionaries used a wide array of strategies as they tried to introduce Christianity into Korea. It may be helpful to identify and discuss a few of the more important strategies they used.

15. *Han* is difficult to translate into a foreign language because it includes such different nuances as are conveyed by the English words *rancor, grudge, hatred, lamentation, regret, grief, pathos, self-pity, fate, mortification,* and so forth. *Han*'s exact meaning can only be grasped experientially.

16. Grayson, "Korea," p. 191.

17. Missionary Statistics of Korean Churches, *Korean Mission Handbook 2003-2004,* KRIM (Korean Research Institute for Mission).

Bible Translation Ministry

Bible translation was a noteworthy distinctive in the mission history of Korea. Before foreign missionaries even began to work within Korea, native believers worked on Bible translation and established a church early on. The Korean people were prepared to receive the gospel and asked missionaries to "come over to Macedonia and help us."[18] Lamin Sanneh says that Christianity has spread principally by a strategy of "mission by translation," which "makes the recipient culture the true and final locus of the proclamation."[19] This is certainly true of the Korean mission.

The Bible was translated via the joint efforts of Koreans and foreign missionaries in neighboring countries and was made available in Korea before the arrival of foreign missionaries. Later, when they discovered that the Korean people had their own alphabet, *Hangul,* missionaries translated the Bible into Korean, which allowed the populace to easily read it and learn it. The Korean churches' love of the Bible fueled the rapid growth of the church. And the translation of the Bible was a key factor contributing to the quick independence of the Korean church from foreign missionaries. It is hard to deny that this Bible-centered faith made a great contribution to the shaping of Korean Presbyterianism.

Nevius Mission Method

One well-known strategy for Korean mission was the adoption of the Nevius method, with its three basic principles: self-propagation, self-government, and self-support. Dr. John Livingston Nevius, a Princetonian who was a missionary in China, visited Seoul, Korea, in 1890. He spent two weeks discussing the methods of mission with young missionaries in Korea, and these missionaries then adopted his method as the main mission strategy.[20] The focus of the method in Korea, however, was not nearly so much on self-support or self-government as it was on the Bible classes. Dr.

18. David J. Bosch, *Transforming Mission: Paradigm Shifts in Theology of Mission* (Maryknoll, NY: Orbis Books, 2003), p. 289.

19. Lamin Sanneh, *Translating the Message* (Maryknoll, NY: Orbis Books, 2002), p. 29.

20. See the thesis of Yong Kyu Park, *Korean Presbyterianism and Biblical Authority: The Role of Scripture in the Shaping of Korean Presbyterianism, 1918-1953* (Ann Arbor, MI: UMI, 1991), ch. III, fn. 18.

Yong-Kyu Park says that the Nevius method implanted three things in the Korean church: a strict Sabbath observance, biblical conservatism and dogmatism, and an antiliberal stance.[21] Although negative evaluations of the Nevius method have been proposed, one cannot deny that the Nevius method was very effective in the early stages.[22]

Mission Field Comity Arrangement

The Mission Field Comity Arrangement is another distinct feature of the missionary work in Korea. In 1882 the missionaries set geographical boundaries for denominations to avoid conflicts and to facilitate cooperation and efficient mission activities.[23] This arrangement was based on the following points:

1. Joint occupation for an open port or city with more than 5,000 people.
2. Prohibition of other denominations in a city of under 5,000 if a quasi-mission base is already established.
3. Priority on expansion of mission base in the areas with no existing missionary presence.
4. Requirement to have the pastor's recommendation letter if a person were to change churches.
5. Mutual respect and adherence to other churches' rules and regulations.

According to these principles, the Presbyterians and Methodists divided the country between them: Southern Presbyterian took up the middle and southwest province; Canadian Presbyterians the north province; Australian Presbyterians the south province with the center of Pusan; South Methodist Church the east-middle province with the center of Wonsan. After this arrangement, any overlapping local mission work was arranged as a joint enterprise. This arrangement helped reduce unnecessary friction among various denominations and minimized the waste of fi-

21. Park, *Korean Presbyterianism*, pp. 81-82.
22. Yong Kyu Park, "Nevius Methods as a Mission Strategy in the Korea Mission Field," *Presbyterian Theological Quarterly* 69, no. 3 (Fall 2002): 58, fn. 4.
23. Young Jae Kim, "The Trend of World Mission and Mission Strategies in Korea": http://www.user.chollian.net/~ikcho102/nm6-2.htm [accessed Dec. 1, 2004].

nancial resources. But this arrangement can be criticized because it has contributed to a power struggle among denominations based on regional differences; it has also contributed to the fragmentation of churches.[24] Another of the comity arrangement's negative results for the Korean church was the regionally disproportionate distribution of a denomination. For instance, although the Korean Methodist Church began its mission work around the same time that the Presbyterian Church did, it could not plant churches beyond the central region of Korea.

Education and Social-Medical Diaconia[25]

Verkuyl says that "[t]he kingdom does not only address the spiritual and moral needs of a person, but his material, physical, social, cultural and political needs as well. For this reason Jesus came not only as one who preaches but also as one who serves *(diakonos)*."[26] Early missionaries in Korea emphasized this point of mission. At first, the missionaries became quickly involved in education. Knowing about the Korean's zeal for education, missionaries began to establish schools such as Baejae boys' school and Ewha girls' school; they hoped to enable illiterate Koreans to read the Bible. These schools facilitated the rapid expansion of Christianity among the common people. Currently, "thirty-one Korean universities claim a Christian origin, of which three are considered among the top five universities in the country."[27]

Besides their involvement in education, the missionaries also carried out medical diaconal activities. Before Underwood and Appenzeller arrived in Korea, Dr. Horace N. Allen arrived (1884) and began work there as a medical missionary. Allen established the first general hospital (Kwanghye-won) on April 10, 1885. Since then, missionaries have established many

---

24. Chang Young Kim, "Mission Comity and Nevius Mission Methods": http://www.ncjeil.or.kr/jboard/?p=detail&code=3ncjeil&id=88&page=6 [accessed Nov. 27, 2004].

25. Johannes Verkuyl suggests four ways and means God uses in communicating his good news: communicating the gospel, fulfilling diaconal responsibility, establishing fellowship, and serving the cause of righteousness and justice. Verkuyl, *Contemporary Missiology: An Introduction,* ed. and trans. Dale Cooper (Grand Rapids: Eerdmans, 1978), pp. 205-25.

26. Verkuyl, *Contemporary Missiology,* p. 211.

27. Grayson, "Korea," p. 1040.

hospitals and medical clinics. Some Korean churches, supported by American mission societies, were active in medical missions, especially during the Korean War, In addition to these efforts, many churches also operated orphanages and nursing homes, and they did pioneering work in helping the disabled.

Contributing to Social and Political Justice

The churches in Korea did not neglect the responsibility of working toward social and political justice. When the Christian gospel was introduced to Korea, the Korean people welcomed it as a liberating gospel for those who had suffered, not only at the hands of foreign countries such as China and Japan, but also from the conservative Confucianism in the eighteenth and nineteenth centuries. Strong evidence can be found of Christian leadership in the independence movement in 1919; moreover, Christianity was the biggest conceptual influence behind the independence movement.

Christianity was faithful in its responsibility to work for justice during Japanese rule. In the midst of an increasingly severe oppression and the efforts of Japanization, Christian leaders were on the front lines of the anti-Japan and independence movements. This phenomenon later reemerged in the process of the anti-Communist movement, as well as the anti-military government movement that challenged President Park's regime. The churches became an active democratic force in Korea, and church leaders moved to the forefront of the movement for democracy. As a result, Christianity gained social credibility, and Korean people became more open to Christianity.

Developing a Contextual Missiology for the Missional Church in the GAPCK

A Review of the Theology and Missiology in the Current GAPCK

The GAPCK, the biggest denomination in Korea, has adopted Reformed theology that is rooted in Calvinism as its foundational principle, and the

Westminster Confession of Faith, together with the *Larger and Shorter Cate-chisms,* as its doctrinal standards. In *The Book of Constitution,* the GAPCK states that the denomination adopts these as the doctrinal standards be-cause Reformed theology and the above documents best represent a cor-rect interpretation of Scripture.[28] The Calvinist tradition's emphasis on the Bible existed from the beginning of the Presbyterian mission in Korea. Most of the early Presbyterian missionaries held conservative theological views, and one of those was the recognition of the absolute authority of the Scripture.[29] The emphasis on Scripture can be seen in the influence of the missionaries from the Northern Presbyterian Church, who stood in the line of the Old School Princeton tradition: Charles Hodge, B. B. Warfield, and J. Gresham Machen. From the missionaries of the Northern Presbyterian Church, the theology of the inerrancy of the Bible was intro-duced into Korea. Dr. Hyung-Nong Park and Yoon-Sun Park took the lead in this theological stance: they rejected Karl Barth's Neo-orthodoxy and higher criticism of the Bible.

Besides the emphasis on Scripture, another prominent characteristic of Calvinism is its emphasis on God's sovereignty. This became the theo-logical bedrock of the GAPCK. Surprisingly, the emphasis on God's sover-eignty appeared as an evangelistic fervor.[30] The people in the GAPCK be-lieved that, because an unbeliever's repentance depends on God's sovereignty, their only responsibility was to present the gospel. They be-lieved that, because God already had responsive people everywhere in the world, all they needed to do was present the gospel. God would then be the one to bring people to repentance. As a result, they had a boldness and pas-sion in their evangelism, and that evangelistic fervor was undoubtedly an important factor behind the enormous church growth that Korea wit-nessed. Predestination and the theology of God's sovereignty went well with the Korean people's underlying belief in heavenly destiny; therefore, it was easy for Korean Christians to embrace these views.[31]

The ecclesiology of the GAPCK is based on Calvin's ecclesiology and has not shown much development in the Korean Presbyterian Church.

28. *The Book of Constitution* (Seoul: General Assembly Press, 1993), p. 19.

29. Yong Kyu Park, "The Roots of the Korean Presbyterian Church," *Presbyterian Theological Quarterly* 68 (Fall 2001): 277.

30. Hyung Nong Park, "The Theological Heritage of the Korean Presbyterian Church," *Presbyterian Theological Quarterly* 43 (Fall 1976): 13.

31. Park, "The Theological Heritage," pp. 16-17.

John Calvin's great work, the *Institutes,* consists of four parts: God the Father, Jesus the Son, the Holy Spirit, and the church. Jung-Uck Hwang, a professor at Hanshin University in Korea, says that "[this] indicates how important Calvin found ecclesiology."[32] John Calvin's views of the church are based on God's choosing a people, and they are established in confessing Jesus as the Christ (Matt. 16:16). He finds the essence of the church in the mystical union with Christ.[33] While Luther emphasizes people as the "communion of saints," Calvin, who stresses God's sovereign authority, sees the church as the institution that God sets up for God's elected people.[34] Calvin makes a distinction between the visible church and invisible church; this view originates with Augustine. The mystical union with Christ happens in the true church, the church that is invisible to people but known to God; but it is shown in the visible church through the confession of faith, the proclamation of the Word, the administration of the sacraments, church structure, and polity. Although Calvin recognizes the necessity of a differentiation between the visible and invisible church, he notes the practical impossibility of severance between the visible and invisible church because the two are inseparable.[35]

The Reformation era at the time of Calvin established an ecclesiology in the context of opposing the Roman Catholic Church. Consequently, Calvin emphasized the identifiable signs of *a true church* as the ministry of the Word and the administration of sacraments.[36] Calvinists tend to emphasize the purification of the church rather than its unity or services, which reflects the frame of mind of the Reformation era. Importing Calvinism and its inclination toward an ecclesiological emphasis, the GAPCK also tends to emphasize the purification of the church rather than its unity or services.

The understanding of church in Calvinistic terms has significant implications for an understanding of church leadership. True church leader-

32. Jung-Uck Hwang, "Calvin's Ecclesiology and the Reality of the Korean Presbyterian Church," *Theology Research* 46 (Dec. 2004): 244-45.

33. Chul Won Suh, "The Reformed Ecclesiology," *Presbyterian Theological Quarterly* 63 (Fall 1996): 223-25.

34. Young Jae Kim, "Preface of Author," in Otto Weber, *Die Treue Gottes in der Geschichte der Kirche,* Korean trans. by Young Jae Kim (Seoul: Poongman, 1985), pp. 9-10.

35. Weber, *Die Treue Gottes,* p. 49.

36. John Calvin, *Institutes of the Christian Religion,* bk. IV, ch. 1, trans. Henry Beveridge (Grand Rapids: Eerdmans, 1989), 289-92.

ship is to be found in the proclamation of the Word; this is based on the logic that the proper administration of the church happens when God's Word is properly proclaimed, because the Holy Spirit works through the Word of God.[37] Accordingly, the senior pastor is at the center of the church leadership, and preaching is the most important practice in the exercise of leadership. Recently, limitations of Reformed ecclesiology have surfaced in view of its lack of sufficient theological rigor in projecting a vision for mission. Since the emergence of the Lausanne Committee for World Evangelization (LCWE) in 1974, the emerging ecclesiology is in need of a theology of church that articulates its social responsibility with regard to evangelism.

The missiology of the GAPCK focuses on developing Reformed missions. Calvin's theology views mission as a responsibility of the church. In contrast to the common perception that Calvin lacks any understanding of missions, Reformed theology has a rich understanding of missions.[38] It is incorrect to say that Calvin's view of predestination lacks a treatment of missions.[39] Calvin says that the proper proclamation of God's Word is one of the signs of the true church, which includes spreading the gospel. The sense of responsibility for a church to be a steward of the gospel, which is conferred by the Lord himself, underlies Calvin's argument for the proclamation of God's Word as a sign of the true church. Proclamation of the gospel is also the final step of missionary work (Rom. 10:17). Calvin's theology demands an invitation to the Holy Spirit's redemptive work in every aspect of society — in politics, in the economy, and in the culture. Logically, the command for evangelism leads to the command to reform society and culture.[40] Dutch theologian Abraham Kuyper represents Calvin's posture on missions well when he emphasizes the principle of authority of domain (sphere sovereignty) in Calvinism, which is the recognition of God's sovereign authority in every domain of human life.[41]

37. Suh, "The Reformed Ecclesiology," p. 233.

38. K. S. Latourette, *A History of the Expansion of Christianity* (Grand Rapids: Zondervan, 1937), pp. 25-26; Stephen Neill, *A History of Christian Mission* (London: Penguin Books, 1986), pp. 187-89; Herbert Kane, *A Concise History of the Christian World Mission* (Grand Rapids: Baker, 1978), pp. 73-75.

39. Seong Uck Kim, "John Calvin and His Missionary Concern," *Presbyterian Theological Quarterly* 69 (Fall 2002): 337-52.

40. Calvin, *Institutes*, II, 233-47.

41. Sung Tae Kim, "The Conception of Mission in Modern Missiology," *Presbyterian Theological Quarterly* 66 (Fall 1999): 139.

Developing a Missiological Ecclesiology

It is important to begin with a reconsideration of ecclesiology. The ecclesiology of the GAPCK has been interested in the dichotomy between the visible church and the invisible church. This reveals an unnecessary overemphasis on the invisible church, and it is too simplistic and deficient in its understanding of the visible church, or the institutional aspect of the church. Also, Reformed ecclesiology has tended to overemphasize Christology as the basis of its ecclesiology. Kevin Giles points out the limited role of pneumatology in Reformed ecclesiology:

> The Spirit has been as an extra or addendum in Christocentric ecclesiology. . . . The church has a historical beginning in the incarnation, death, and resurrection of Christ, but the Spirit of Christ enables it to grow as the body of Christ, and to adapt to the ever-changing circumstance of subsequent history.[42]

Christocentric Reformed ecclesiology tends to focus on the salvation of an individual rather than on the demonstration of the kingdom of God; thus it can lead to individualism of faith and individualism in the local church.[43] This is the reason why the conservative churches in Korea, along with the GAPCK, have been very passive in social and public services and social justice work. The church needs a trinitarian approach in order to understand ecclesiology properly. Giles says:

> All three persons of the Trinity are involved in the emergence and life of the Christian community. The Father sends the Son to redeem a people for himself, the Son dies on the cross to effect this redemption, and the Spirit is given by the Father through the Son to the redeemed community, the church.[44]

A trinitarian ecclesiology is far more effective in understanding the nature and function of the church and its ministry: it not only allows the church to overcome underlying hierarchical thinking with regard to gen-

---

42. Kevin Giles, *What on Earth Is the Church? An Exploration in New Testament Theology* (Downers Grove, IL: InterVarsity Press, 1995), pp. 221-22.

43. Miroslav Volf, *After Our Likeness: The Church as the Image of the Trinity* (Grand Rapids: Eerdmans, 1998), pp. 196-97.

44. Giles, *What on Earth Is the Church?* p. 221.

der and various offices, but it also enables the mission of the church to be viewed and practiced in the broader perspective of proclamation and the demonstration of God's sovereign authority all over the world. A trinitarian ecclesiology, however, need not weaken the Christological center of its ecclesiology. It does not lead to a denial of Christ's death on the cross as the only way to salvation, because the meaning of the cross is even more fully explicated within a trinitarian framework.

The Korean church's missiology needs to have a revised understanding based on a trinitarian ecclesiology. The GAPCK has made tremendous efforts to fulfill its mission responsibility within the Calvinistic Reformed theology, based on the Great Commission (Matt. 28:18-20). Although the Korean church has not used the term "missional church," it has been widely accepted that evangelism was the main purpose of the church's existence, and the Korean church was missional from the beginning — at least in this regard. So far, the Korean church has considered evangelism as the primary responsibility of the church and the highest calling for every believer. This was shown in the Korean church's overwhelming interest in world mission: Korean churches have sent many missionaries overseas in the past several decades. It is crucial to incorporate this insight back into an understanding of the very nature of the church.

Starting as a missional church was inevitable for the Korean church because it needed to take root in a soil where the gospel had not yet been heard. However, the church must now examine the past (rather than enjoying past successes), learn from it, and look forward to the future. The stagnation of church growth, which is now common in Western churches, is also beginning to be seen in Korea. The lack of a proper understanding of the nature of the church and its missional nature have resulted in stagnation in mission. In other words, the church has wrongly considered mission and evangelism to be one of the ministries and programs of a church, a program to bring about church growth, rather than considering it to be part of the very nature of the church. In his book *The Essence of the Church*, Craig Van Gelder points out:

> Those who start with a theology of the church and proceed to mission usually make mission a functional task of the church. This is especially true of churches influenced by the modern missions movement. Within this movement, the church is viewed in institutional terms,

with mission being one of several tasks the church undertakes on God's behalf.[45]

But Van Gelder suggests a new understanding of church:

> It is my conviction that we need to move beyond trying to find the "next" church that will help us be successful one more time. We need to rediscover something more basic about what it means to *be* the church.[46]

This is defining the church to be, by its nature, missional. David Bosch says that mission has its origin in the heart of God, who sent his beloved Son into this world in order to save this world. "This is the deepest source of mission. It is impossible to penetrate deeper still; there is mission because God loves people."[47] According to Stephen B. Bevans, mission is "prior to the church, and constitutive of its very existence."[48] Therefore, the church needs to realize that its missionary nature derives from a trinitarian basis, that God has called it into ministry in this world through Jesus' death on the cross, and has sent it into this world under the leading of the Spirit.[49]

Developing a Contextual Missiology

Even if the Korean church rediscovers the essential nature of the church, its mission will have but limited impact without a proper understanding of and interaction with the context in which the church operates. Thus it needs to have a proactive response to the changing context in order for it to make progress toward developing a missional church in Korea. Because cultures are diverse, and because theology is always relative to the context, contextualization is necessary.[50] When the gospel is communicated

---

45. Craig Van Gelder, *The Essence of the Church* (Grand Rapids: Baker, 2000), p. 32.
46. Van Gelder, *Essence of the Church*, p. 24.
47. Bosch, *Transforming Mission*, p. 392.
48. Stephen B. Bevans and Roger P. Schroeder, *Constants in Context: A Theology of Mission for Today* (Maryknoll, NY: Orbis Books, 2004), p. 13.
49. Van Gelder, *Essence of the Church*, p. 98.
50. Eun Soo Chae, "Contextualization in Mission," *Presbyterian Theological Quarterly* 64 (Winter 1997): 18.

through local forms and symbols, listeners are much more receptive.[51] For contextualization to be effective, Louis Luzbetak argues, it should go to "the very roots of culture," that is, at the psychological or cognitive level.[52] Mission work in Korea is a good example of this. When Korean people met the foreign missionaries from America for the first time, Christianity was as foreign to them as the missionaries professing it were. But when the American missionaries presented the gospel, it penetrated the hearts of the Koreans because the heart of the gospel and the heart of the Koreans connected at the deepest level.

It is worthwhile to note here that the mentality of *Han* is similar to the mentality of the Israelites in the Old Testament. It can be said that the Hebrew people had a form of *Han* shaped through their checkered history just as Koreans had. As a minority group of people surrounded by strong nations, the Hebrews suffered under the ancient superpowers — Assyria, Babylon, Greece, and Rome. The Old Testament reflects the *Han* of the Hebrew people. Thus God promised a land, Canaan, to the Hebrews, who were filled with *Han,* and God offered numerous material blessings contingent on their obedience to him. We can see the mentality of *Han* among the Israelites in the fact that one-third of the psalms are laments, and over forty of the psalms contain imprecatory contents.

In addition, the ministry of Jesus focused on the *Han* of the Galileans under the oppression of Rome and King Herod, especially that of marginalized people, such as women, children, the "sinners," and those who were sick and disabled. Jesus' teaching in the parable of Luke 18:1-8 reflects the *Han* of the Galileans. When Korean people read the Bible, they were able to identify with the Hebrew people without difficulty. This was probably one of the major reasons why Korea is perhaps the only country in East Asia where Christianity took easy root in its soil. Thus understanding *Han* is a key to understanding Korean Christianity and its churches.

But, if Christianity in Korea was well contextualized at the conceptual level, why is the Korean church now facing a plateau despite its increased experience, knowledge, resources, and zeal for evangelism and church growth? One of the main reasons for this plateau may lie in the fact that the gospel is not matched to the present context at the deepest level. In

---

51. Eun Soo Chae, "Contextualization in Mission," p. 18.

52. Louis J. Luzbetak, *The Church and Cultures: New Perspectives in Missiological Anthropology* (Maryknoll, NY: Orbis Books, 1998), p. 75.

other words, the *Han,* which underlies the Korean mentality and which serves as an important characteristic of the soil for receiving the gospel, is being changed into a different shape.

The churches need to rediscover renewed contextual meanings of *Han.* The new sources of *Han* are such things as the sense of lost identity, the sense of fragmentation and estrangement, and the social conflicts between the haves and have-nots in the modern and postmodern society. With an increasing dependence on the Internet for information, people are losing their face-to-face connections within communities and are failing to form a sense of healthy identity. The Korean church needs to better research and understand its present context, a context that is changing at the deepest levels. It needs to study once more the relationship between the context and the gospel, and also between the church and culture.

Developing a Missional Church Polity

The GAPCK adopted Presbyterian church polity from the United States. Presbyterian church polity finds its basis in the Bible (Rom. 12:8; 1 Cor. 12:28; 1 Tim. 5:17), but its institutional origins are in Calvin. Dr. Chang Sup Shim articulates the reason that Calvin adopted the system of elders:

> First, it was to prevent the tyranny of the papacy; second, to resist anarchistic deinstitutionalization of church promoted by the extremely radical reformers; and third, to make church governance and administration be independent from Geneva city's interference.[53]

The system of elders that was institutionalized by Calvin developed into congregational Presbyterianism through the Westminster Assembly of Divines in 1643; it was later imported to Korea via American missionaries. The governance system of eldership was very likely a contributor to rapid growth of the Presbyterian Church in Korea because this rule of eldership appealed to Koreans, who had grown up in a patriarchal environment. But elders became the subject of respect and admiration more by the position they represented than by the ministry they performed. In this regard, elder

53. Chang Sup Shim, "What Is the Origin of the Presbyterian Church Polity?" a lecture presented at the Forum of The Korean National Association of Christian Pastors Council of Pastors for Church Renewal, April 28, 1997.

governance, as a representative governance system, also became a model for democracy.

The Church Session, the basic church court, is the core of the Presbyterian Church governance system (consisting of the General Assembly, Presbytery, and the Church Session). The membership of the Church Session includes ruling elders and a teaching elder, who is the ordained pastor. The role of the moderator of the Church Session gave the senior pastor disproportionate power, indicating that the GAPCK puts the most emphasis on the proclamation of the Word. The responsibility of ruling elders is to cooperate and support the teaching elder's responsibility to proclaim the Word well. The Church Session played a huge role in effectively spreading the gospel by maintaining the relationship of mutual respect and cooperation, and thereby being an example of Christian brotherhood inside and outside the church.[54]

Unfortunately, the relationship of mutual respect and cooperation between pastors and elders has gradually, over time, degenerated into a relationship of distrust and conflicts. The conflicts stem mainly from unclear roles concerning the responsibility of the ruling elders. In the Korean Presbyterian church, deacons handle most of the church business, and the pastors or seminary-trained staff carry out worship, teaching, and counseling ministries. The responsibilities that are set out by the constitution for the ruling elders are threefold: representatives of the congregation, supporters of the ordained pastor, and helpers in the church members' spiritual growth. However, these responsibilities are now mostly carried out by the ordained pastor. As a result, the ruling elders do not have much significant work to do in the church, and that position has thus become primarily an honorary position. Nevertheless, ruling elders exercise power in the Church Session, where major decisions are made regarding the church's direction and ministries.

In the Korean church, responsibility and authority are focused in the ordained pastor, yet the governance system revolves around elders. It is natural in this context to witness conflicts between ordained pastors and elders. As a result of such conflicts and tensions, the Church Session often fails to become an effective operational group administered by team leadership. Instead, it becomes an organization that hampers the growth of the

---

54. Sung Chul Hwang, "Problems and the Resolution of Church Council in Korean Presbyterian Church Polity," *Presbyterian Theological Quarterly* 64 (Summer 1997): 225.

church. In fact, it can be said that true elder governance as prescribed in the Book of Order is not being practiced in Korea. This shortcoming may be a repeat of the mistaken tendency of the eldership to disappear during the Middle Ages, after the emergence of strong bishop leadership in the second century.

It is also important to re-examine Presbyterian church polity, especially in light of the function and roles of the elders and the Church Session. The present context of the Korean church is considerably different from the context when Calvin instituted elder governance. At the time of Calvin, one of the main functions of the Church Session was the exercise of church discipline in order to preserve the purity of the church. Church discipline is hardly practiced today. The present context is also significantly different from the time when the Presbyterian faith was first introduced to Korea. Although eldership and the Church Session of the Korean Presbyterian Church are based on biblical guidelines and are specified by the Presbyterian constitution, the governance system needs to reflect continual changes in the context. Calvin himself pointed out that the elder system is not the permanent and only form of a biblical church polity. In his exegesis of 1 Corinthians 14:34-37, Calvin says that the external governance of the church needs to be adaptable to changing context and that church polity and an administrative system are morally neutral, and thus should not constrict our conscience.[55]

Because the role of church structure and polity is to serve effectively the ministries of the church, the polity and organization of the church should be adapted to the most effective form in which a new generation may engage in the mission of the church. This mission is to convey the gospel to a given context. Most of all, in light of the recovered understanding of the missional essence of the church, church polity needs to be examined and considered for proper changes. "A missional ecclesiology will always include organizational forms, but one should not see these as the essence of the church. Organization needs to serve, not determine the nature of the church with its duality of being both divine and human."[56] Needs (or requests) for a reform of the present eldership and Church Ses-

---

55. Chang Sup Shim, "What Is the Origin of the Presbyterian Church Polity?"

56. Inagrace T. Dietterich, "Missional Structures: The Particular Community," in Darrell L. Guder, ed., *Missional Church: A Vision for the Sending of the Church in North America* (Grand Rapids: Eerdmans, 1998), p. 222.

sion are coming forward; other reform issues include the tenure system,[57] the sabbatical year system,[58] the spirit and practice of partnership in an ordained pastor,[59] and putting an end to the patriarchal authoritarianism of elders.[60] However, these changes do not address fundamental matters of contextualization; they serve as temporizing policies. Instead, what is called for is a reconsideration of the organizational structure and leadership that is congruent with the missional essence of the church. One possible alternative would be to consider the logic of Local Missional Congregations, the Mobile Missional Structure, and the connectional processes suggested by Van Gelder.[61] Within this structure it is naturally conceivable that the Church Session would serve as a connectional process, and eldership could be redefined to renew the spirit of eldership intended by the Book of Order.

Conclusion

This chapter has explored the possibility of building a missional church based on Calvinist Reformed theology in the context of the Korean church. The Korean soil, where the seed of the gospel fell, was a society dominated by traditional religions such as Shamanism, Buddhism, and Confucianism. What seemed like rocky or thorny soil became fertile through the sacrificial services and sufferings of God's servants. The blood of martyrs firmly established the church, along with effective mission strategies such as Bible translation, the Nevius method, the Mission Field Comity Arrangement, Educational-Medical Services, and contributions to social justice. However, since the era of the church's establishment and rapid development, Korean society has undergone rapid changes.

In the midst of this societal change, the church itself seems to have become disoriented and increasingly unclear about its identity. By examining Calvinist Reformed theology, ecclesiology, and missiology within the

---

57. Byung Ho Sohn, *A History of Presbyterian Churches* (Seoul, Korea: Evangelion Press, 2000), p. 459.

58. Hwang, "Problems and the Resolution," p. 246.

59. Jang-sik Lee, "Reformation of John Calvin and Korean Presbyterian Church," *Christian Thoughts* 244, no. 21 (Oct. 1978): 48.

60. Hwang, "Problems and the Resolution," p. 245.

61. Van Gelder, *Essence of the Church*, pp. 162-79.

GAPCK, I have explored how this denomination might develop a contextual missiology. I have offered a proposal that would establish a missional ecclesiology based on a trinitarian understanding of God's mission. In light of this, the church must acknowledge that there are additional details that require consideration, such as the question of how a Reformed theology in Korea might interface with a missional ecclesiology, the need to develop a contextual missiology, and a reconsideration of how to construct missional church polity. This challenge is worth the time and consideration that is required, so that the gospel can once again seep into Korean hearts and minds, riding a fresh folk tune, a new "Arirang."

CHAPTER 7

An Old New Church in the Marketplace:
The Evangelical Lutheran Church in America (ELCA)
into the Twenty-First Century

Mary Sue Dehmlow Dreier

> *The church of Christ in every age*
> *Beset by change but Spirit led*
> *Must claim and test its heritage*
> *And keep on rising from the dead.*[1]

Introduction

The long awaited resolution was on the floor of the Ninth Biennial
Churchwide Assembly of the Evangelical Lutheran Church in America
(ELCA), held in August 2005. It would take a two-thirds vote of the 993
voting members present to change the church's expectations of ros-
tered leaders to include openly partnered gay or lesbian pastors. Numerous amendments were being proposed, considered, and defeated.

And then they walked in. With quiet but determined steps, members of Good Soil in support of the resolution filed in and stood silently along the front of the assembly floor. These were the people being discussed, along with some of their supporters. Now the
proceedings fell silent as well.

They stood there. Real people whose lives were on the line. They
stood there as uninvited intruders into the assembly's voting arena,

---

1. F. Pratt Green, "The Church of Christ, in Every Age," in *The Lutheran Book of Worship* (Minneapolis: Augsburg, 1978), p. 433.

and yet they were the very people whose future ministry would be decided by these voters. They stood there as unwelcome disrupters of an orderly process, and yet they were the very pastors whose ministries, livelihoods, homes, and families had already been disrupted by ELCA Visions and Expectations that varied from their own.

The voting members sat there — real people whose church lives were on the line. They sat there, stunned and anxious, and yet responsible to vote on behalf of five million ELCA members who were counting on them. They sat there prepared to face this difficult vote, and yet they were nervous and cautious about how to proceed, especially at this moment.

The assembly faltered. Should the proceedings continue or not? Should the Good Soil folks be asked to leave or allowed to stay? ELCA Presiding Bishop Mark Hanson asked them to leave; but when they chose to stay, he led the proceedings forward. So they stood there for at least two hours, until the assembly defeated their cause 490-503. Then they left as peaceably as they had come.[2]

This is a poignant snapshot of the current ELCA. It is a church straining with the tension of accepting gays and lesbians at the Lord's Supper but not onto the clergy roster — unless they remain celibate. It is a church attempting, through legislative due process, to address real people whose everyday lives have become public illustrations of contemporary social issues. Actually, not one but three proposals on sexuality came before that Churchwide Assembly. A first recommendation, overwhelmingly adopted by a vote of 851-127, urges the ELCA to find ways to "live together faithfully in the midst of disagreements"; a second recommendation, by a vote of 670-323, denied creating formal rites for blessing same-sex relationships and instead entrusted them into the pastoral care of pastors and congregations.[3] All of this has important implications for the church.[4]

2. The event occurred on August 12, 2005, at the Ninth Biennial Churchwide Assembly of the ELCA in Orlando, Florida, and was reported by numerous news media, including *The Lutheran,* the official magazine of the ELCA; see Ann Hafften et al., "Churchwide Assembly," *The Lutheran* (October 2005): 12-14. The narrative report of the event represented here was written by the author of this chapter.

3. "A Brief Summary of Actions: Ninth Churchwide Assembly" (Chicago: Evangelical Lutheran Church in America): http://www.elca.org/assembly/05/summary [accessed Sept. 8, 2005].

4. Throughout this essay I will use the term "congregation" to denote the local wor-

There is another important glimpse of the ELCA from that Churchwide Assembly in August 2005 that is less dramatic but is helpful to investigate in regard to the sexuality proposals and, specifically, the Good Soil incident. Proposals were adopted for restructuring the churchwide organization, as well as its system of governance. Basically, the Churchwide Assembly approved a design of program units, offices and service units, and created a governance structure of program committees to work with the various units. These actions were intended "to achieve the goal of the reformation of this church *for mission*" (italics added).[5] And the design proposal was aptly titled, "Faithful Yet Changing: *Design for Mission* through the Churchwide Organization of the Evangelical Lutheran Church in America" (italics added).[6] The clear intent behind these efforts was to align the ministries and decision-making of the institution with its new mission and vision statements,[7] so that the church might become "even more effective in accomplishing, with God's help and guidance, God's mission through this church."[8]

One gets important insights into the ELCA by placing the sexuality and the restructuring proposals side by side. The ELCA was formed in 1989 after a series of mergers throughout the twentieth century between dozens of predecessor church bodies. These bodies straddled the Atlantic Ocean: they had one foot still in the Western European Reformation tradition and the other firmly planted in American soil and culture — as the ELCA still does today. This precarious posture is both its historical strength and part

---

shiping community and the term "church" to denote the community of baptized Christians in general and any of the variety of corporate ecclesiastical bodies comprised of such local worshiping communities.

5. "Report for the Church Council on Governance," Oct. 7, 2004 (Chicago: Evangelical Lutheran Church in America, Executive Committee of the Church Council), "Introduction": http://www.elca.org/planning/governance1116.pdf [accessed Oct. 14, 2005].

6. "Faithful Yet Changing: Design for Mission through the Churchwide Organization of the Evangelical Lutheran Church in America" (Chicago: Evangelical Lutheran Church in America): http://www.elca.org/planning/restructuring1116.pdf [accessed Oct. 14, 2005].

7. These official statements of the ELCA were adopted in the 2003 Churchwide Assembly; see "Mission Statement and Signature Phrase of the Evangelical Lutheran Church in America" (Chicago: Evangelical Lutheran Church in America): http://www.elca.org/planning/mission.html [accessed Oct. 14, 2005]; see also "Vision Statement of the Evangelical Lutheran Church in America" (Chicago: Evangelical Lutheran Church in America): http://www.elca.org/planning/vision.html [accessed Oct. 14, 2005].

8. "Report on Governance."

of its current challenge. At the ELCA's core is a tension between confessionalism and contextualization, between Reformation ecclesiology and the institutional upheavals of postmodernity.[9]

Here is a confessional church trying to structure itself institutionally for mission within Reformation traditions and the changing challenges of its twenty-first-century context. Viewed together, these proposals demonstrate some of the underlying missional questions that face the ELCA today. What is God calling the ELCA to be and to do? Who are the people to whom it is called and sent? What is its mission in the context of the United States at this time?[10] How will it deliberate and position itself to act on that mission? In other words, what is a *contextual missiology* for the ELCA in the twenty-first century?

These missional questions represent the shift that began midway through the twentieth century regarding the church's understanding of mission: "Mission as geographical expansion gave way to an understanding of mission as the task of the whole church."[11] The theological discipline of missiology, the "conscious, intentional, ongoing reflection on the doing of mission,"[12] has also experienced a shift, and it is becoming a nec-

---

9. The cultural milieu of today is commonly defined by the term "postmodernity." Although it is not universally endorsed, I will use this term in this chapter as one denotation for the present context, which is in many ways a departure from "modernity," and thus presents a new era of mission for the church. For background on postmodernity, see Steven Best and Douglas Kellner, *The Postmodern Turn* (New York: Guilford Press, 1997); Darrell L. Guder, ed., *Missional Church: A Vision for the Sending of the Church in North America* (Grand Rapids: Eerdmans, 1998); and Stanley J. Grenz, *A Primer on Postmodernism* (Grand Rapids: Eerdmans, 1996).

10. I use the term "United States" and "U.S." throughout this essay to designate the United States of America. I also use the terms "America" and "American," reluctantly, to refer to the United States because of their prevalence both in the literature and in common usage, though I want to acknowledge that the sphere of the Americas in reality includes many nations in South, Central, and North America. I believe it is necessary to make this acknowledgment in order to develop a sensitive and responsible contextual missiology in the twenty-first century.

11. Mike Goheen, "Toward a Missiology of Western Culture": http://www.deepsight.org [accessed Oct. 26, 2004]. For a general description of this development of a missional identity for the church, see Guder, *Missional Church*, and George R. Hunsberger and Craig Van Gelder, *The Church between Gospel and Culture: The Emerging Mission in North America* (Grand Rapids: Eerdmans, 1996).

12. Alan Neely, "Missiology," in *Evangelical Dictionary of World Mission*, ed. A. Scott Moreau (Grand Rapids: Baker, 2000), p. 633. Neely and Findeis (see fn. 13) provide well-

essary part of the concrete realities of local churches that seek various contextual ways of living the faith and doing theological reflection.[13] If the overall mission of the ELCA is to be effective, that church body needs a well-formulated contextual missiology.

Formulating a contextual missiology for the ELCA is the goal of this chapter. I will begin by defining the particular spiritual marketplace lens I am using to focus this chapter. Using this lens, I will explore the historical context of American Protestantism in general, and the ELCA in particular, along with theoretical notions of innovative change in organizations and the hermeneutical possibilities of communicative action over legislative due process. From this background perspective, I will propose a contextual missiology that envisions the ELCA as a missionary, public, global, confessional, and imaginative church participating in God's twenty-first-century mission in the United States.

U. S. Religion as Marketplace

Americans love to shop. The Mall of America in Bloomington, Minnesota, with more than 520 shops, plus theme park, restaurants, aquarium, and movie theaters, is one of the top tourist destinations in the nation.[14] And right in the middle of it all is the River Church, offering "a safe place to figure out what life is about" and competing for its own market share by dispensing religious goods and services to passersby from one of the storefronts.[15] This should not offend us. Congregations have been along the corridors of the American market since colonial times.

In a compelling analysis in their book *The Churching of America*

---

researched dictionary sketches of missiology. For a thorough examination of missionary paradigms throughout Christian history, see David Bosch, *Transforming Mission: Paradigm Shifts in Theology of Mission*, American Society of Missiology Series, no. 16 (Maryknoll, NY: Orbis Books, 1991). A look at the emerging future of missiology is presented by John Roxborogh, "After Bosch: The Future of Missiology," Princeton Currents in World Christianity Seminar, Feb. 2, 2001: http://roxborogh.com/missiology.htm [accessed Oct. 14, 2005].

13. Hans-Jürgen Findeis, "Missiology," in *Dictionary of Mission: Theology, History, Perspectives*, ed. Karl Muller et al. (Maryknoll, NY: Orbis Books, 1997), p. 301.

14. Mall of America, "Media: Mall Facts": www.mallofamerica.com/about_moa_faqs .aspx [accessed Nov. 26, 2004].

15. "Media: Mall Facts."

1776-1990: Winners and Losers in Our Religious Economy, Roger Finke and Rodney Stark illuminate how the religious environment of the United States became a spiritual marketplace.[16] The supermarket of religious choice first developed through the colonial separation of church and state, and created a "free market religious environment that exposed religious organizations to relentless competition."[17] Principles of (1) supply and demand, (2) winners and losers, and (3) competition in a free-market religious economy have, therefore, not only helped shape our nation but have uniquely shaped the religion that has grown up in this nation (Finke and Stark, pp. 2, 18). According to the language of religious economies, "where religious affiliation is a matter of choice, religious organizations must compete for members" (p. 17). This spirit of competition was thus formative in the shaping of American Protestantism: just as economic consumerism has advanced steadily in the United States, the consumerist religious marketplace has also expanded to large proportions.[18]

This lens of the U.S. spiritual marketplace is particularly useful in shedding light on the religious history of America because, according to Finke and Stark, "well-established deductions from the principles of supply and demand can illuminate what might otherwise seem a very disorderly landscape" (p. 18). But this lens does more than provide order; a marketplace mentality is part of the DNA of United States–grown religion and, as such, subtly and pervasively influences how churches do business and why. The marketplace is not itself our focus, but it is the lens I use to help us get a clearer picture of the religious horizon, to discern the powerful

16. The conceptual frameworks of the marketplace and religious economy represent just one lens through which to explain the religious landscape. There are many others that can be useful in exploring other aspects of that landscape, but the contextual missiology presented here will be framed through the particular challenges that come into view through this lens.

17. Roger Finke and Rodney Stark, *The Churching of America 1776-1990: Winners and Losers in Our Religious Economy* (New Brunswick, NJ: Rutgers University Press, 1992), p. 2.

18. Wade Clark Roof, *Spiritual Marketplace: Baby Boomers and the Remaking of American Religion* (Princeton, NJ: Princeton University Press, 1999), pp. 9-10. Roof identifies three aspects of that spiritual marketplace that are particularly significant for understanding the mission field in which the ELCA was planted: (1) large sectors of the population are involved; (2) there is an emphasis on the self — self-understanding and self-reflexivity — because of pluralism, relativism, and ontological uncertainties; and (3) creative currents are activating deep energies and commitments out of a deep hunger for genuine and satisfying self-transformation.

competitive impulses within the church, and to identify the related realities that challenge the missional church in this context.

I will use this approach with caution. In the American capitalist society, the marketplace represents a formative, symbolic language of the culture. And in any missionary endeavor, learning the language is an important step in translating the gospel to address the people.[19] Focusing the conversation by way of marketplace dynamics in no way *advocates* for a church consumerist culture that commodifies the gospel in pursuit of a large bottom line in which people are the currency of success. However, an effective missiology for the ELCA in the twenty-first century must be able to *function within* this American spiritual marketplace, and must be aware of its dynamics, potentials, and dangers.

As I have previously observed, the ELCA has one foot in Europe and the other in North America. It is a story of both looking backward and looking ahead, a story in which issues of its Reformation identity from the past and its missional identity for the future continue to live in lively tension, which is both challenge and opportunity. How the ELCA will function — and possibly flourish — in the contemporary spiritual marketplace will be, in large part, determined by its ability to see this tension as a productive position for mission.

U.S. Protestantism in Context

A religious history of Protestantism in the United States is a highly complex and intricate story. However, from its general historical contours, there were three historical disestablishments of certain aspects of American religion that are important to note: (1) the separation of church and state; (2) the nationwide acknowledgment of non-Protestant religions; and (3) the decline of mainline religious institutionalism.[20] A brief examina-

---

19. Two influential discussions of the relationship between translation and mission are Lesslie Newbigin, *Foolishness to the Greeks: The Gospel and Western Culture* (Grand Rapids: Eerdmans, 1986), and Lamin Sanneh, *Translating the Message: The Missionary Impact on Culture*, American Society of Missiology Series, No. 13 (Maryknoll, NY: Orbis Books, 1989).

20. Craig Van Gelder, "A Great New Fact of Our Day," in George R. Hunsberger and Craig Van Gelder, eds., *The Church between Gospel and Culture: The Emerging Mission in North America* (Grand Rapids: Eerdmans, 1996), pp. 63-65, presents the typology of three disestablishments used in this analysis.

tion of each of these three phenomena and their implications for U.S. Protestantism in general will provide the necessary historical backdrop for understanding the religious marketplace environment in which the ELCA was shaped.

Separation of Church and State: Disestablishment No. 1

Christians arriving from Europe tended to preserve the old ways they had practiced in the old country, even those who were dissenters in search of religious freedom. Many came from countries still living within the Constantinian charter, in which state religions were established by law and therefore enjoyed official favor and status.[21] Although four of the thirteen original colonies never officially established the church, the rest of the colonies did, and their churches enjoyed the privileges of legal establishment.[22] However, the practical necessities of building one nation out of separate colonies with differing political structures and religious establishments soon broke the Constantinian pattern.[23] Among other things, the separation of church and state helped accomplish the political agenda of uniting the colonies into one nation.[24]

Once the new government no longer ensured their existence or their success, according to Finke and Stark, the colonial denominations were

21. Martin E. Marty, *Righteous Empire: The Protestant Experience in America* (New York: The Dial Press, 1970), p. 35.

22. Marty, *Righteous Empire*, pp. 39-40. Those four were Rhode Island, Delaware, Pennsylvania, and New Jersey. According to Finke and Stark (p. 40), "The two potentially most powerful religious bodies in colonial America, the Congregationalists and the Episcopalians, rested upon legal establishment. The Episcopalians enjoyed legal establishment in New York, Virginia, Maryland, North and South Carolina, and Georgia; the Congregationalists were established in New England."

23. The religious pluralism in the middle colonies, especially Pennsylvania, led to the imagination of separating church and state while allowing religious freedom. This idea was then picked up as the preferred approach to religion in the uniting of the colonies; see Sydney E. Ahlstrom, *A Religious History of the American People* (New Haven: Yale University Press, 1972), pp. 110-12.

24. Marty, *Righteous Empire*, p. 44. The U.S. Constitution was radically new in that it was silent about commitment to God and included only a clause forbidding religious tests for public office. The First Amendment forbade federal establishment of religion and guaranteed free exercise of religion.

unable to cope with the consequences of religious freedom and the rise of a free-market religious economy, and they went into a slow process of disestablishment and decline (Finke and Stark, p. 54). The very loss of once-privileged status actually exacerbated that decline (p. 40). This environment of religious freedom, however, sparked a new kind of religiosity and fanned the flames of two significant and unique American religious phenomena, the Great Awakening and the Second Great Awakening, which were to have a formative influence on the religious development of this new nation.

The soul-shaking expectancy of the Great Awakening (1740s) ushered in a renewed emphasis on the Christian experience of conversion and regeneration as a new bond of fellowship, one that transcended the fine points of doctrine. There were two major themes in the preaching of the Great Awakening: "the necessity of spiritual rebirth and demands for upright living."[25] Revivals became a major means by which people of diverse types responded to America's changing moral, religious, intellectual, and social conditions. The pietism of the Great Awakening, blended with Puritanism, became the foundation of American evangelicalism. "Only through that convulsive outburst of piety did 'American Evangelical Protestantism' become aware of itself as a national reality and alive to its culture-shaping power."[26] In the developing American spiritual marketplace, the Great Awakening demonstrated that there was an immense "market opportunity" for more robust and less secularized religion, the fruits of which were not incorporated into the mainline colonial denominations.[27]

The revolutionary era (1770s), however, was a period of decline for American Christianity as a whole, with the Enlightenment worldview gaining influence. Then came the Second Awakening, beginning at the turn of the century and becoming powerful by the 1820s. It was different in many ways from the first one. It was a calm act of God resulting in renewed spiritual seriousness and reformation of morals, conducted by settled ministers in their own parishes and not the sensational itinerants of the Great Awakening.[28] The results of the Second Awakening were the

25. Randall Balmer and Lauren F. Winner, *Protestantism in America* (New York: Columbia University Press, 2002), p. 43.

26. Ahlstrom, *Religious History,* p. 6.

27. Finke and Stark, *Churching of America,* p. 51.

28. Ahlstrom, *Religious History,* pp. 417-18.

transformation of "slumbering churches" and the creation of an "evangelical united front" that became a force in the country (Ahlstrom, p. 7).
In addition, a new kind of religious institution arose: the voluntary association of private individuals for missionary, reformatory, or benevolent
purposes, that is, missionary societies, publication and education societies, moral reform societies, and those addressing humanitarian interests
(Ahlstrom, pp. 422-28). These flourished in the free-enterprise environment and brought new competitive dynamics into the American spiritual
marketplace.

Boosted by the Great Awakening and the Second Great Awakening,
evangelicalism blossomed during the first half century of the United
States' existence as a nation as, ironically, "a kind of national church or national religion."[29] With participation in congregations done on a voluntary
basis apart from civil authorities, all churches were now on the same footing. Even though religion lost the security of de facto establishment, "Protestants could compete with each other without danger to society" (Marty,
p. 44). New religious enterprises began to take shape, and there was a gradual emergence of a "strange piecemeal empire" that became known as the
"Protestant empire" (Ahlstrom, p. 123).

Without the order of civil authority, new churches forged their own
kind of order through networks of denominations, local congregations,
educational institutions, and agencies (Marty, p. 67). Denominations were
a key building block in the construction of the Protestant empire, giving it
some shape and jurisdictional order. They became the "fundamental
church structure of this country,"[30] and have been heralded by church historian Marty as the most basic administrative change in the church in
fourteen hundred years (Marty, pp. 67-68). Sociologically, the social-
contract theory of voluntary associations became deeply embedded in U.S.
denominations,[31] and they developed the distinctive character of "a voluntary association of like-hearted and like-minded individuals, who are
united on the basis of common beliefs for the purpose of accomplishing
tangible and defined objectives" (Richey, p. 71).

---

29. Marty, *Righteous Empire*, p. 67.
30. Russell E. Richey, ed., *Denominationalism* (Nashville: Abingdon, 1977), p. 136.
31. Craig Van Gelder, *The Essence of the Church: A Community Created by the Spirit*
(Grand Rapids: Baker Books, 2000), p. 69.

Catholics and Jews in the Empire: Disestablishment No. 2

But there was a problem within the Protestant empire: not everyone was Protestant, or even Christian, though the Supreme Court still spoke of the United States as a "Christian nation" as late as 1931.[32] If the separation of church and state was the first disestablishment of U.S. Protestantism, the second disestablishment came with the growing acknowledgment in the early to middle part of the twentieth century of two significant non-Protestant religious communities: the Roman Catholics and the Jews.[33]

Roman Catholics did remarkably well in America because they "became an extremely effective and competitive religious firm when forced to confront a free market religious economy" (Finke and Stark, p. 110). They actually have the longest history of any Christian denomination in the United States, and today they are the largest by far.[34] Nevertheless, the significance of Catholicism only slowly dawned on the consciousness of America. It was not until World War II and the Cold War, when Americans strove for a unified national wartime identity, that the flourishing Roman Catholic presence became undeniable. With the election of John F. Kennedy to the presidency in 1960, Catholics were finally included both symbolically and substantively in the public milieu, bringing to an end the Great Puritan Epoch, which had begun back in 1558 (Ahlstrom, p. 1079). Unity now had to be defined *through* religious diversity — not in spite of it.

The Jewish contingent of the American population also achieved

32. Martin E. Marty, *Modern American Religion,* vol. 3: *Under God, Indivisible 1941-1960* (Chicago: University of Chicago Press, 1996), p. 54.

33. Will Herberg, *Protestant — Catholic — Jew: An Essay in American Religious Sociology,* rev. ed. (Garden City, NY: Doubleday, 1960), offers a detailed analysis of the "American way of life" as the common religion of the United States made up of three fundamental subdivisions: Protestantism, Catholicism, and Judaism. A common civil religion gradually emerged as the reformulation of the earlier Protestant empire in terms of religious plurality, the result of the blending of religious streams begun in this second disestablishment.

34. According to Eileen W. Lindner, ed., *Yearbook of American and Canadian Churches 2004* (Nashville: Abingdon Press, 2004), p. 11, the Roman Catholic Church has 66,407,105 adherents; the next largest is the Southern Baptist Convention at 16,247,736. Richard Ostling, in "America's Ever-Changing Religious Landscape: Where We've Come From and Where We're Going," *Brookings Review* (Spring 1999): 12, asserts that the Roman Catholic Church today, as the biggest denomination in the United States, has become "a federation of fiefdoms," with varying loyalties and opinions, much like the loosely connected denominations of the Protestant empire.

recognition during this struggle for unity in the middle to late twentieth century, with the added impetus of three identifiable events that helped move the Jews from the margins to the nation's "third faith": (1) the Holocaust; (2) the birth of the state of Israel; and (3) suburbanization, which dispersed Jews into communities where they were a diffused presence among non-Jewish Americans.[35] In many communities, joint church and synagogue activities began to appear. The National Conference of Christians and Jews advanced opportunities for Jews to become more central in American religious life.[36] Judaism could no longer be ignored, and thus was ushered into the three-way religious limelight.[37]

The cultural reality of America was becoming an acknowledged interfaith ethos, and the Protestant empire was gasping its final breaths. The shared identity of U.S. citizens as Americans was critical to national identity after World Wars I and II and the Cold War, and the individual identity of each separate religion became important to the ongoing success of all three in this new diverse religious economy.[38] The disestablishment of the unifying identity of a national Protestant religion dramatically altered the religious marketplace: it changed from one target audience to three, which were all integral to the success of the real operative faith of the American people, that is, "the American Way of Life."[39]

Decline of Mainline Institutionalism: Disestablishment No. 3?

Disestablishment No. 1, the separation of church and state, created the free religious environment into which the American spiritual marketplace was

---

35. Marty, *Under God*, pp. 54-55.

36. Marty, *Under God*, pp. 62-63.

37. Ostling ("Ever-Changing Religious Landscape," p. 12) contends that the diffusion of Jews into non-Jewish populations has had deleterious effects for U.S. Judaism, which today has an aging and shrinking population base with fewer people carrying Judaism as their religious identification.

38. Marty, *Under God*, p. 277.

39. Herberg, *Protestant — Catholic — Jew*, pp. 75, 87. Herberg (p. 211) even asserts that his analysis is almost without exception: "The three religious communities — Protestant, Catholic, Jewish — are America. Together, they embrace almost the entire population of this country." There were, of course, other religions. Finke and Stark suggest that their growth and visibility were "artificially thwarted" by the Protestant empire; see Finke and Stark (*Churching of America*, pp. 242-44) for their analysis of the effects these dynamics specifically had on Asian religions in the United States.

born. Disestablishment No. 2, the recognition of non-Protestant subdivisions within that marketplace, opened that marketplace to mainline diversity. Disestablishment No. 3, the critique and resulting decline of mainline institutionalism, deconstructed and reframed the marketplace itself.

It began in the "turbulent sixties" — that momentous watershed decade, that turning point in American history, that moment of truth for "the nation with the soul of a church" (Ahlstrom, p. 1079). It was a time of both contrasts and of convergence of many sources for change. On the one hand, there were rich natural resources and technological advancements that generated vast productive power, postwar optimism and idealism, expanding educational resources, including universities, and flourishing communities of faith. On the other hand, a number of events and movements dramatically redefined social consciousness. Turbulence erupted with the assassinations of the Kennedys and Martin Luther King, and the escalating Vietnam War. Vatican II and an unpopular encyclical condemning birth control stirred things up in the Roman Catholic Church, while two epochal Supreme Court decisions cut into Protestant political power (Ahlstrom, p. 1080).[40] The civil rights movement (which later transitioned into the black power movement), the feminist movement, and the ecological movement created significant momentum for change.

The United States became "a country wracked by fear, violence, racism, war, and moral hypocrisy" (Ahlstrom, p. 1087). There were growing doubts about the supernatural, swiftly growing awareness of vast contradictions between professed ideals and actual realities, and increasing doubts about institutional capability in general — whether ecclesiastical, political, social, or educational — to rectify the country's woes. "The sense of national failure and dislocation became apparent to varying degrees in all occupational groups and residential areas" (Ahlstrom, p. 1087).

The religious marketplace was in upheaval. Mainline churches, formerly the mainstay of the Protestant empire, were thought to be outdated, irrelevant, morally disintegrating, and materialistic.[41] And these mainline churches were in rapid decline. In sharp contrast and providing

---

40. The Supreme Court cases referred to were: Baker v. Carr, 369 U.S. 186 ("one man — one vote," 1962), which weakened rural political strongholds; and Engel v. Vitale, 370 U.S. 421 (unconstitutionality of religious ceremonies in public schools, 1962), which decisively curtailed prevailing Protestant practices.

41. Thomas C. Reeves, *The Empty Church: The Suicide of Liberal Christianity* (New York: The Free Press, 1996), p. 133.

a corrective to some of this disillusionment with mainline denominations, conservative churches were actually growing.[42] Comparing these
times to the first and sixteenth centuries, Eugene Smith of the World
Council of Churches observed: "The nontraditional search for God in our
time may yet produce changes in institutional Christianity as far-reaching
as in those fateful centuries."[43]

Alternatively, many people embarked on nontraditional religious
quests that showed a strong interest in spirituality but little interest in
Christianity or its institutional forms. As people began exploring spiritual
venues outside the church, the spiritual marketplace complied by produc-
ing new spiritual malls replete with new product lines, unfamiliar imports,
and surprising innovations. Historian Thomas Reeves recalls the words of
Robert Terwilliger, an Episcopal priest from New York: "There is a revival
of religion everywhere — except in the church."[44] Religious pluralism had
made its home within American religion.

So far, this chapter has traced the development of the American religious marketplace in light of two awakenings and three disestablishments
in American religion. In *Vital Signs: The Promise of Mainstream Protestantism,* however, three historical theologians suggest a different interpretation
of this development: they rename the third disestablishment a third
"awakening," because they identify transformations that have led to
"deeper insights into the richness of the Christian faith and the complexity
of human life."[45] It is an intriguing suggestion given the vibrant spirituality evident today in the pluralistic religious marketplace in the United
States, which offers diverse opportunities for renewal and revitalization.

42. Reeves, *Empty Church,* p. 134. For a portrait of the evangelicalism that emerged, see
Randall Balmer, *Mine Eyes Have Seen the Glory: A Journey into the Evangelical Subculture in
America,* 3rd ed. (New York: Oxford University Press, 1989). Ahlstrom presciently notes that
in the "Bible belt," in the lower middle classes and ethnic minorities, and in organized labor
groups, "an inchoate conservative tendency could be noted, though no one could say what
this frightened and perplexed multitude portended as a political force" (Ahlstrom, p. 1094).

43. Erwin L. Lueker et al., eds., "Youth Work, *LCMS,*" *The Christian Cyclopedia* (St.
Louis: Concordia Publishing House, 2000): www.lcms.org/ca/www/cyclopedia [accessed
Sept. 15, 2005].

44. Reeves, *Empty Church,* p. 156.

45. Milton J. Coalter et al., *Vital Signs: The Promise of Mainstream Protestantism*
(Grand Haven, MI: FaithWalk Publishing, 2002), pp. 106-7. Milton J. Coalter, John M.
Mulder, and Louis B. Weeks have summarized the research on American mainstream Prot-
estantism in the twentieth century and offer hope and insight for the future.

U.S. Lutheranism in Context

The unique story of the immigrant Lutherans as they embarked on their American adventure and entered the religious marketplace of the United States fits well into the wider context of U.S. Protestantism. Lutherans discovered in America an attractive transplanted Reformation environment, as well as a "New World extension of Christendom" (Ahlstrom, pp. 13, 83). Like many who came to America out of state churches in Europe, Lutherans were habituated to having ecclesiastical matters ordered by authorities; so they immediately began to create new church structures that represented these hierarchical traditions — often with an American twist.[46]

The German Lutherans at Halle sent Rev. Henry Melchior Muhlenberg (1711-1787) to assist American churches. Muhlenberg became firmly committed to a pietistic understanding of the faith. He was instrumental in the formation of the Pennsylvania Ministerium (August 1748), considered by historian Sydney Ahlstrom to be "the most important single event in American Lutheran history" because it outlined a synodical organization and prepared a book of common worship that drew on the church's liturgical tradition (Ahlstrom, pp. 258-59). The main lines of Lutheran organizational development were thus laid down in Philadelphia, the area that would witness its greatest colonial growth.

As I have observed above, the Lutherans consciously nurtured their roots in Europe while they planted new start-up churches in the United States. From their beginnings to the present day, Lutherans in America struggled with how to live in this new land. How much should they plunge into the freewheeling Americanization of religion, and how much should they be governed by their roots?[47] Theirs is a story of looking back and looking ahead, a story in which issues of identity through the past and mission into the future have lived together in characteristic Lutheran tension.

The Lutherans' use of the German language is a helpful way to understand how they dealt with these issues within the diverse and developing Protestant empire, because "behind every other problem loomed the

---

46. Lutheran immigrant stories create a rich tapestry of European traditions and Americanization. For an example of the unique developments and adaptations by one Lutheran ethnic group, see Mark A. Granquist, "The Swedish Ethnic Denominations in the United States: Their Development and Relationships, 1880-1920" (Ph.D. diss., University of Chicago, 1992).

47. Granquist, "Swedish Ethnic Denominations," p. 1.

language question."[48] At first, Americanization seemed to move swiftly forward for them. Starting with the formation of the Pennsylvania Ministerium and under the instrumental leadership of Muhlenberg, Lutheran leaders began to think in terms of "an American church with an American ministry and an American future" (Ahlstrom, p. 259). In 1807 the Ministerium of New York, presided over by Muhlenberg's own son-in-law, changed its official language from German to English.

However, as time passed, acculturation, patriotic fervor, and the American Enlightenment modified the Lutherans' "firm but practical concern for the historic Lutheran confessions" (Ahlstrom, p. 519). Some did not want those modifications. For many, true piety and German culture were inseparable, and thus opposition arose to the momentum of Americanization that was causing a decline in "Lutheran consciousness."[49] With the tercentenary of Luther's 95 Theses in 1817, confessional and unionist tendencies were at odds. Renewed German immigration during this period heightened the growing contention (Ahlstrom, p. 756). In 1837, the New York Ministerium reversed the 1807 decision establishing the English language and reinstated German as the official language for the church (Ahlstrom, p. 522).

The church had taken a step backward. And this was a posture that was to become familiar to Lutherans, who were becoming increasingly dissatisfied with the theological and moral stance of the Protestant mainstream in America — especially when its actions were "overtly nativistic" (Ahlstrom, p. 513). In 1850, C. P. Krauth, professor at Gettysburg Seminary, published a conservative manifesto issuing the following call to his fellow Lutherans:

> Too ignorant have we been of our own doctrines, and our own history . . . and we have taken pride in times past in claiming a paternity in every reputable form of Christianity, and have denied our proper parentage, in our mendicancy for foreign favors. Shame that it has been so! . . . Let us go back to our father's house (Ahlstrom, p. 523).

"Our own doctrines." "Our own history." "Our proper parentage." "Our father's house." These phrases drew the battle lines among Lutherans

---

48. E. Clifford Nelson, ed., *The Lutherans in North America* (Philadelphia: Fortress Press, 1975), p. 95.

49. Nelson, *Lutherans in North America*, p. 95.

in America, creating an ecclesiastical civil war even as the national Civil War was brewing. The unlegislated ecclesiastical freedom of the American spiritual marketplace allowed for contentions among Lutherans to grow, eventually resulting in secessions from the General Synod and the formation of new congregations, seminaries, and synods on the basis of disagreements. By 1870, two competing Lutheran organizations had replaced the unified church Muhlenberg had envisioned. Ahlstrom says, "'American Lutheranism' as a dominating tendency was a thing of the past" (p. 525).

Even so, its numerical growth had not yet reached its zenith. No other Protestant communion "was so thoroughly transformed by the later nineteenth-century immigration as was the Lutheran" (Ahlstrom, p. 756). They numbered a half-million in 1870, and their numbers had almost quintupled by 1910. They settled in virtually every section of the country, contributed to western expansion, and formed many independent new churches, while at the same time they maintained "an underlying unity of faith and practice which was probably unequaled among America's large communions except in the Roman Catholic Church" (Ahlstrom, p. 761). Yet many Lutheran immigrants maintained strong theological ties to their homeland traditions, continuing to look to those homelands for the needed supply of pastors and worship materials in their native languages.[50]

Becoming an American Lutheran Church

According to E. Clifford Nelson, the theology of American Lutheranism in the early twentieth century was concerned predominantly with three major issues: the authority of the Bible, unionism, and attitudes toward secret societies (Nelson, p. 458). In fact, when the United Lutheran Church dealt with the question of lodge membership in the 1930s, it was "the first time on American soil a major church body definitely committed to the Lutheran confessions sought to take an evangelical position in relation to contemporary questions" (Nelson, p. 463). American Lutherans were finally starting to look around and address the theological challenges of becoming a truly American church on American soil.

This was a missional moment for Lutherans, the tentative beginnings of making the theological reconstructions that would eventually bring

---

50. Nelson, *Lutherans in North America,* pp. 365-68.

them more actively into the American spiritual marketplace. It was a minor breakthrough, because at first "Lutheran reconstructionists remained solidly confessional and exhibited an anxiety about modernism" (Nelson, p. 465). Nevertheless, modernism — and eventually postmodernism — could no longer be ignored by the Lutheran confessional churches. It was a big step forward, full of theological challenges and possibilities.

But the ties these Lutheran churches had with each other, chiefly through their common roots in the Augsburg Confession, continued to be one of their major considerations. The Lutherans have had a checkered history of internal disagreements and dissolutions, yet they have constantly sought means for intersynodical cooperation through mergers and extensions of fellowship (Ahlstrom, p. 761). In their efforts to achieve a greater degree of unity within American Lutheranism itself, the question that challenged them was whether confessional unity required theological uniformity (Nelson, p. 471).[51] Lutherans were divided on this issue and its ramifications for both their own internal unity and for their participation in the ecumenical movement that emerged in the twentieth century.

The formation of the ELCA is a story of such intersynodical mergers, a gradual grafting together of some of the diverse branches of Lutheran fellowships throughout the twentieth century.[52] The details paint a picture of Lutheranism as a church phenomenon that has continued to spend much of its life concerned with its own *familial* relationships. The attention to mergers indicates the unflagging desire among Lutherans to participate in a more unified witness to Christ in the world; and the attention to mergers *within* their own Lutheran ranks indicates their concern for continued confessional unity on the basis of the Lutheran articles of faith.

Today Lutherans of the ELCA continue to look backward and forward, to herald the value of their historical roots even as they shape a unique American church. Early in the life of the ELCA, however, the young church began earnest ecumenical negotiations outside Lutheranism, a direction that signaled a new church attempting a new course.

51. This was, and continues to be, a key challenge, with these dynamics evident in the previously cited 2005 ELCA Churchwide Assembly.

52. The online archives of the ELCA catalog carefully detail the dozens of independent churches whose mergers eventually formed the ELCA. See "Key to Predecessor Church Bodies of the Evangelical Lutheran Church in America," Archives of the Evangelical Lutheran Church in America: ELCA History: http://www.elca.org/archives/churchbodykey.html [accessed Oct. 13, 2004].

Toward a Contextual Missiology for a Twenty-First-Century ELCA: Theoretically Informed

The twenty-first-century contextual missiology for the ELCA proposed in this essay has been designed from the perspective of two theoretical frameworks: (1) the sect-church cycle of understanding the formation phases of church bodies in relationship to their environments proposed by Roger Finke and Rodney Stark in *The Churching of America 1776-1990*, and (2) the diffusion theory of organizational change defined by Everett Rogers in *Diffusion of Innovations*. The resulting theoretical framework provides insights and possibilities for an effective contextual missiology.

Church Cycles and Choices

According to Finke and Stark, religious bodies are continually engaged in a natural sect-church process, "an endless cycle of sect formation, transformation, schism, and rebirth" (p. 42). Sects are religious bodies that sustain beliefs and practices at variance with their environment, creating tension between themselves and that religious environment with which they are at odds. New religious bodies tend to begin with sect formation and, if they attract a following, gradually undergo transformation and become churches. Once established, churches tend to shift their emphasis: from the originating high tension with their environment toward peace within the environment to which they now appeal for the membership needed to maintain themselves. Those desiring a higher-tension faith become increasingly discontented within the church environment, to the point that a schism takes place and, with it, the rebirth that leads to the formation of a new sect. And the cycle begins again (Finke and Stark, pp. 40-42). As denominations increasingly adopt the reasonable and sociable aspects of becoming and maintaining status in the mainline, they are also "always headed for the sideline" through decline (p. 275).

This sect-church cycle is predicated on the freedom of choice and varieties of options available in the spiritual marketplace. Finke and Stark have made three observations: (1) in a consumer economy people will shop for religion like other objects of choice, in a cost-benefit-risk assessment. (2) religion as a collectively produced commodity has socially generated rewards and engenders confidence through interaction with others;

(3) rather than deterring participation, stigmas and sacrifices actually increase commitment, involvement, and satisfaction with member benefits and rewards. Finke and Stark's research indicates that churches that flourish in this religious marketplace will maintain sect-like tension with their environment by maintaining significant costs to participation and by incorporating dissenting or marginalized groups into their larger frameworks. The authors attribute the sect-like success of the Roman Catholic and Southern Baptist churches to these characteristics (pp. 198, 273).

Arguably, the members of Good Soil who support the acceptance of partnered gays and lesbians into the ELCA clergy roster may be thought of as in sect-like tension with the ELCA institutional environment. There is a fear of schism in the ELCA over this issue. Attempts to maintain unity have forced it to live with a certain tension between its members and American culture, which is also conflicted over this issue. In Finke and Stark's terms, the ELCA churchwide deliberations have entailed cost-benefit-risk assessments regarding the inclusion of gay or lesbian pastors, as well as consideration of the related stigmas and sacrifices.

As the ELCA seeks to strengthen both its missional and institutional viability through restructuring efforts, the opportunity to incorporate the sect-like group represented by Good Soil may actually provide an avenue for renewal that may reverse the tendency of this mainline denomination to continue migrating to the sidelines. Living in the tension between confessionalism and contextualization, the ELCA has an impulse to keep the scales even by welcoming gays and lesbians in every way other than acceptance onto the clergy roster, thus maintaining the traditions of its inherited Reformation ecclesiology.[53] But perhaps an understanding of the rigorous American spiritual marketplace within the sect-church cycle can provide the ELCA with the courage necessary to envision a promising new future not motivated by institutional survival or clouded by fears of schism.

Diffusion of Innovations

In addition to understanding the sect-church cycle, we may find it helpful to understand how systems themselves change: *diffusion theory* can pro-

53. Van Gelder, *Essence of the Church*, p. 69.

vide that theoretical framework. According to Everett Rogers's *Diffusion of Innovations*, the advantages of change are assimilated into a system through the gradual diffusion and adoption of innovations, known as diffusion theory.[54] There are four essential elements in the diffusion of an idea: (1) the innovation, and (2) its communication from one individual to another, (3) in a social system, (4) over time. An "innovation" is an idea that is perceived as new, and "diffusion" is the process by which it is adopted (Rogers, pp. 19-20). The "rate of adoption" is the relative speed with which an innovation is adopted by members of a social system such as a church (p. 146). Most desirable innovations require considerable time lag for rational adoption (p. 3), and "overadoption" occurs when a new idea is adopted too quickly under irrational conditions (p. 147).[55]

Some have alleged that the recent ELCA restructuring efforts are simply analogous to the rearrangement of the deck chairs on the Titanic — that is, neither transforming nor enduring. If we consider both the restructuring and the sexuality proposals together, however, we may see the ELCA as maintaining its institutional denominationalism and, at the same time, living in a certain prophetic tension between conservative and liberal tendencies among its members and within the American religious culture. Continued attention to the sexuality issue may indicate that the diffusion of innovations is beginning within the ELCA, and that this issue, rather than threatening its viability, may reverse the momentum of a mainline church headed for the sidelines.

Toward a Contextual Missiology for the Twenty-First-Century ELCA: Communally Discerned

When the Good Soil advocates stood silently before the ELCA Churchwide Assembly, one institutional dilemma was painfully clear: it is difficult to

---

54. Everett M. Rogers, *Diffusion of Innovations* (New York: The Free Press, 1962). Merton P. Strommen has applied this theory to church change via an "Innovation Study" presented in *The Innovative Church: Seven Steps to Positive Change in Your Congregation* (Minneapolis: Augsburg, 1997).

55. One example of the detrimental consequences of overadoption can be seen in the radical institutional changes to the Walther League, the youth organization of the Lutheran Church–Missouri Synod (LC–MS), which were adopted in 1968: they led to disaffiliation with the LC–MS by 1977, and to complete dissolution of the Walther League by 1989.

face one another over difficult and divisive contemporary issues when committed to a legislative process dictated by Robert's Rules of Order. The proposal receiving the most intense attention was the amendment regarding "Visions and Expectations," the ELCA document that outlines clergy expectations.[56] Embedded in the issue were all the main elements of Reformation ecclesiology: Word and sacraments, ordination, ministerial authority, and procedures for placing and governing pastoral leadership.[57] With its focus on the hierarchical administration of the life of the church, this ecclesiology dictated how the Assembly could and would discuss the very lives of the people standing before them. Ironically, the church was trying to engage in honest dialogue with the very people whom the process itself had silenced.

Many credit the presiding bishop, Mark Hanson, with setting the tone and showing the way through this difficult encounter with grace, sensitivity, and humor. One woman was deeply moved by the fact that his visionary leadership had steered the whole Assembly toward reconciliation and unity amid many fears of contention and schism. She stepped to one of the microphones and passionately expressed her heartfelt gratitude and hope: "Bishop, if you can do it, we can do it!" And then the presiding bishop had to rule her "out of order" according to parliamentary procedure. Perhaps such a legislative process may not be the best way for the ELCA to proceed if the church is to discern its course in the postmodern twenty-first century.

Jürgen Habermas's theory of communicative action offers an alternative. He says that the potential for emancipatory change lies in communicative, discursive rationality and in practices that embody that communicative rationality, such as the democratic public sphere. The same could apply to the democratic *ecclesiastical* public sphere, such as the ELCA gathered in its Churchwide Assembly. Unlike instrumental reason, which relies on its own objectivity as a self-preserving mechanism, communicative rationality enables discussion and self-reflection that constitutes a "symbolically structured lifeworld" in which "communicative reason does not simply encounter ready-made subjects and systems; rather, it takes part in

56. "Vision and Expectations: Ordained Ministers in the ELCA" (Chicago: Evangelical Lutheran Church in America): http://www.elca.org/candidacy/vision_ordained.html [accessed Oct. 14, 2005].

57. Van Gelder, *Essence of the Church*, p. 69.

structuring what is to be preserved."[58] Habermas fashions his linguistic communicative paradigm, the theory of communicative reason and action, in order to free postmodernity from domination and reclaim life together in communication.[59]

When we apply Habermas's theories to the deliberative processes of the church, the possibilities for communal discernment go beyond decision-making toward creating a communicative ethos, in which all people and perspectives are welcomed into discussion and reflection. This risks change for the sake of creating a dynamic church that can only be mutually constituted; and this allows for something new to emerge for the entire community, something that would not be known without communicative rationality.

When Good Soil stood for two hours before the ELCA's Churchwide Assembly, they framed a snapshot of the present that was embedded with seeds of hope for the future. This church body might become something it could not be, and will not become, without the inclusion of these participants in structuring its future. It is a picture of possibilities.

Toward a Contextual Missiology for a Twenty-First-Century ELCA: Theologically Framed

In a small monograph that was published posthumously and entitled *Believing in the Future,* David Bosch proposed four general contours of a missiology for postmodern Western culture: he envisioned a church that is missionary, public, global, and confessional.[60] I would like to add one more to Bosch's four: a church that is *imaginative.* I will use these five categories as the basic ecclesiastical framework for proposing a contextual missiology for the ELCA. They will provide both definition and structure as we examine the potential viability of the ELCA as a missional denomination in the twenty-first century.

58. Jürgen Habermas, *Theory of Communicative Action,* vol. 1: *Reason and the Rationalization of Society,* trans. Thomas McCarthy (Boston: Beacon Press, 1981), p. 398.

59. Gary M. Simpson, *Critical Social Theory: Prophetic Reason, Civil Society, and Christian Imagination,* Guides to Theological Inquiry (Minneapolis: Fortress Press, 2002), p. 87.

60. David J. Bosch, *Believing in the Future: Toward a Missiology of Western Culture,* Christian Mission and Modern Culture (Harrisburg, PA: Trinity Press International, 1995).

1. *Missionary Church*

Bosch says: "Because God is a missionary God, God's people are mission-ary people" (Bosch, p. 32). Mission is God's work growing out of God's trinitarian nature.[61] The missionary church "has no reason to exist other than critically to accompany the *missio Dei*" (p. 32). A "delightful renais-sance" of the doctrine of the Trinity has helped anchor the recent focus on *missio Dei* in the rich trinitarian theological and biblical tradition.[62]

The ELCA has always been trinitarian, holding to the historic creedal confessions of the church. Yet its understanding of the Trinity has taken a theological back seat to its Christological emphasis on the theology of the cross. A trinitarian emphasis does not detract from a Christological em-phasis; it is, in fact, the essence of a deeper understanding of the theology of the cross.[63] Bringing together the depth of both theological traditions, Trinity and theology of the cross, the ELCA is poised to contribute a dis-tinctively "missionary theology of the cross" to the growing understanding of being God's missionary church as Bosch envisioned.

The "missionary church" could easily become entrepreneurial only to get its market share and be successful among the vendors of spiritual goods and services. This missionary theology of the cross, however, em-powers the Lutheran church to function within the spiritual marketplace rather than to ignore it, flee from it, or disparage it. With a missionary the-ology of the cross at its core, the ELCA might courageously enter the mar-ket square of the world's empires, resisting the temptations to preach a prosperity gospel and, instead, proclaiming good news to the spiritually

---

61. Van Gelder, *Essence of the Church*, p. 33: As mission theology, a contextual missiology "links the missionary nature of the church to an understanding of the mission of the Triune God." See also Jürgen Moltmann, *The Trinity and the Kingdom: The Doctrine of God*, trans. Margaret Kohl (Minneapolis: Fortress Press, 1993); Gary Simpson, "No Trinity, No Mission: The Apostolic Difference of Revisioning the Trinity," *Word & World* 15, no. 3 (1998): 264-71, for further discussion regarding how the trinitarian understanding of God defines the nature and mission of the church.

62. Patrick Keifert, "The Trinity and Congregational Planning: Between Historical Minimum and Eschatological Maximum," *Word & World* 15, no. 3 (1998): 282.

63. The irreducible interconnectedness of the Trinity on the cross, through the suffer-ing of God in Jesus, defines the *missio Dei* in the world for the sake of the world. Gary Simpson proposes that, in the "reciprocal dependence of the Father and the Son through the Spirit, the crucified God is the one and only trustworthy God" (Simpson, "No Trinity," p. 271).

penniless wandering in the marketplace. As such, it is the foundation for the remaining four contours proposed here for an ELCA contextual missiology.

2. Public Church

Bosch says that the missionary church is not recruiting folks to a certain brand of religion but "alerting people to the universal reign of God" (Bosch, p. 33). He contends that historically the church has been tempted to try to establish a Christian society or to withdraw completely from the public realm (pp. 33-34). Instead, using Wilbert Shenk's term, it must be involved in a "missionary encounter" with God's world (p. 35).

Modernity relegated Lutheranism — along with the rest of the church — to the private sphere and away from the public sphere. Many are happy with this situation because they are comfortably rooted in Christendom. Presiding Bishop Mark Hanson, speaking at Luther Seminary in St. Paul, noted that churches often want leaders to protect them *from* the world rather than prepare them *for* the world.[64] In addition, encountering the world of the spiritual marketplace has caused survival anxiety among mainline denominations like the ELCA, which have competed less successfully in this marketplace than have some of their conservative counterparts.

Yet the *missio Dei* leads the church into the public sector, and the church has an opportunity to reclaim the marketplace as a rich civic environment for sharing the gospel of Jesus Christ for the common good of the neighbor and the life of the world.[65] In *Critical Social Theory*, Gary Simpson suggests that missional congregations can be public companions that "*create, strengthen, and sustain* the moral fabrics that fashion a life-giving and life-accountable world."[66] It may surprise some that Lutheranism has a rich theological tradition for publicly living out its vocation in

64. Bishop Hanson presented these thoughts in a Hein-Fry Lecture delivered at Luther Seminary, St. Paul, Minnesota, on March 23, 2006.

65. Craig Van Gelder notes that, as the modern private church is led into the postmodern public square, it is indeed struggling to reposition itself in relationship to this new context. He observes two prevalent but conflicting postures: (1) rallying all the forces of consumerism to reach target markets; or (2) disengaging from the dominant cultural milieu (Van Gelder, "A Great New Fact," pp. 66-67).

66. Simpson, *Critical Social Theory*, pp. 144-45.

the world.[67] Exploring and then mobilizing its vocational legacy, the ELCA might not only discover new avenues of life-giving public companionship but might also recover its long-held, life-giving understanding of the baptismal promise and calling.

3. Global Church

According to Bosch, a contextual missiology for the twenty-first century must actively partner with the Third World church in becoming a global church (p. 36).[68] He says that the West has been complicit in the economic plight of the Third World, and thus he challenges the Western church to act responsibly and with respect toward those churches (pp. 36-39). In addition, he says that Third World theologies are essentially missionary theologies, unlike those in the West, and that these "Third World theologies may become a force of renewal in the West as we grope toward a missiology of Western culture" (p. 36).

Existing structures, such as the ELCA's Reformation ecclesiology, maintain the dominance of the wealthy West and consequently prevent ecclesiastical embodiment of the true international, interracial, and uniting activity of the *missio Dei* for the sake of the world. James Scherer makes the point that we should give high priority to designing structures that represent this missional reality,[69] rather than maintaining ecclesiological traditions that detract from the church's ability to respond missionally to the actual economic imbalances of the global marketplace. The global spiritual marketplace cannot ignore the global economy; the church is called into the world to reflect the *missio Dei*.

The Global Mission Unit of the ELCA, following the lead of its predecessor, the Division for Global Mission (DGM), operates within a missiological vision that embraces many of the characteristics Bosch and

---

67. For two revealing and empowering explorations of this, see Marc Kolden, *Christian's Calling in the World,* Centered Life Series (St. Paul: Luther Seminary Centered Life, 2002); Cynthia D. Moe-Lobeda, *Public Church: For the Life of the World,* Lutheran Voices (Minneapolis: Augsburg Fortress, 2004).

68. Bosch uses the term "Third World," but a more desirable alternative is now "Majority World," which is more reflective of realities acknowledged today.

69. James A. Scherer, *Gospel, Church, and Kingdom: Comparative Studies in World Mission Theology* (Minneapolis: Augsburg, 1987), p. 238.

Scherer envision. It is a model for mission called "accompaniment," which it describes as "walking together . . . with neither companion ahead or behind, above or below, the other. . . . *Accompaniment* implies companionship of mutual respect . . . [and] holds the potential to create a radical shift in power within today's global relationships."[70] For example, DGM sought to divest itself of residual attitudes and patterns of behavior marked by domination and subordination in order to more completely establish relationships of true mutuality in mission with companion churches and agencies, giving appropriate attention to *their* priorities.

Quite significantly, the ELCA has the vision of living into this paradigm throughout the whole church and not just in its global relationships. This theology of accompaniment was one of the goals for the 2005 ELCA-wide restructuring efforts: "The churchwide organization pledges itself to live into this model."[71] To do so would facilitate one of its greatest, most necessary, and most life-giving changes: a true global paradigm integrated into the mainstream church.

4. Confessional Church

In Bosch's vision for a contextual missiology for the twenty-first century, the church articulates who it is authentically and confidently (Bosch, p. 44). Bosch challenges the church to stay centered on Christ amid cultures of idolatry — modern and postmodern. He continues: "The New Testament church flowed from its encounter with the crucified and risen Christ. . . . The Christian missionary of today either shares in that same experience or is no Christian missionary" (p. 44).

Denominations no longer command the allegiance they did in the past, because denominational identities are less important to the average church shopper in the spiritual marketplace. With increased ecumenical partnerships between denominations coming into play, the tendency is to blur and downplay denominational distinctions in order to arrive at unity. Meanwhile a panoply of diverse spiritual voices, Christian as well as non-

70. "Global Mission in the Twenty-first Century: A Vision of Evangelical Faithfulness to God's Mission" (Chicago: Evangelical Lutheran Church in America), 12: http://www.elca.org/globalmission/policy/gm21full.pdf [accessed March 12, 2006].

71. "Faithful Yet Changing," Section Two: Goals of Restructuring, no. 6.

Christian, clamor for attention. The present pluralistic religious market-place needs a missional church that is also a confessional church, a unique voice that is able to clearly proclaim that Jesus Christ makes a difference for the world. Gallup polls support the need for a confessional church, noting that Americans want to get from church a relationship with Jesus Christ that has real impact on their day-to-day lives.[72] In market terms, the very identity of the church is its niche in the spiritual marketplace.

The ELCA is such a confessional church. Its strong confessional identity positions it well for the twenty-first-century missional demands that require clarity that denominations in general have difficulty achieving.[73] Article VII of the Augsburg Confession is cited as formative for ELCA ecumenical affairs and provides confessional clarity here: "For the true unity of the church it is enough to agree concerning the teaching of the Gospel and the administration of the sacraments."[74] As the twenty-first-century ELCA discovers the missional advantages of its confessional core, it may explore with increasing confidence its positive position in the spiritual marketplace.

5. Imaginative Church

In addition to Bosch's four categories, I propose to add a fifth: a contextual missiology for the twenty-first century invites the church to cultivate its *imagination* for God's future activity.

The cultivation of the Christian imagination of a congregation provides the important link between its life of spiritual discernment/theological reflection and the practical realities of being a missionary, public, global, and confessional church. Unfortunately, according to Patrick Keifert, "the shared Christian imagination of most congregations has very little past and almost no future. They are imprisoned in a very present now."[75] In an effective missiology for the twenty-first century, the imaginative church must be deeply historical and courageously visionary. This

72. Reeves, *Empty Church*, p. 187.

73. Richey, *Denominationalism*, pp. 9-10.

74. *Augsburg Confession*, Lat. 7:2, in *The Book of Concord: The Confessions of the Evangelical Lutheran Church*, ed. and trans. Theodore G. Tappert (Philadelphia: Fortress Press, 1959), p. 32.

75. Keifert, "The Trinity and Congregational Planning," pp. 284, 285.

involves deep listening to the Word of God in Scripture, tradition, culture, society, and in the personal and communal experience of the faithful. With its enduring tension between confessionalism and contextualization, the ELCA might well glimpse and grow into this deeper tension between God's primeval and eschatological imagination for the world. Grounded in God's Word in this present in-between time but not imprisoned by it, the ELCA can creatively navigate the postmodern terrain of relativity, plurality, and subjectivism.[76]

The imaginative missional church, faithful to the *missio Dei* as it lives into the reign of God, practices hospitality.[77] This is more than a series of well-orchestrated tactics. It is the deep-seated, eschatological conviction that the congregation draws its life from the hospitality of God and creates its present behavior on the basis of its future, that is, "on the basis of those who do not yet belong to Christian community, but whom the congregation believes God is calling to belong."[78] Welcoming churches are not focused on their own market-driven attractiveness and attractions; welcoming churches are focused on their welcoming God, who calls, gathers, enlightens, sanctifies, and sends them out on a path full of hope and promise.

In summary, a contextual missiology for the twenty-first-century ELCA envisions a missional, public, global, confessional, and imaginative church that is led by the *missio Dei* into the spiritual marketplace. Undeterred by competitive religious voices, this church extends the hospitality of God in public ways with all God's people and to all God's people and, through its confessional clarity, engages the commerce of consumerism with the grace of the cross and an eschatological vision of the reign of God for the sake of the world.

Conclusion: Ready for Mission!

With its headquarters looming comfortably in the Chicago skyline, the ELCA appears to be well-situated in American culture. Gone are many of the tensions of the immigrant Reformation churches in a foreign land; and

76. Best and Kellner, *Postmodern Turn,* pp. 4-23.
77. See Patrick Keifert, *Welcoming the Stranger: A Public Theology of Worship and Evangelism* (Minneapolis: Fortress Press, 1992).
78. Keifert, "The Trinity and Congregational Planning," p. 289.

gone are many of the particular tensions with which its predecessor churches contended. Yet the ELCA today is living in the current tensions between confessionalism and contextualization, rooted in its Reformation identity and now sent into a new era of mission in the American spiritual marketplace of the twenty-first century. Its history illustrates that Lutheranism has long lived within such a tension and has not sought easy solutions to complex faith issues, neither in its Reformation birthplace nor in its American home.

From the perspective of Roger Finke and Rodney Stark's sect-church cycle, the ELCA may be developing the capacity to incorporate dissenting groups and thus maintain the sect-like tendencies that help reverse the migration of a mainline denomination to the sidelines in the religious marketplace. In its proposals on sexuality and restructuring, the ELCA may have begun the diffusion of necessary innovations, as described by Everett Rogers, for the gradual emergence of an effective twenty-first-century missional church. The poignant encounter between Good Soil and the 2005 Churchwide Assembly exposes the difficulties of communally addressing issues within the judicatory milieu of Robert's Rules of Order. Envisioning the possibilities described by Jürgen Habermas, the ELCA might begin to transform its deliberative processes into communicative action through which the Spirit will shape its life and community in new ways. The ELCA is well positioned to live into the new tensions of being a missional church in the twenty-first-century spiritual marketplace. But the truth will be told in how that actually plays out in reality. Inspired by David Bosch's theological vision of a missionary, public, global, and confessional church, with the added component of becoming an imaginative church, the ELCA may lay claim to its missional calling in God's world for the sake of that world.

CHAPTER 8

A Contextual Missiology for the Southern Baptist Church in Taiwan: Reviewing the Past and Envisioning the Future

James Tzu-Kao Chai

Introduction

Because God is calling and sending every church into its particular context to participate in God's mission *(missio Dei)*, every church needs to think and act both contextually and missiologically. This is the guiding premise of this essay: that the Southern Baptist Church in Taiwan (TSBC) needs to review its past missions, to develop a contextual missiology, and to envision its future mission missiologically and contextually.

To reflect on the church's mission contextually, a church needs to define its context carefully. Therefore, I will in the first section provide an understanding of the context of Taiwan, especially the social, economic, political and religious issues since World War II. It is also helpful to review how the church has historically participated in God's mission in Taiwan. Therefore, this chapter will review the history of Taiwanese Protestant missions in general, and the TSBC's history of missions in particular. To review the church missiologically, I wish to incorporate a missional church perspective in order to offer a theological framework to help critique past missiologies as well as envision a contextual missiology for the future of the TSBC.

Defining the Context

In this first section I will provide an overview of Taiwan from historical, demographic, social, economic, political, and religious perspectives with a particular focus on the period between World War II and the present. In addition, I want to identify some of the opportunities and challenges that the church of Taiwan faces at the present time.

The Historical and Demographic Setting

The land area of the island of Taiwan is only 35,980 square kilometers, making it slightly smaller than Maryland and Delaware combined. It is strategically positioned and thus it readily became involved in the competition of colonial powers. Colonization greatly influenced Taiwan's society, and it is important to understand this history. During the late sixteenth and early seventeenth centuries, European countries such as Portugal, Spain, and Holland built strongholds in Taiwan. At that time, China officially occupied Taiwan, but China did not pay much attention to this island until Japan expressed interest in it during the late nineteenth century.

After China lost the first Sino-Japanese War (1894), Taiwan became Japan's colony. During its fifty years of Taiwan colonization (1895-1945), Japan had the opportunity to improve bureaucratic administration, land surveys, transportation, health care, and school systems. In 1945, following the second Sino-Japan War, Taiwan was returned to China. In 1949, after the end of the civil war between the Nationalist Party (KMT) and the Communist Party in China, the KMT withdrew from China and relocated on Taiwan. Following World War II, the KMT used its military, political, and economic strength to dominate Taiwan for almost fifty years.

Like the United States, Taiwan is a country of immigrants. Most people either came because they were seeking new land or because they were refugees from China. Today these immigrants represent four major groups: aborigines, Minnan, Hakka, and Mainlanders. Table 1 on page 221 shows the composition of these four groups.[1]

---

1. This table was revised from Qing-Rong Yu, "The Voice of The Hakka People": http://home.pchome.com.tw/life/mihau/hakkavoice.htm [accessed April 29, 2003].

Table 1. The Four Major Immigrant Groups
and the Christian Percentage in Taiwan

Major Groups	Population	Percentage in Taiwan	Christian Population	Christian Percentage
Aborigines	700,000	3.0%	98,000	14.0%
Minnan (Taiwanese)	15,300,000	66.5%	306,000	2.0%
Hakka	3,700,000	16.1%	7,400	0.2%
Mainlanders	3,300,000	14.4%	165,000	5.0%
Total	23,000,000	100.0%	576,400	2.5%

Two of these groups need to be highlighted. The Minnan, the largest group, came to Taiwan from southern China beginning in the early seventeenth century and through the nineteenth century. Minnan residents speak Taiwanese, a dialect of southern China. From 1945 to 1949, during the civil war in China, Mainlanders came to Taiwan; they speak Mandarin Chinese. Since the KMT government was made up of Mainlanders, they established Mandarin Chinese as the official language.

The history of immigration and colonization has greatly influenced Taiwanese society. Since each immigrant group brought its own historical traditions, uniting them was difficult. In addition, most of the political regimes that gravitated to Taiwan came with their own dominant cultural perspective. Because of this, the earlier residents of Taiwan gradually lost their cultural identity over time.

The Social, Economic, and Political Setting: Post–World War II to the Present

After World War II, Taiwan shifted from a high-fertility, agricultural, and colonized society to a low-fertility, industrial society with an active social civic movement.[2] Scholars divide the history of post–World War II Taiwan

2. Albert Hermalin, et al., "The Social and Economic Transformation of Taiwan," in Arland Thornton and Hui-Sheng Lin, eds., *Social Change and the Family in Taiwan* (Chicago: The University of Chicago Press, 1994), pp. 49-87.

into three periods on the basis of this economic transformation: the post-war rehabilitation period (1945-1961); the export-oriented industrial period (1961-1973); and the industrial upgrading period (1973-present).[3] In each period, the general trend of postwar Taiwan was toward industrialization, urbanization, and a democratic society. Table 2 compares the general features of each period.

Table 2. Comparison of the Three Periods in Postwar Taiwan

Postwar rehabilitation period	*Export-oriented industry period*	*Industrial upgrading period*
Chaotic	Military dominant	Democratization
Agricultural	Labor-Intensive	High-Technical
Rural	Suburban	Urban

Postwar Rehabilitation

World War II brought great destruction to Taiwan. Toward the end of the war, as a result of the constant bombing by Allied forces, almost 80 percent of its infrastructure had been destroyed. In 1945, inflation rose 3500 percent. In 1949, after the Nationalist Party (KMT) lost China to the Communists, the KMT relocated to Taiwan, bringing a sizable number of experts and money to help with the rehabilitation.[4] U.S. support also contributed a good deal: from 1949 to 1967, U.S. economic and military support amounted to $4.2 billion (USD).[5] The loss of China to the Communists and the bloody experience of the Korean War promoted a global anti-Communist postwar atmosphere, which led the U.S. government to recognize the KMT government as its partner in Asia.[6]

One important factor affecting Taiwan's economy was that all major change was initiated by the government. Without competition from large corporations and capitalists, the KMT government had absolute authority

3. Thornton and Lin, *Social Change*; see also Thomas B. Gold, *State and Society in the Taiwan Miracle* (Armonk, NY: M. E. Sharpe, Inc., 1986).
4. Hermalin et al., "Transformation of Taiwan," p. 62.
5. Hermalin et al., "Transformation of Taiwan," pp. 62-63.
6. Gold, *State and Society*, p. 58.

and the necessary resources to control the economic direction of Taiwan.[7] One of the important projects in this period was land reform, which the government implemented by releasing land from landlords to farmers. Some scholars note that this project successfully promoted a better distribution of social welfare and resulted in high agricultural production, which in turn resulted in transferring the agricultural surplus to industry.[8] But other scholars criticized this project because it sacrificed the landowners and the role of agriculture in order to promote industry, leading to a decline in the rural areas.[9]

Not only had the viable infrastructure been destroyed by the end of World War II, but cultural values, norms, and identity were also changed under the regime of the KMT government, which came to Taiwan in 1949. After the colonial period under Japan ended, people in Taiwan needed to search for a new identity: it was the identity of being Chinese, and it included learning Mandarin. During this transitional period, conflicts were common. On February 28, 1947, the tragic 228 Incident occurred. It began as a dispute over the issue of a tobacco monopoly, but it soon shifted to an islandwide demonstration against the KMT's corrupt military dominance and economic monopoly. The government used the military to put down the demonstration, and in that process it arrested many social elites and killed many intellectuals for no good reason. Some historians believe that this government reaction to the demonstration was a pretext to destroy the social intellectuals.[10] The 228 Incident was one of the most important events in postwar Taiwan: it furthered the hostility between the Minnan and the KMT government, as well as between the Minnan and the Mainlanders. The 228 Incident also increased the gap between Minnan churches (especially the Presbyterian Church in Taiwan) and Mandarin churches.

Export-Oriented and Labor-Intensive Industry Period

From 1961 to 1973, the economic character of Taiwan was primarily export-oriented, that is, the production of goods was mainly for earning foreign

7. Gold, *State and Society*, p. 64.

8. Hermalin et al., "Transformation of Taiwan," pp. 63-66.

9. Gold, *State and Society*, pp. 64-67.

10. Murray Rubinstein, "Christianity and Democratization in Modern Taiwan," in Philip Clart and Charles B. Jones, eds., *Religion in Modern Taiwan: Tradition and Innovation in a Changing Society* (Honolulu: University of Hawaii Press, 2003), p. 215.

exchange. From 1962 to 1972, exports grew from 13 percent to 43 percent of the Gross Domestic Product (GDP). Industries became labor-intensive during that period. With the fertility rate rising rapidly in the 1950s, the population between the ages of fifteen and twenty-four increased 80 percent, which provided many cheap laborers for industry. However, the unemployment rate also advanced sharply in the early 1960s, as urbanization dramatically increased.

The government established some Export Production Centers (EPC) around Taiwan during this period. These EPCs attracted surplus laborers from the rural areas to industry. Good transportation systems and the placement of the EPCs near rural areas made it possible for rural residents to work in industry without changing where they lived, and this moderated the pace of urbanization. In 1964, in an effort to prevent the population from growing too fast, the government initiated an islandwide family planning project, and this was successful in slowing down the birthrate by the 1970s.[11]

Industrial Upgrading Period

In the 1970s, Taiwan's economy was affected by two oil shocks and an international economic recession. The KMT government reacted by initiating a ten-year project to stimulate the economic growth rate. This project involved developing heavy industry, an infrastructure of transportation, and a nuclear electricity plant. In the 1980s, with increasing energy but also rising labor costs, the KMT launched a high-tech industry project.[12] In the 1990s, many companies that had been initially attracted to Taiwan because if its cheaper labor now moved their plants to mainland China, which created a greater economic dependence on China for the island. With the shift of industrial activity to China, many Taiwanese businesspeople had to move away from their families in Taiwan, which caused family problems.

From the early 1970s, with the changing attitude of the U.S. government toward China, Taiwan encountered serious diplomatic setbacks. In 1971, the United Nations Security Council approved China to replace Taiwan in its role on the Security Council. The following year, then U.S. President Richard Nixon visited China and issued the Shanghai communiqué, which further eroded relations between the KMT and the United States.[13]

11. Hermalin et al., "Transformation of Taiwan," p. 74.
12. Hermalin et al., "Transformation of Taiwan," pp. 78-81.
13. Rubinstein, "Christianity and Democratization," pp. 225-26.

This was followed, in 1975, by the death of Chiang Kai-shek (leader of the KMT), and the severing of the relationship between Taiwan and the United States in 1978.

In view of the deteriorating diplomatic situation of the 1970s, voices for self-determination began to argue that the future of Taiwan should be decided only by the Taiwanese people, especially those who had lived in Taiwan before 1945, and not by the Mainlander KMT government or by U.S. politicians. During the 1980s, this self-determination movement shifted to a quest to build a new and independent nation.[14] In 2000 the KMT lost its first presidential election to a young political party, the Democracy and Development Party (DDP); and in 2004, the DDP presidential candidate was re-elected with the slogan "Yes! Taiwan." This seemed to indicate that more than half of the Taiwanese people desired a more radical quest for national identity. However, with the DDP promoting an independent Taiwan, the military threat from China also rose: for reasons of nationalism and national security, China feels that it cannot allow Taiwan to be independent. Therefore, military tension on both sides of the Taiwanese Strait has reached a new high point.

Religious Setting

Early Chinese immigrants usually brought religious idols with them to Taiwan. Chinese folk religion, known in Taiwan as "Taiwanese popular religion," consists of a mixture of magic, ancestor veneration, and devotion to plural divinities. It shows influences from other religions, such as Taoism, Buddhism, Confucianism, and traditional animistic beliefs and practices. These folk religions usually mixed religious syncretistic characteristics with the Chinese cultural tradition; this was often a hindrance to those who converted to Christianity. Today, by the far the largest number of Taiwanese believe in Chinese folk religion (51 percent), followed by Buddhism (21 percent), Taoism (10 percent), and new religions (7 percent). Christianity represents only 2.5 percent of the Taiwanese population.[15]

---

14. Rubinstein, "Christianity and Democratization," pp. 225-26.

15. David B. Barrett et al., eds., *The World by Countries, Religionists, Churches, Ministries*, vol. 1 of *World Christian Encyclopedia: A Comparative Survey of Churches and Religions in the Modern World*, 2nd ed. (Oxford: Oxford University Press, 2001), p. 723.

Table 3. Comparison of Religious Background in Taiwan

Folk Religion	50.7%
Buddhism	20.9%
Taoism	10.2%
New Religions	6.8%
Christianity	2.5%

In the 1960s a folk religion renaissance came about. Some sociologists argue that societal changes such as the industrialization and urbanization of society prompted people to seek religion. However, most of these religion-seeking people did not favor Christianity. Rather, they participated in traditional religious observances, such as popular folk religions and temple festivals that were familiar in their hometowns.[16] For example, the *Yigundao,* a popular folk religion, tended toward "a conservative morality and attempted to develop an indigenous Chinese tradition-based response to modernization."[17] The revival of popular religions has proved to be the greatest challenge to the Taiwanese Christian church.

Opportunities and Challenges for the Church in Context

The above discussion has defined the context of Taiwan from the perspective of several different dimensions. This context offers both opportunities and challenges for the church. If the church is to participate in God's mission in this context, then it needs to engage these opportunities and respond to these challenges. The diverse histories and cultures of the various immigrant groups have an impact on not only the country but also the churches inside the country. Churches often find it difficult to develop common ground on which to cooperate. The church needs to reflect theologically on the identity of Taiwan's peoples, and needs to help people respect diversity and cooperate with one another. The economic and industrial improvements brought forth many social problems, such as increasing

16. Rubinstein, "Christianity and Democratization," p. 224.

17. Murray A. Rubinstein, *The Protestant Community on Modern Taiwan: Mission, Seminary, and Church* (Armonk, NY: M. E. Sharpe, 1991), p. 51.

environmental damage, a rising criminal rate and divorce rate, and growing speculations in real estate and stocks. The church needs to respond to these problems theologically and to find ways to participate in improving the quality of life for everyone.

As Taiwan's people worry about the military tension between Taiwan and mainland China, the church needs to reflect theologically on this issue as well. On the one hand, the church needs to bring God's peace to people; on the other hand, the church needs to offer a practical strategy for the country. The church needs to think about how to preach the gospel within the context of religious pluralism. The church needs to learn why and how some folk religions contextualize their strategies; and it needs to understand what other religions believe in order to have a better dialogue with them.

Overview of the Protestant History of Mission in Taiwan

In this section I will highlight important events and movements in the history of Protestant missions in Taiwan. I will show how the social, economic, and religious setting of Taiwan affects the church and how the church in Taiwan might respond to these challenges.

Early Dutch Missions in Taiwan in the Seventeenth Century

In 1624, Dutch missionaries became the earliest Protestant community in Taiwan. By the 1660s, at least twenty-nine Dutch clergymen were serving on this island and actively spreading the Christian faith. G. Candidius and R. Junius were the most famous among them, and they did make some progress in spreading the faith. "Hundreds of converts were won, schools were established, and catechists employed to instruct the neophytes and the children . . . and a translation was made of at least the gospel of Matthew."[18] The large majority of the converts were aborigines. Unfortunately, the Manchu regime that was then resident in China drove the last Dutch missionaries out of Taiwan in 1683. As Kenneth Scott Latourette points

18. Kenneth Scott Latourette, *A History of the Expansion of Christianity,* vol. 3, *Three Centuries of Advance* A.D. *1500–*A.D. *1800* (New York: Harper, 1939), pp. 359-60.

out, "The Christianity which was so dependent upon Dutch prestige disappeared with the regime under whose aegis it had been initiated."[19]

The Presbyterian Missions under the Japanese Regime

Taiwan Presbyterians were the most representative Protestant community from the middle of the nineteenth century to the end of World War II, and they still form the largest Protestant community today. During the past 140 years, the Presbyterians have built an extensive indigenous church in Taiwan, especially among the Minnan (or Taiwanese) group. The early Presbyterian missionaries usually engaged in medical, educational, and Bible-translating ministries. From 1865, the English Presbyterians, led by James Maxwell, extended missions from China to South Taiwan. Another important figure was William Barclay, who contributed to the founding of the two Presbyterian seminaries and who translated the whole Bible into the Taiwanese dialect.[20] In 1871, G. L. Mackay, a Canadian Presbyterian and one of the most influential leaders at that time, began his work in the northern part of Taiwan and laid a solid foundation for a strong indigenous Presbyterian church.[21]

Under Japan's fifty-year colonial rule, the church experienced an increasingly tense relationship with the state. The situation worsened during World War II, to the point that the Presbyterian missionaries felt it necessary to withdraw from Taiwan. The local Presbyterian church was cut off from its founding churches for the duration of the war between Japan and the Allies.[22] Independent of Western support, the congregations faced some challenges, but this helped them become a more indigenous church.

The Rapidly Growing Church of the 1950s

The church in Taiwan experienced rapid growth in the 1950s and early 1960s. Hollington Tong, a Chinese church historian, boldly predicted that

19. Latourette, *History,* vol. 3, p. 360.

20. Latourette, *A History of the Expansion of Christianity,* vol. 4, *The Great Century in Northern Africa and Asia A.D. 1800–A.D. 1914* (New York: Harper, 1939), p. 332.

21. Rubinstein, *The Protestant Community on Modern Taiwan,* p. 19.

22. Latourette, *A History of the Expansion of Christianity,* vol. 7, *Advance Through Storm A.D. 1914 and After,* pp. 400-401.

Taiwan would become a Christian nation in less than half a century.[23] One important reason was that the church had abundant resources during this time. Before the end of the civil war in China in 1949, Taiwan was still seen as a frontier of China; but after the Communists had occupied China, many Western missionaries moved to Taiwan to continue their mission activities. Almost all of the Western missionaries had left Taiwan during World War II; but by the early 1950s, there were more than 300 missionaries working with more than 100 denominations and other parachurch organizations in Taiwan. By 1960, close to 600 Protestant missionaries were participating in missions.[24] In addition, many Chinese church leaders had also immigrated to Taiwan from China. Taiwan seemed to have become an island that was blessed with an abundance of many Christian resources.

Previously Presbyterian, the dominant Protestant community now became multidenominational. Unlike the Presbyterian Church, whose main strength was among the Minnan (Taiwanese), missionaries of other denominations who had come from mainland China usually concentrated on the Mainlanders, because Mainlanders seemed to have a greater openness to the gospel in the chaotic times following World War II. Besides, most of these missionaries could speak only Mandarin Chinese. The speed of conversion was higher during this period than at any other time in the history of the church in Taiwan.[25] The Christian community that had numbered only 51,000 in 1948 had grown to almost 380,000 by 1960.[26] That first full decade following World War II, 1950 to 1960, saw a significant expansion of Presbyterians and other denominations.

Tension between the Presbyterians and the KMT Government

The 228 Incident of 1947 worsened the relationship between the state and the Taiwan Presbyterian Church. This church had a long mission history in Taiwan and deeply identified with the suffering of Taiwanese people

23. Hollington K. Tong, *Christianity in Taiwan: A History* (Taipei: China Post, 1961), p. 240.

24. Tong, *Christianity in Taiwan*, p. 84.

25. Rubinstein, "Christianity and Democratization in Modern Taiwan," p. 213.

26. Allen J. Swanson, *The Church in Taiwan: Profile 1980: A Review of the Past, A Projection for the Future* (Pasadena, CA: William Carey Library, 1981), p. 26.

(mainly the Minnan). After 1949, the KMT government required all people in Taiwan to speak Mandarin, prohibiting the use of other dialects in public. This hindered the use of Taiwanese in the Sunday services and prohibited the dialect translation of the Bible. These regulations deeply hurt the feelings of the Taiwanese people and hindered previous efforts to preserve Taiwanese culture and identity under Japan's colonization.

In the 1970s, the Presbyterian Church made various political announcements that helped initiate the Taiwanese self-determination movement. And these statements further worsened the relationship between the Presbyterian Church and the government.[27] The cooperation between the Presbyterian Church and the Mandarin churches was also hindered by their different attitudes toward the state. Many Mandarin churches tended to have a more conservative attitude toward the government and social justice issues than did the Presbyterian Church, and these political differences were an obstacle to their cooperation for mission.

The Church Growth Movement and New Evangelism Opportunities of the 1970s

Though society settled down in the early 1950s and there was a rapid expansion of the economy and personal income, many church leaders perceived the limits that this expansion brought with it in the 1960s. The stagnation in church membership encouraged leaders to search for solutions. Donald McGavran, the father of church-growth theory, was invited to lead a weeklong seminar on that subject in Taiwan. The Church Growth Society was established after that conference, and four foundational studies were published to analyze the church's stagnation. These books identified some major factors that were hindering church growth in the 1960s: growing indifference regarding the gospel, increasing clericalism, lack of lay training programs, individualism, and the problem of Western subsidy.[28]

In 1975, after the KMT leader Chiang Kai-Shek died, a greater openness to the gospel emerged. Many churches immediately grasped the opportunity to launch a series of campaigns, including a Billy Graham cru-

---

27. Rubinstein, "Christianity and Democratization in Modern Taiwan," pp. 225-27.
28. Swanson, *The Church in Taiwan*, pp. 27-29.

sade and the campaigns of Rev. Lien-Hwa Chow (Chiang Kai-Shek's family pastor). Taiwan Campus Crusade also launched two big campaigns, entitled "I Found" and "Target 80." The Presbyterian Church initiated the "Ten-plus-One Movement" in 1979.[29] Though the effectiveness of these campaigns could not compare to the church growth of the 1950s, they did lead to an increase in conversions.

The Charismatic Movement of the 1980s

In 1979, Taiwanese church leaders began a pilgrimage to visit large churches in Korea, especially the largest church in the world, the Full Gospel Central Church of Seoul. They discovered that prayer was important for church revival. In 1982, the first Prayer Mountain was held in Central Taiwan: it offered more than twenty weeklong prayer and fasting retreats each year. One church historian said that, "with attendance ranging from a few hundred to one thousand and more, this single establishment, more than any other, introduced a new renewal dynamic to numerous churches and Christians in Taiwan."[30] Murray Rubinstein says: "It stands as a bridge between Western and Chinese churches and also serves to unite in spirit those separated by the formal walls of denominations."[31]

Interdenominational Cooperation from the 1990s

Since 1990 there have been some united activities between the Mandarin Church and the Minnan Church (mainly the Presbyterians). In 1990, a 228 Peace Memorial service memorializing the death of the innocents in the 228 Incident was led by a Taiwan Southern Baptist Church (TSBC) pastor (representing the Mainlanders Church) and a Presbyterian Church pastor (representing the Minnan Church), symbolizing the further reconciliation between the Mainlander and Minnan churches.

29. Swanson, *The Church in Taiwan,* pp. 29-31.

30. Allen J. Swanson, *Mending the Nets: Taiwan Church Growth and Loss in the 1980's* (Pasadena, CA: William Carey Library, 1986), p. 32.

31. Murray Rubinstein, "Holy Spirit Taiwan: Pentecostal and Charismatic Christianity in the Republic of China," in Daniel H. Bays, ed., *Christianity in China: From the Eighteenth Century to the Present* (Stanford, CA: Stanford University Press, 1996), p. 358.

In 1991, church leaders initiated a united evangelistic effort, the Target 2000 Evangelism Movement, which had a vision that there would be two million Christians and ten thousand churches in Taiwan (which would send two hundred missionaries overseas) by the year 2000. This vision was not realized by 2000, but it did contribute to significant church growth and marked a new stage in which the Mandarin and Minnan churches worked together for the purpose of evangelism.

Reviewing the History of Missions of the TSBC

Now that I have defined the Taiwan context and have reviewed the history of Protestant missions, in this section I want to review the history of missions of the TSBC. The TSBC is a representative Mandarin-speaking denomination that has some parallels to the other Protestant experiences in Taiwan.

Historical Overview

Unlike Presbyterians, Baptists had no former history in Taiwan before the end of World War II. In 1948, Southern Baptist missionaries in China decided to send missionaries to Taiwan: a Chinese pastor, along with a missionary, began work there. In 1950, immediately after the U.S. government's commitment to support the KMT in Taiwan, the Southern Baptist Convention Foreign Mission Board committed resources to Taiwan. Compared to other Western missionaries who were sent out following World War II, Southern Baptists were among the earliest denominations in Taiwan and had the most support from their American mission headquarters.

In Taiwan in 1949, there was only one Southern Baptist congregation, with fewer than fifty members; by 1961, however, there were thirty-six American missionaries stationed in cities and towns throughout Taiwan, and twenty-six congregations had been built, with a total membership of more than 6,800.[32] But that outlook began to change in the mid-1960s, when the Baptist leaders faced declining growth. In 1961, the TSBC Seminary's enrollment had already fallen to forty-eight, and only three students

---

32. Rubinstein, "Holy Spirit Taiwan," p. 270.

graduated in 1964, a situation that caused the Baptist leadership to seriously re-evaluate its mission.[33] Those leaders implemented some changes during the mid-1970s; at the same time, they proposed and put into action new evangelistic strategies. And in the early 1980s, they launched another evangelistic initiative, the "Know Him" campaign. In the early 1990s, TSBC joined the "Year 2000 Gospel Movement" with other churches in Taiwan. TSBC set the target goal of 500 congregations with 75,000 members by 2000; by 2001, however, the actual number of congregations had only risen to 193, with 23,763 members.[34]

Missiological Overview

Baptist missions in Taiwan were a continuation of the missions they had established in China. Rubinstein points out that the Southern Baptist missionaries had a deep and broad experience of converting the Chinese and in planting indigenous churches.[35] This continuation played out in Taiwan as Southern Baptist missionaries chose as their mission target the immigrants from China who came after 1949. Southern Baptists ministered to immigrants, officers, soldiers, and their families from China; they left the Taiwanese to the Presbyterians. This was because the Baptist missionaries could speak Mandarin Chinese and could identify with these Mainlanders: both they and the immigrants were refugees who were in social and cultural transition. Concentrating on the Mainlanders seemed to be a good strategy because of the growth rate in that decade of the 1950s. But it did not prove effective over the long haul.

The TSBC not only worked with the same ethnic group they had worked with in China, but they also used the same classical and time-proven techniques they had developed in China. Those techniques included: proclaiming the gospel in the pulpit and in public gathering places; distributing tracts; setting up reading centers and bookstores; holding large-scale revival meetings; and organizing summer retreats and Bible

33. Rubinstein, "Holy Spirit Taiwan," pp. 270-73.

34. San-Tsai Zu, ed., Taiwan Christian Church Statistic Report: 2001, Chinese Christian Evangelical Association: http://database.ccea.org.tw/statics/default.htm [accessed May 20, 2004].

35. Rubinstein, "American Evangelicalism in the Chinese Environment," *American Baptist Quarterly* 3 (1983): 270.

camps.[36] In addition, beginning in 1950, Southern Baptist missionaries began to focus on the evangelization of college students. They purchased land in key cities near major colleges, and they established congregations for that purpose.[37] Conscious of the need for the church's revival and for finding ways once again to promote growth, they launched new campaigns. In the 1960s and 1970s they used advertisements to publicize these campaigns; and in the 1980s they used television, as well as radio and newspapers, to broadcast these campaigns.

The missions of the TSBC differed in some points from its early experience in China and Hong Kong. For example, the TSBC did not engage in various kinds of benevolent activities. They also decided early on that they did not have the resources to develop a whole school system like the ones they had established in various places in China. Furthermore, these Southern Baptists were pragmatists: from their experience in China, they knew such school systems had to be registered with authorities and would be subject to regulation, thus hindering their efforts to use these schools for evangelism. The other reason is that they believed that the government had built an effective higher education system in Taiwan.[38] Baptists had also run a number of hospitals in China, but they did not get involved in medical work in Taiwan. They felt that there was little need for the TSBC to develop such a ministry, probably because the Presbyterians, Seventh-day Adventists, and other missionary groups had already developed such work, and also because the government ran an adequate health-care system.[39]

The TSBC's ecclesiology can best be understood by way of the "Baptist Faith and Message."[40] First, a New Testament church is an autonomous local congregation of baptized believers; second, each congregation operates under the Lordship of Christ through democratic processes; third, its scriptural officers are pastors and deacons; fourth, the office of pastor is limited to men as qualified by Scripture. While these criteria worked in the United States, they did not make as much sense in the context of Taiwan, because most congregations in Taiwan did not know the meaning of dem-

---

36. Rubinstein, *The Protestant Community on Modern Taiwan*, p. 66.

37. Tsai Ling-Ming, "The Development and Reflection of Baptist History in Taiwan": http://www.twbap.org.tw/history/index.htm [accessed Feb. 24, 2004].

38. Rubinstein, *The Protestant Community on Modern Taiwan*, p. 67.

39. Rubinstein, *The Protestant Community on Modern Taiwan*, p. 67.

40. Southern Baptist Convention, "The Baptist Faith and Message": http://www.sbc.net/bfm/bfm2000.asp.

ocratic processes or how to skillfully operate the process, and this resulted in many conflicts among members of congregations.[41]

In 1954, TSBC missionaries helped their brethren build a convention in order to promote cooperation among the Baptist congregations and also to help unify new congregational mission efforts. At that time there were only eleven Baptist congregations, with a total membership of 2,200. These local congregations had no ability to think beyond themselves, and thus the convention was directed and supported by the Western leaders.[42] Baptist church polity emphasizes the authority of the local congregations, and thus the convention was under the authority of congregations. This is very different from the polity of those churches that have bishops. The convention is more like a coordinator striving to unite resources, and it serves as a representative of the TSBC. The convention's highest authority is the assembly of all the member congregations. This assembly is held annually, and its participants are the representatives of the member congregations, each congregation being allowed at least two representatives. Today there are about 200 representatives who attend the annual assembly. The assembly approves the budget, elects the executive committee, and votes on other important issues. However, the majority of the decisions are made by the executive committee, which is made up mostly of fulltime pastors, with very few lay leaders.

Just one year after the board had decided to create a permanent mission on the island, the TSBC made the decision to train Chinese leaders. In 1952, Southern Baptist Seminary training was begun in Taipei to train local pastors and teachers. Swanson observes that the early beginnings of theological training contributed heavily to the rapid growth of the Baptist church.[43] The seminary depended a great deal on mission subsidy; however, from 1989 on, the American mission board began to decrease its financial support by 10 percent each year, ending their support in 1998. Rubinstein observes that, in early 1990, the seminary's curriculum was very similar to that of U.S. seminaries: it emphasized the biblical languages, church history, and systematic theology, but it paid little attention to the realities of the Taiwanese environment.[44] Before 1990, the faculty had a siz-

41. Tsai Ling-Ming, "Baptist History in Taiwan."

42. Tsai Ling-Ming, "Baptist History in Taiwan."

43. Allen J. Swanson, *Taiwan: Mainline versus Independent Church Growth* (South Pasadena: WIlliam Carey Library, 1973), p. 110.

44. Rubinstein, *The Protestant Community on Modern Taiwan*, p. 78.

able number of teachers from the United States; most of the local faculty members were without Ph.D. degrees. In recent years the faculty situation has improved: many Ph.D. graduates are coming from both the Asia Baptist Seminary and Baptist seminaries in America.

Unlike the tense relationship between the Presbyterian Church and the KMT government, the relationship between the TSBC and the state was good. The KMT government was friendly toward the Mandarin-speaking denominations and missionaries: it understood that the missionaries had to be accommodated to please the United States, because many missionaries belonged to politically conservative and anti-Communist denominations. These missionaries were, in turn, an important lobbying group for the KMT authorities. On its side, the TSBC agreed with the strong anti-Communist beliefs of the KMT, and many had faith in the KMT's leader, President Chiang Kai-Shek.[45]

Engaging the Missional Church Perspective in Developing a Contextual Missiology

A contextual missiology for the Southern Baptists should be built on a solid theological foundation of a missiological ecclesiology. In this section I will engage the missional church perspective to critique the past missiologies of the TSBC and to help envision a contextual missiology for this church. The missional church perspective draws from a missionary, or "sending," understanding of God, and it is informed by the church's missionary nature and its participation in God's mission in the world. Before I unpack this further, I want to clarify the term "mission." In contrast to the use of the word "missions" in the previous discussion, where it referred to the practice and efforts of the church, the term "mission," or "missional," used in relationship to church, has a broader meaning. The mission church, or missional church, shifts from "missions" to "mission" and integrates that concept to become the focus of the whole church, especially an understanding of the church's very nature and its relationship to the world.

45. Rubinstein, *The Protestant Community on Modern Taiwan*, p. 34.

A Missionary God and Missio Dei

The sending, or missionary, nature of God is emphasized by Karl Barth, Lesslie Newbigin, and Craig Van Gelder when they speak of the church's participation in God's mission in the world. Barth argues that it is primarily God who engages in mission by sending God's self in the mission of the Son and the Spirit. The church can be in mission authentically only in obedience to God as being in mission. Barth's concept was taken up by Karl Hartenstein, who in 1934 coined the term *missio Dei.*[46]

Newbigin found that missions from the West were primarily founded on an emphasis on Christology rather than on the whole Trinity. "The church centric view of missions has perhaps been too exclusively founded upon the person and work of Christ and has perhaps done less than justice to the whole Trinitarian doctrine of God."[47] His understanding of God's mission also emphasizes the role of the Holy Spirit. Newbigin argues that it is the Spirit who thus bears witness in the life of the church and is not confined to the church's limitations. "It is the clear teaching of the Acts of the Apostles, as it is the experience of the missionaries that the Spirit goes, so to speak, ahead of the Church."[48]

Van Gelder emphasizes that God is a sending and missionary God. All persons in the Godhead are involved in mission, through creation, re-creation, and the final consummation. The Father sends the Son; the Father and the Son send the Spirit; the Father, Son, and Spirit send the church into the world.[49] This missional understanding of church shifts the church's identity from an institution that organizes for mere surviving to one that participates in God's redemptive mission in the world.[50] Because the church is missionary by nature and sent into the world, Van Gelder urges the church to pay attention to the issues of the gospel and cultures.

46. Stephen B. Bevans and Roger P. Schroeder, *Constants in Context: A Theology of Mission for Today* (Maryknoll: Orbis Books, 2004), p. 290.

47. Lesslie Newbigin, *Trinitarian Faith for Today's Mission* (Richmond, VA: John Knox Press, 1964), p. 31.

48. Newbigin, *Trinitarian Faith,* p. 49.

49. Van Gelder, *The Essence of the Church: A Community Created by the Spirit* (Grand Rapids: Baker, 2000), p. 96.

50. Van Gelder, "From Corporate Church to Missional Church: The Challenge Facing Congregations Today," *Review & Expositor* 101 (2004): 425-50.

Missional Church Perspective

The missional church perspective is that it provides a missiological under-standing of ecclesiology, which bridges doctrines about the Triune God (especially an emphasis on *missio Dei*) with a theology of the church (ecclesiology). The missional church perspective broadens the church's horizon through an understanding of her missionary nature. I want to highlight two books that relate the missional church perspective. *Missional Church* develops a missiological ecclesiology for the church: the church's nature and vocation is as God's called and sent people.[51] "Mission is not just about a program of the church, it defines the church as God's sent people. Our challenge today is to move from church with mission to missional church."[52] While this book is particularly designed for churches in the North American context, it can also help churches in other contexts to reflect on these issues.

Van Gelder's *The Essence of the Church* reflects on the church's nature, ministry, and organization from a missional church perspective. He argues that the church, which is missionary by its very nature, is the community created by the Spirit to participate in God's mission in the world. Van Gelder insists that the church's nature, ministry, and organization must be put in the correct sequence. The ministry of the church needs to serve the nature of the church; the organization of the church needs to serve the ministry of the church. Van Gelder also points out that leaders in both local and mobile missionary structures are important for a missional church. In order to participate in God's mission effectively, leaders in both local and mobile levels need to engage in better communicative and connective processes in their decision-making design.[53]

Now I want to summarize some implications of a missional church perspective to inform a contextual missiology for the TSBC.

A. A missional church needs to understand its missionary nature to participate in Gods' mission.

B. A missional church, as a missionary entity sent into the world, needs

---

51. Darrell L. Guder, ed., *Missional Church: A Vision for the Sending of the Church in North America* (Grand Rapids: Eerdmans, 1998), p. 11.

52. Guder, ed., *Missional Church*, p. 6.

53. Van Gelder, *Essence of the Church*, pp. 179-83.

to pay attention to context. It must translate the gospel into a given culture. A missional church must be sensitive to and respond to the changes of the context.

C. A missional church needs to have a missional understanding of church leaders as a gift to the church, given to help the body of Christ participate in God's mission *(missio Dei)*.

D. A missional church needs to have an interdependent church polity so that congregations can cooperate with each other rather than only caring about themselves. The church needs to understand the role and purpose of the judicatory level in assisting congregations to participate in God's mission in local areas.

Envisioning a Missional TSBC for the Future

In the previous section I reviewed the past practice and theology of mission by the TSBC. This section will critique its past missiologies and envision a contextual missiology for the TSBC within a missional church perspective.

A. A missional TSBC needs to reflect on the nature of the church from a missional church perspective. The TSBC needs to reflect on its nature and its theology of mission from a missional church perspective. The church's present understanding of its nature and theology of mission seems to stand on the grounding of the Great Commission alone rather than on an understanding of God's mission in the world as reflected in the Bible as a whole. Its missiological emphasis is too narrowly focused on evangelism and church growth rather than on participating in the Spirit's leading the church into mission for the sake of God and for the sake of the people of Taiwan. In addition, it lacks a perspective on how to participate in social justice and mercy for the sake of people in Taiwan. For example, the TSBC does not engage in any benevolent activities in Taiwan. Furthermore, the church seemed to be silent in the tragedy of the 228 Incident and during the uncertainty of the society in the 1970s.

A missional church knows that the nature of the church should build on an understanding of God's missionary nature, and its theology of mission needs to focus on participating in God's mission in the world more than on just evangelism and church growth. God sends God's own Son into the world to redeem the world and also sends the Spirit to create the church. The Spirit is at work in and through the church, and leads the church to participate in God's mission rather than to do missions on its own on behalf of God.

As the church of Taiwan emerges in the twenty-first century, it needs to interpret Scripture carefully, and it needs to reflect on the historical development of its theology of mission in order to develop a holistic theology of mission. The church must not only proclaim the faith about Jesus; it must also participate in social justice to its neighbors. The church should engage in such benevolent activities in the society, not only for pragmatic reasons but also because it is a part of the church's way of participating in God's mission. In addition, the church needs to have a more theological understanding of the role and the work of the Spirit, and it must develop the capacity to discern the Spirit's leading.

B. A missional TSBC must be contextual and must respond to the needs of the context. A missional church must translate the gospel message into its context. The missionary nature of the church makes it sensitive to social changes in order to participate in God's mission more faithfully. However, the message and the ministry of the TSBC in the past seems to have been more Western than contextual. Many strategies simply repeated what they had done in the past in China. They even used the same methods based on traditional American evangelical assumptions.[54] The reason for the church's decline was not only that it lacked good evangelism methods; it also resulted from people feeling that the gospel message and church life did not relate to people's lives. In addition, the TSBC was too passive in its responding to the opportunity and challenges of society.

The Southern Baptist Church in the emerging mission in Taiwan needs to focus on the issue of the gospel and cultures. The church should also be sensitive to the emerging postmodern culture, responding to its opportunities and challenges. For example, the church needs to respond to the quest for a more relational and networking relationship among people that is related to the postmodern by engaging a relational networking in the society and using small groups rather than big campaigns for evangelism. In addition, the gospel message proclaimed in a pluralistic society should use narratives, story, and life examples in its preaching. In addition,

---

54. Swanson, *The Church in Taiwan: Profile 1980*, p. 26.

the church needs to pay closer attention to the needs of society and respond to its challenges. As the people in Taiwan continue to seek their identity and struggle with the conflict between different groups, experiencing the uncertainty under China's military threat, and worshiping false gods, there are opportunities and challenges for the TSBC to participate in God's mission in this context.

C. A missional TSBC needs to have a missional understanding of church leadership and its formation.   The TSBC needs to reflect on the issues of church leadership and the formation of leaders from a missional church perspective. In lacking a missional understanding of leadership, the church can easily perceive leaders to be for the sake of the church rather than to be participating in God's mission for the sake of the world. In addition, the Baptist church polity, with its emphasis on the equality of all persons, can result in a very weak image of leadership. Pastors usually struggle and even suffer in the church polity of a democratic and independent local church. The identity and authority of pastors in this polity is weak and unclear. In addition, the ordination of pastors is still limited only to males, and this hinders opportunities for gifted female pastors. Furthermore, the weak image of church leaders also hinders the church from intentionally forming potential leaders. In addition, it tends to train leaders to fit ministry inside the church rather than to lead and equip congregations to respond to the needs of the context. The result is leaders with an inward focus who direct programs.[55]

To envision a contextual missiology for the church in the twenty-first century, the church needs to know that leadership is God's gift to the church so that it can participate in God's mission in the world. The church needs to develop both men and women who have character and gifts to be developed as leaders of congregations in mission. This involves reflecting on leadership and leadership formation issues from a missional church perspective, revising the polity of congregationalism with a more missional and contextual perspective, and enrolling and training more women for leadership roles.

D. A missional TSBC needs to have interdependent church polity and a theological understanding for the Convention.   The church needs to re-

---

55. Swanson, *The Church in Taiwan: Profile 1980*, pp. 114-15.

flect on the role of the convention from a missional church perspective and have a more interdependent church polity. The Baptist church polity emphasizes local congregations and tends to hinder them from having a vision beyond themselves. Congregations do not envision that the convention is important for forming a missional church; and thus many congregations do not support the convention financially. Many local pastors have less intentionality and are too busy to play an active role at the convention level. In addition, church polity seems to lack a theological basis for forming a stronger convention. These factors result in a weak convention in the TSBC, one that does not have the capacity to support local churches and to initiate new ministries in new mission fields.

To envision a contextual missiology for the TSBC, it is essential to note that a mobile missionary structure is also necessary for supporting and forming missional congregations. The congregations need to be taught that they have responsibility to contribute both financially and in growing gifted leaders to the convention level. In addition, in order to have stronger leaders at the convention level, the TSBC seminary needs to expand its formation of leaders to include leaders of the convention. The seminary needs to help the TSBC to develop a more interdependent church polity, because the seminary has more capacity to reflect theologically and has more authority to address this issue. In addition, it needs to amend the current church's constitution by adding basic responsibilities for Baptist congregations and offering some limited authority to the convention.

Conclusion

As the Southern Baptist Church is preparing to celebrate sixty years of mission in Taiwan, it is an appropriate time to reflect on its past and to envision a missiology for its future. In this chapter I have tried to propose a missional church framework that challenges the TSBC to participate in God's mission while engaging its unique and dynamic context. For the TSBC to participate in God's mission in Taiwan in the twentieth-first century, the church needs to reflect on its missional nature with its ministry that needs to engage and respond to the challenges of its context. In addition, the church should have a missional understanding of church leadership, a more mutual interdependent church polity, and a more missional understanding for the Convention.

This project is a continuing process, because the relationship between the context of Taiwan and the church is a dynamic interaction. The church needs to always seek to be missional and contextual. Whenever the church stops to reflect missiologically on its mission, it can easily lose perspective on the essence and purpose for which the missionary God calls ands send it into the world. In addition, since the context is always changing, the church's contextual missiology must engage these changes in its context and respond to the needs of the people within it.